Johannesburg &
Kruger National Park

Lizzie Williams

Credits

Footprint credits

Editor: Stephanie Rebello
Production and layout: Emma Bryers
Maps: Kevin Feeney

Publisher: Patrick Dawson
Managing Editor: Felicity Laughton
Advertising: Elizabeth Taylor
Sales and marketing: Kirsty Holmes

Photography credits

Front cover: LOOK-foto/Superstock
Back cover: Marka/Superstock

Every effort has been made to ensure that the facts in this guidebook are accurate. However, travellers should still obtain advice from consulates, airlines, etc, about travel and visa requirements before travelling. The authors and publishers cannot accept responsibility for any loss, injury or inconvenience however caused.

The content of Footprint *Focus Johannesburg & Kruger National Park* is based on Footprint's *South Africa Handbook*, which was researched and written by Lizzie Williams.

Printed in Spain by GraphyCems.

Publishing information

Footprint *Focus Johannesburg & Kruger National Park*
2nd edition
© Footprint Handbooks Ltd
January 2015

ISBN: 978 1 910120 11 8
CIP DATA: A catalogue record for this book is available from the British Library

® Footprint Handbooks and the Footprint mark are a registered trademark of Footprint Handbooks Ltd

Published by Footprint
6 Riverside Court
Lower Bristol Road
Bath BA2 3DZ, UK
T +44 (0)1225 469141
F +44 (0)1225 469461
footprinttravelguides.com

Distributed in the USA by National Book Network, Inc.

Kruger wildlife:
Page 1: Superstock: Gallo Images/Gallo Images. Page 3: Superstock: NaturePL/NaturePL. Page 4: Superstock: Kim Walker/Robert Harding Picture Library. Page 5: Superstock: Minden Pictures/Minden Pictures. Page 6: Superstock: Mint Images/Mint Images; Tibor Bognár/age fotostock; Prisma/Prisma. Page 8: Superstock: age fotostock/age fotostock. Page 9: Superstock: imageBROKER/imageBROKER; Minden Pictures/Minden Pictures; Radius/Radius. Page 10: Superstock: age fotostock/age fotostock; imageBROKER/imageBROKER; Mint Images/Mint Images. Page 11: Superstock: Biosphoto/Biosphoto; imageBROKER/imageBROKER; Westend61/Westend61. Page 12: Superstock: Minden Pictures/Minden Pictures. Page 14: Superstock: Kerstin Layer/Mauritius; NaturePL/NaturePL. Page 15: Superstock: age fotostock/age fotostock; Bill Gozansky/age fotostock. Page 16: Superstock: Cusp/Cusp

Contents

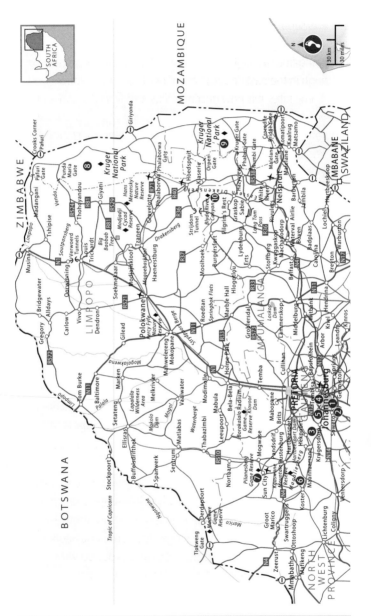

Since its sudden birth in 1886 when a hapless Aussie discovered gold on the Highveld, Johannesburg has dominated the country, morphing from a rough frontier town into a financial metropolis. Although in the past, Joburg has suffered from much-publicized high crime rates, it is now dusting off its dodgy reputation and drawing back visitors in droves. Regeneration and crime-busting programmes have seen formerly run-down areas transformed into attractive places to visit and live in, while attractions include some of South Africa's finest cutting-edge museums, such as the Apartheid Museum and the Cradle of Humankind. There are numerous other historical and cultural sights, as well as mega-shopping malls, excellent restaurants and sophisticated nightlife.

Just 50 km to the north, South Africa's capital Pretoria couldn't be more different from vibrant Joburg. Founded as a Voortrekker settlement and today's seat of government, it has instead a rather staid and conservative atmosphere, albeit softened by wide streets lined with jacaranda trees which bloom a regal purple in spring. The North West Province is known first and foremost as the home of Sun City, a huge entertainment complex and one-time gambling haven which was once the most visited site in South Africa. Gambling aside, a good reason for visiting is the Pilanesberg Game Reserve, which offers the chance of seeing the Big Five at a malaria-free altitude, while the Magaliesberg Mountains make a pleasant few hours excursion from Johannesburg or Pretoria.

To the east, the province of Mpumalanga is home to the magnificent Kruger National Park, one of the best places in Africa for game viewing. While it's entirely possible to see the Big Five in one afternoon, a longer stay allows visitors to fully appreciate the wilderness of the park. West of Kruger, the Panorama Region is well worth a detour. This mountainous area is dotted with quiet agricultural towns, clustered along the top of the spectacular Blyde River Canyon.

Planning your trip

Best time to visit Johannesburg and Kruger National Park

Johannesburg and Pretoria, with an average altitude of over 1500 m, are in Gauteng Province, which sits on South Africa's elevated inland plateau known as the Highveld, which has a moderate climate and long sunny days for most of the year. During summer (November-February), daytime temperatures average around 25°C while nighttime temperatures rarely dip below 15°C. However, it is in summer that the Highveld gets most of its rainfall and can experience dramatic electrical thunderstorms during the afternoon, although they usually disappear as quickly as they arrive. The best time to appreciate the beautiful colours of the millions of trees in Johannesburg and Pretoria is during spring (September-October) and autumn (March-April). Winter (May-August) in the cities is mild and dry with temperatures of about 20°C during the day, but at night it can drop down to 4°C. The winter months are the best time of year for game viewing, when vegetation cover is at a minimum and a lack of water forces animals to congregate around rivers and waterholes. Summer has its advantages too and, after the summer rains arrive from November onwards, Kruger is transformed into a beautiful green landscape. Animals will be in good condition after feeding on the new shoots, and many young summer-born animals are around, which in turn attract the predators. However, the thick vegetation and the wide availability of water means that wildlife is far more widespread and difficult to spot.

All over the country December and January, followed by Easter, are by far the busiest periods for domestic tourism. The schools and universities shut and these are the times for special events and festivals. Kruger in particular is a very popular family destination over Christmas and New Year. Despite being cooler, July and August are also popular with overseas visitors as they coincide with the European school holidays. Be sure to book car hire and accommodation well in advance during these times. For further advice visit www.weathersa.co.za.

Getting to Johannesburg and Kruger National Park

Air

The three main international airports in South Africa are: **OR Tambo International Airport** in Johannesburg, page 27, **Cape Town International Airport** in Cape Town, and **King Shaka International Airport** in Durban. OR Tambo (renamed from Johannesburg International Airport in 2006 after the late anti-Apartheid activist Oliver Tambo) is the regional hub with numerous

Don't miss…

Numbers relate to the map on page 4.

daily flights to and from Europe, North America, Asia and Australia. Most flights to South Africa first arrive in Johannesburg, (although some international carriers also fly directly to Cape Town and Durban), and if you are connecting in Johannesburg to the other domestic cities, regardless of your eventual destination, immigration is done at Johannesburg, which usually means you have to pick up your luggage from international arrivals and check in again at domestic departures. Jet lag is not an issue if flying from Europe to South Africa as there is only a minimal time difference.

There is a far-reaching and efficient domestic service and numerous daily flights connect Johannesburg with South Africa's major cities; all of which are within a couple of hours' flying time of each other. Most airlines also operate regional flights to the capital cities of South Africa's neighboring countries. By booking early online, good deals can be found with all the airlines. You can either book directly or through the national booking agency **Computicket**, www.computicket.com, T011-340 8000, or in South Africa, at any of their kiosks in the shopping malls or any branch of **Checkers** and **Shoprite** supermarkets.

British Airways Comair ① *T011-441 8600, www.britishairways.com*, has daily flights between Johannesburg and Cape Town, Durban, Bloemfontein, East London, George, Hoedspruit, Nelspruit and Port Elizabeth, as well as regional flights between Johannesburg and Harare, Mauritius, Nairobi, Windhoek, Livingstone and Victoria Falls. **Kulula** ① *T0861-585 852 (in South Africa), T011-921 0111 (from overseas), www.kulula.com*, also owned by British Airways, is a no-frills airline with daily services between Johannesburg and Cape Town,

Durban, George, East London and Port Elizabeth. On a code-share agreement with BA, they also fly to the above regional destinations. **Mango** ⓘ *T0861-162 646 (in South Africa), T011-359 1222 (from overseas), www.flymango. com*, another no-frills operator owned by SAA, has daily flights between Johannesburg and Cape Town, Durban, George and Port Elizabeth and also has flights to Zanzibar. **South African Airways (SAA)** ⓘ *T0861-359 722 (in South Africa), T011-978 1111 (from overseas), www.flysaa.com*, covers all the country's major centres and has flights to most southern African cities in conjunction with both its subsidiaries SA Airlink and SA Express.

With a huge choice of routes and flights, you need to book well in advance for the best fares, especially over the Christmas and New Year period which is the peak summer holiday season in South Africa. For live flight information visit the **Airport Company of South Africa**'s website, www.acsa.co.za, or phone T0867-277888.

Rail

There are no international rail services between South Africa and its neighbouring countries, but South African long-distance passenger trains operate on a number of routes which all start and finish in Johannesburg. The network is run by **Shosholoza Meyl** ⓘ *T0860-008 888 (in South Africa), T011-774 4555 (from overseas), www.shosholozameyl.co.za*. Shosholoza means 'to push forward' or 'to strive' and is the name of a popular traditional African song favoured particularly by hard-working men whose job it was to lay railway lines. Most of South Africa's major cities are linked by rail but train travel is very slow, and as all travel overnight, they arrive at some stations en route at inconvenient times. However, the services are popular and seats should be reserved well in advance. The trains have sleeping carriages, with coupés that sleep two or four people with a wash basin, fold-away table and bunk beds. The trains generally don't have a problem with security but, if you leave your compartment, make sure a train official locks it after you. Refreshments are available from trolleys or dining cars, but don't expect brilliant food and it's a good idea to take extra snacks.

The routes are: **Johannesburg–Cape Town** (Wednesday, Friday and Sunday daily in both directions, 27 hours); **Johannesburg–Durban** (daily, Friday, Wednesday and Sunday in both directions, 13 hours); **Johannesburg–East London** (Wednesday, Friday and Sunday in both directions, 17 hours); **Johannesburg–East London** (Wednesday, Friday and Sunday in both directions, 17 hours); **Johannesburg–Port Elizabeth** (Wednesday, Friday and Sunday in both directions, 20½ hours); **Johannesburg–Musina** (Wednesday and Friday, Thursday and Sunday in the opposite direction, 12 hours); and **Johannesburg–Komatipoort** (Wednesday and Friday, Thursday and Sunday in the opposite direction, 11 hours).

Shosholoza Meyl also operates a more upmarket service, the **Premier Classe** ① *T011-774 5247, www.premier.co.za*, between Johannesburg and Cape Town (25 hours), Johannesburg and Durban (14 hours), both twice a week, and Johannesburg and Port Elizabeth (25 hours), once a week. This is a pleasant alternative to flying if you have the time, and the carriages are a lot nicer than the regular train, with two-bed coupés and extras such as dressing gowns, toiletries and 'room service', and there's a good restaurant car serving breakfast, high tea and dinner; fares include all meals. Vehicles can be taken on the trains, which gives the option of taking the train in one direction and driving in the other. If the journey is more important than the destination, then old-fashioned luxury trains operate much like five-star hotels on wheels. **The Blue Train** ① *T021-334 8459, www.bluetrain.co.za*, is considered to be southern Africa's premier luxury train. The wood-panelled coaches feature luxury coupés with en suite bathrooms, elegant lounge cars and fine dining in the restaurant car. It runs between Pretoria and Cape Town (27 hours), and Pretoria and Durban (20 hours). **Rovos Rail** ① *T012-315 8242, www.rovos.co.za*, is a similar luxury train and runs between Pretoria and Cape Town and Durban with occasional longer rail safaris between Pretoria and Victoria Falls in Zimbabwe.

Road

Bus **Greyhound** ① *T083-915 9000 (in South Africa), T011-276 8550 (from overseas), www.greyhound.co.za*, and **Intercape** ① *T0861-287 287 (in South Africa), T012-380 4400 (from overseas), www.intercape.co.za*, are the two long-distance bus companies that cover routes across South Africa's borders. The coaches are air conditioned and have a toilet; some sell refreshments and show DVDs. They will stop at least every four to five hours to refuel and perhaps change drivers and give passengers a chance to stretch their legs and buy snacks and drinks at a petrol station takeaway. For long journeys, the prices are reasonable (though the no-frills airline tickets can be competitive). All bus tickets can be booked directly with the bus companies or through the national booking agency **Computicket** ① *www.computicket.com, T011-340 8000*, or in South Africa, at any of their kiosks in the shopping malls or any branch of **Checkers** and **Shoprite** supermarkets.

Greyhound runs services between Johannesburg/Pretoria and Maputo in Mozambique, and Harare and Bulawayo in Zimbabwe. **Intercape** runs services between Johannesburg and Windhoek in Namibia, and between Pretoria and Gaborone in Botswana, Pretoria and Bulawayo and Victoria Falls in Zimbabwe, which then continue to Livingstone, Lusaka and Ndola in Zambia, and Pretoria and Harare in Zimbabwe, which then continue to Blantyre and Lilongwe in Malawi.

Car If crossing any international borders in a private car, you must have a registration document, insurance and a driving licence printed in English with a photograph. With the exception of Zimbabwe, you should be able to take a hire car from South Africa into all the bordering countries, though check with the rental company first. You will need a letter of permission to take a car across a border if it is not registered in your name, and a ZA sticker (available from car rental companies or any AA shop in South Africa – usually found in the shopping malls). Botswana, Namibia, Lesotho, Swaziland, Mozambique and South Africa are all part of SADC's (Southern Africa Development Community) joint customs agreement, so if you are in your own car travelling on a carnet, you only have to produce this when crossing your first or last border to the SADC countries.

Transport in Johannesburg and Kruger National Park

Air

In Johannesburg, domestic and regional flights operated by the above airlines arrive and depart at **OR Tambo International Airport** (see above and page 27), and some airlines also operate domestic flights to and from Gauteng's second airport, **Lanseria International Airport** (see page 28).

The three principal airports serving Kruger are **Kruger Mpumalanga International Airport** (see page 122), 25 km north of Nelspruit near Kruger's Numbi and Malalane gates; **Phalaborwa Kruger Gateway Airport** (see page 122) 2 km from Phalaborwa and within easy reach of many of Kruger's gates; and **Eastgate Airport** (see page 122) at Hoedspruit, close to Orpen Gate. **Of the above airlines, British Airways Comair,** has daily flights between Johannesburg and Hoedspruit and Nelspruit, and **South African Airways** (SAA), has daily flights (operated by its subsidiaries SA Airlink and SA Express) between Johannesburg and Hoedspruit, Nelspruit and Phalaborwa. Charter flight airlines also use these airports.

Rail

On the long-distance rail service run by **Shosholoza Meyl** (above), between Johannesburg and Komatipoort (Wednesday and Friday, Thursday and Sunday in the opposite direction, 11 hours), trains stop in Nelspruit en route. However, the arrival and departure times in Nelspruit are at inconvenient times late at night/early hours of the morning.

Road

Bus and coach The Baz Bus ⓘ *reservations Cape Town T021-422 5202, www. bazbus.com,* is a hop-on, hop-off bus that offers a convenient and sociable alternative to the main long-distance bus services. It is specifically designed for backpackers visiting South Africa and remains one of the most popular ways of seeing the country on a budget. One of the best aspects of the service is that the bus collects and drops off at backpacker hostels. There are a few exceptions where the bus will drop off on a main road, and the hostels will then meet you for an extra charge, but you must arrange this in advance. The Baz Bus route is **Cape Town–Durban** along the coast, and **Durban–Johannesburg** via the Drakensberg, with an extra shuttle from Johannesburg to Pretoria if there is the demand. Visit the website for the full timetable.

Tickets are priced per segment, for example from Durban to Johannesburg. You are allowed to hop off and on the bus as many times as you like in the given segment, but must not backtrack. This is where the savings are made, since the other long-distance bus companies charge high prices for short journeys. For long distances without stops, the other buses may be better value.

The three main intercity coach companies are **Greyhound** ⓘ *T083-915 9000 (in South Africa), T011-276 8550 (from overseas), www.greyhound.co.za*, **Intercape** ⓘ *T0861-287 287 (in South Africa), T012-380 4400 (from overseas), www.intercape.co.za*; and **Translux** ⓘ *T0861-589 282 (in South Africa), T011-774 3333 (from overseas), www.translux.co.za*. They run between towns and popular destinations, and to some cities in South Africa's neighbouring countries (see page 9). You can book directly or through the national booking agency **Computicket** ⓘ *www.computicket.com, T011-340 8000*, or in South Africa, at any of their kiosks in the shopping malls or any branch of **Checkers** and **Shoprite** supermarkets. The coaches are air conditioned and have a toilet, and will stop at least every three to four hours to give the passengers a chance to stretch their legs and buy refreshments. Long-distance buses are more than twice as fast as the trains.

Car hire Hiring a car for part, or all, of your journey is undoubtedly the best way to see South Africa; you get to travel at your own leisurely pace and explore more out-of-the-way regions without being tied to a tour or a timetable. Driving isn't challenging; the roads are generally in excellent condition and, away from the major urban centres, there is little traffic. Petrol, not a major expense, is available 24 hours a day at the fuel stations in the cities and along the national highways; an attendant fills up, washes the windscreen and, if necessary, checks oil, water and tyre pressure, for which a tip of a few rand is the norm. Parking is easy and the sights and shopping malls have car parks. For street-side parking in the cities and towns, you pay a uniformed attendant between 0800 and 1700. Parking costs on average around R5-7 per hour. In less formal places and at night, you pay a 'car guard' about the same to watch over your car – they are usually identified by a badge or work vest. Driving is on the left side of the road and speed limits are 60 kph in built up areas, 80 kph on minor roads and 120 kph on highways. Speed traps are common. Remember that if you are caught by a speed camera, the fine will go to the car hire company who have every right to deduct the amount from your credit card, even if it is some time after you have left South Africa.

The minimum age to rent a car is usually 23. A driver's licence (with a translation if it's not in English) and a credit card are essential. Tourist offices usually recommend large international organizations such as **Avis** or **Budget**, but there are a number of reliable local companies, and it is worth asking at hotels for recommendations. Most of the larger companies have kiosks at the airport and partner with the airlines, so it's also possible to book a car online with your flight.

There is a range of vehicles to choose from, from basic hatchbacks and saloon cars, to camper vans and fully equipped 4WD vehicles. Costs for car hire vary considerably and depend on days of the week, season, type of vehicle and terms (insurance, excess, mileage, etc). A compact car starts from as little as R250-350 per day; a fully equipped 4WD or camper van with tents and equipment from R800-1300 per day. If this is shared among a group of four it's the most affordable way to get around. The cost of fuel is about two-thirds of what Europeans are used to, but distances travelled can be considerable so longer holidays will run up a hefty fuel bill.

In the event of an accident, call your car hire company's emergency number. For emergency breakdown and traffic update information contact the **Automobile Association of South Africa** ① *T083-84322, www.aa.co.za.*

Hitchhiking This is not common in South Africa and is not recommended as it can be very dangerous. Women should never hitch, under any circumstances, even in a group. If you have to hitch, be very wary of whom you accept a lift from; a car with a family or couple is usually the best option.

Minibus taxis The majority of South Africa's population travel by minibus taxis and, in many areas, including inner cities, they are the only way of getting around. However, the accident rate of such vehicles is notoriously high, with speeding, overcrowding and lack of maintenance being the main causes. There is also the problem of possible robbery, especially at the taxi ranks, and so many visitors and locals are wary of using them.

Nevertheless, minibus taxis remain the cheapest and most extensive form of transport in the country. Many routes have experienced little or no crime, but you should exercise extreme caution and always ask people in the know before using them.

Taxis Regular taxis are not hailed in the street, and except in the major cities there are few taxi ranks in South African towns so it's normal to phone for one; any hotel or restaurant can do this for you. Taxis are metered and charge R11-14 per kilometre. Groups should request a larger vehicle if available as these can carry up to seven people. Some can accommodate wheelchairs.

Where to stay in Johannesburg and Kruger National Park

There is a wide variety of accommodation in the region from top-of-the-range five-star hotels, luxury game lodges and tented camps that charge R3000-8000 or more per couple per day, to mid-range safari lodges and hotels with air-conditioned double rooms for R1500-3000, to guesthouse or B&Bs that charge R500-1500 and dormitory beds or camping for under R200 a day. Generally, there are reasonable discounts for children and most places offer family accommodation. During the popular domestic tourism seasons and the long school holidays such as Christmas, New Year and Easter, reservations should be made well in advance, especially for the parks and along the coast. All accommodation in South Africa is graded a star value by the **Tourism Grading Council of South Africa** ① *www.tourismgrading.co.za*, and the website has comprehensive lists in all categories. There are numerous other resources for independently booking accommodation in South Africa; comprehensive accommodation information can be found on the regional tourism websites listed in each area, and exploring the websites of **AA Travel Guides** ① *www.aatravel.co.za*, **SA-Venues** ① *www.sa-venues.com*, and **Sleeping Out** ① *www.sleeping-out.co.za*, is a good start.

Hotels South Africa offers a wide variety of hotels. There are some delightful family-run and country hotels, boutique hotels with stylish interiors in the cities and towns and, for those who enjoy the anonymity of a large hotel, chains such as **Tsogo Sun**, **Protea** and **City Lodge**. Many of the more upmarket hotels offer additional facilities such as spas, golf courses and some fine restaurants, which are almost always open to non-guests. Every small town also has at least one hotel of two- or three-star standard: often aimed at local business travellers, these can be in characterless buildings and the restaurants may serve bland food, but they nevertheless represent good value.

Guesthouses Guesthouses can offer some of the most characterful accommodation in South Africa with interesting places springing up in both cities and small towns. Standards obviously vary enormously; much of what you'll get has to do with the character of the owners and the location of the homes. Some are simple practical overnight rooms, while at the more luxurious end, rooms may be in historic homes filled with antiques and offering impeccable service. Breakfast is almost always included and, in some, evening meals can be prepared if you phone ahead. For listings look at the websites of the **Guest House Association of Southern Africa** ① *www.ghasa.co.za*, or the **Portfolio Collection** ① *www.portfoliocollection.com*.

Backpacker hostels Apart from camping, backpacker hostels are the cheapest form of accommodation, and a bed in a dormitory will cost as little as R120 a

Price codes

Where to stay

$$$$ over US$350 $$$ US$150-350
$$ US$75-150 $ under US$75

Prices refer to the cost of a double room, not including service charge or meals unless otherwise stated. See page 22 for exchange rates.

Restaurants

$$$ over US$30 $$ US$15-30 $ under US$15

Prices refer to the cost of a two-course meal for one person including a soft drink, beer or glass of wine.

---

night. Some also have budget double rooms with or without bathrooms, while others have space to pitch a tent in the garden.

You can usually expect a self-catering kitchen, hot showers, a TV/DVD room and internet access. Many hostels also have bars and offer meals or nightly *braais*, plus a garden and a swimming pool. Most hostels are a good source of travel information and many act as booking agents for bus companies, budget safari tours and car hire. The **Baz Bus** (see page 10) caters for backpackers and links most hostels along the coast between Cape Town and Durban, and some on its route between Durban and Johannesburg via the Drakensberg. **Coast to Coast** ⓘ *www.coastingafrica.com*, publishes a free annual backpackers' accommodation guide and is available in all the hostels.

Camping and caravan parks Camping is the cheapest and most flexible way of seeing South Africa. Every town has a municipal campsite, many of which also have simple self-catering chalets.

As camping is very popular with South Africans, sites tend to have very good facilities, although they may be fully booked months in advance, especially during the school holidays in the most popular game reserves and national parks. Even the most basic site will have a clean washblock with hot water, plus electric points and lighting. All sites have *braai* facilities, with charcoal, wood and firelighters available in campsite shops. Some sites also have kitchen blocks. At the most popular tourist spots, campsites are more like holiday resorts with shops, swimming pools and a restaurant – these can get very busy and are best avoided in peak season.

Camping equipment is widely available in South Africa if you don't want to bring your own. Lightweight tents, sleeping bags, ground mats, gas lights, stoves and cooking equipment, etc, can be bought at good prices in all the major cities and some car hire companies rent out equipment. **Cape Union**

Mart ⓘ *www.capeunionmart.co.za*, is a quality outdoor adventure shop for gear, as well as outdoor clothing, and branches can be found in the larger shopping malls across the country.

Self-catering Self-catering chalets, cottages or apartments are particularly popular with South African holidaymakers. However they are rarely found in the cities, but the choice is enormous in the national parks and along the coast. The quality and facilities vary, from basic rondavels with bunks, to chalets with a couple of bedrooms and fully equipped kitchens. They can be excellent value and the cost could be as little as R100-200 per person per day and are ideal for families or a group of friends on a budget. The self-catering accommodation in Kruger ranges from simple huts that share communal bathrooms and kitchens with campers to spacious multiple bedroom units with at least two bathrooms and quite often have a view of a river or floodplain for game viewing. While the larger rest camps in Kruger have supermarkets, restaurants and petrol stations, most camps are rather more basic. But all have a reception desk or office where you can arrange guided walks and game drives, and perhaps a small shop selling maps, basic food provisions and firewood. National parks across South Africa are under the jurisdiction of **South African National Parks** (**SANParks**) ⓘ *central reservations, 643 Leyds St, Groenkloof, Pretoria, T012-428 9111, www.sanparks.org.*

Luxury game lodges The most famous luxury game lodges are on private game reserves adjoining Kruger, although there are many others around the country. Their attraction is the chance to combine exclusive game viewing in prime wilderness areas, with top-class accommodation, fine dining, vintage wines and a spectacular natural setting.

The cost of staying in a luxury game lodge varies from R3000-8000 or more per couple per day. This includes all meals, most drinks and game-viewing activities. In order to get the most from the experience, guests tend to stay for at least two nights. The lodges are often isolated and not easily accessible by road so many reserves offer shuttle transfers from the nearest city, and some have their own airstrips where charter aircraft can land. For details of the luxury reserves around Kruger National Park, see pages 144-148.

Food and drink in Johannesburg and Kruger National Park

Food
South African food tends to be fairly regional, although a ubiquitous love of meat unites the country. As well as quality steak and Karoo lamb, South Africa offers plenty of opportunities to try an assortment of game such as ostrich or springbok. One of the first local terms you are likely to learn will be *braai*, which quite simply

South African dishes

Bobotie A Cape Malay dish similar to shepherd's pie but with a savoury custard topping instead of mashed potatoes, and the mince stew is mixed with fruit.

Boerewors A coarse, thick sausage made from beef or game meat and usually cooked in a spiral on the *braai*. The word is a combination of 'farmer' and 'sausage' in Afrikaans.

Bredie The Afrikaans word for 'stew' usually made with mutton, cinnamon, chilli and cloves and cooked for a very long time. *Waterblommetjie bredie* is meat cooked with the flower of the Cape pondweed (tastes a bit like green beans).

Cape brandy pudding Also known as tipsy tart, this warming winter pudding was probably concocted soon after brandy was distilled in the Cape in 1672. Dates and nuts are added to this syrupy dish.

Frikkadels Beef or lamb meatballs, usually made with nutmeg and coriander and baked or deep fried.

Koeksisters A popular sweet snack, which is (sometimes) plaited, made of deep-fried sugary dough and then coated in honey and cinnamon. The name is derived from the Afrikaans *koek* (cake) and *sissen* (to sizzle).

Mealie A *mealie* is a maize cob, and *mealie meal* is maize flour, which is mostly cooked to a fairly stiff consistency known as *pap* ('porridge' in Afrikaans). The staple diet for much of the black South African population, and eaten for breakfast with milk, butter and sugar or as a main meal with meat and tomato stew.

Malva pudding A traditional caramelized dessert made with apricot jam and sponge and usually served with custard. A twist is to soak the sponge in dessert wine.

Melktart A baked custard tart, with a biscuit shell and dusted with cinnamon. Popular at *braais* (after all the meat).

Potjiekos Stews cooked over coals in three-legged cast-iron pots of the same name. The word means 'little-pot food' in Afrikaans, and is thought to originate from the Voortrekkers who hooked the pots under their wagons, and then heated them up again after adding ingredients collected during the day.

means barbecue. The *braai* is incredibly popular, part of the South African way of life, and every campsite, back garden and picnic spot has one. Given the excellent range of meat available, learning how to cook good food on a *braai* is an art that needs to be mastered quickly, especially if you are self-catering.

A local meat product which travellers invariably come across is *biltong* – a heavily salted and spiced sun-dried meat, usually made from beef but sometimes made from game. Non-red meat eaters and vegetarians need not despair though as most fruit and vegetables are grown in South Africa (and indeed exported) and there is an excellent choice of local produce. Fish and seafood is plentiful also and the likes of Cape salmon and West Coast mussels come from South Africa's Atlantic coast, while prawns, sea bass and snapper come from Mozambique.

Supermarkets have a similar selection of groceries to that found in Europe and in most cases considerably cheaper, especially meat and fresh fruit and vegetables. There are several large supermarket chains, and the larger ones also feature extensive counters for pre-prepared food, hot meals, pizzas and sandwiches (in some, even sushi). Across the region there are also plenty of farmers' markets (and often on the roadside, padstalls – Afrikaans for 'farmstalls'), for tasty home-made goodies, organic vegetables, wine and olives.

Drink

South Africa is a major player in the international market and produces a wide range of excellent wines. The Winelands in the Western Cape has the best-known labels but there are a number of other wine regions dotted around the country. South Africa also produces a range of good beer. Major names include Black Label, Castle and Amstel. Windhoek, from Namibia, is also widely available and more popular than some South African beers. Home-brewed beer, made from sorghum or maize, is widely drunk by the African population. It has a thick head, is very potent and not very palatable to the uninitiated.

No liquor may be sold on Sundays (and public holidays) except in licensed bars and restaurants. The standard shop selling alcohol is known as a bottle store, usually open Monday-Friday 0800-1800, Saturday 0830-1400 (some may stay open until 1600). Supermarkets do not sell beer or spirits, stop selling wine at 2000, and don't sell alcohol on Sundays. A bottle of wine and beer bought from a bottle store starts from an affordable R30 and R10 respectively.

Soft drinks Tap water in South Africa is safe to drink. Bottled mineral water and a good range of fruit juices are available at most outlets – the Ceres and Liquifruit brands are the best. Another popular drink is Rooibos (or red bush) tea – a caffeine-free tea with a smoky flavour, usually served with sugar or honey, that is grown in the Cederberg Mountains in the Western Cape.

Eating out

South Africa has an excellent variety of restaurants that represent every kind of international cuisine as well as a good choice of quality South African dishes. Johannesburg in particular is a culinary hotspot given that Joburgers themselves love dining out and expect high standards of food and service. Eating out can be very good value, and a two-course evening meal with wine in a reasonable restaurant will cost under R300 for two people; generally you can be assured of good food and large portions. For the budget traveller there

South Africanisms

English, the official language, is understood and spoken by the majority of South Africans, but it is peppered with a host of other commonly used words; some borrowed freely from Afrikaans (similar to Dutch) and the numerous African languages, while others are completely fabricated slang that is uniquely South African.

Bakkie A utility/pick-up truck.
Babbelas A hangover.
Born frees South Africans who were born into a democratic South Africa – that is, after 1994.
Braai Barbeque; usually a metal grill where you light your own fire underneath with wood or coals.
Bushveld A terrain of grassland dotted with thick scrubby trees and bush. Veld means 'field' in Afrikaans.
Dop or doppie Drink, usually alcoholic.
Dorp Afrikaans for 'town', although usually refers to a small urban centre with just a few farmers wandering around.
Eish Used to express surprise, wonder, frustration or outrage. An isiXhosa word but now used across all the languages.

Fundi Expert or skilled person. Derived from isiZulu for great honour or wisdom.
Howzit How is it going?
Ja Yes. From Afrikaans and pronounced *yaa*.
Ja-Nee Yes-no (*yaa-near*), but actually means so-so or maybe.
Jol To have fun or party; can refer to anything from a picnic to an all-night rave.
Lapa Thatched shelter, usually without walls, for entertaining, especially when *braaiing*.
Lekker Nice, good, great, cool or tasty.
Kopjie A hill or outcrop of rocks, and a common feature on wide open plains.
Madiba The universal affectionate name for Nelson Mandela (it was his clan name).
Now-now and just-now Widely used to indicate concepts of time.
Robot Traffic lights.
Shebeen Township pub. Once set up at the back of someone's home and illegal under Apartheid.
Stoep A veranda in front of a house.
Traffic circle A roundabout.
Yebo Yes, for sure; derived from isiZulu.

are plenty of fast-food outlets, and almost every supermarket has a superb deli counter serving hot and cold meals.

A great starting point for choosing a restaurant is the **Eat Out** website ⓘ *www.eatout.co.za*, which features South Africa's best choice of restaurants, or you can buy the latest edition of their magazine, available at **CNA** and **Exclusive Books**. **Dining Out** ⓘ *www.dining-out.co.za*, is another excellent resource and provides hundreds of reviews and contact details for restaurants throughout the country.

Essentials A-Z

Accident and emergency

Police, T10111; **medical**, T10177; **fire**, T10111. All emergencies from a cell phone, T112.

Children

South Africa is a popular family holiday destination with plenty to do, and there are significant discounts on accommodation, transport and entry fees. You will find plentiful supplies to feed and look after your little ones, and many restaurants have kids' menus. Hygiene throughout the country is good; stomach upsets are rare and the tap water everywhere is safe to drink.

Most accommodation options welcome families; many hotels have family or adjoining rooms, there are plenty of self-catering chalets or apartments, and children love camping, either with your own camping equipment or an upmarket tented camp.

In Kruger and the other parks, seeing animals on safari is very exciting for children, especially when they catch their first glimpse of an elephant or lion. However, small children may get bored driving around a hot game park all day if there is no animal activity. Keep them interested by providing them with their own animal and bird checklists and perhaps their own binoculars and cameras. While in the bush, be sure to protect your children from the sun's intense rays, and be aware of the potential dangers of wild animals, snakes and insects.

Disabled travellers

Facilities for disabled travellers are generally of a high standard and the airports are fully wheelchair accessible and can provide wheelchairs for less mobile travellers. Modern hotels have specially adapted rooms, but it is worth enquiring in advance at older hotels or more remote places. Most **SANParks** (www.sanparks.org) accommodation in Kruger now has at least one unit that has been adapted for use by mobility impaired guests (book well in advance), while a number of the campsites have accessible ablution blocks.

Almost all shopping malls, museums and tourist attractions have ramps or lifts and disabled parking right by the entrance. Some Johannesburg attractions, such as **Constitution Hill** (page 50), the **Apartheid Museum** (page 52) and **Maropeng** (page 64), have been designed for wheelchair-users to get around. **SANParks** have equipped as many as possible with facilities like boardwalks, hides, museums and picnic sites throughout Kruger with ramps for wheelchairs.

The more modern transport – for example, **Johannesburg's City**

Sightseeing (page 84) and **Rea Vaya** (page 84) buses, and the **Gautrain** (page 29) between OR Tambo International Airport and Johannesburg and Pretoria – are accessible for wheelchairs. With notice, the larger car hire companies, such as **Avis**, **Budget** and **Hertz**, can organize cars with hand controls. **Avis** can organize for one to be picked up at **Skukuza Rest Camp** in Kruger (www.avis.co.za).

Customs and duty free

The official customs allowance for visitors over 18 years includes 200 cigarettes, 50 cigars, 250 g of tobacco, 2 litres of wine, 1 litre of spirits, 50 ml of perfume and 250 ml of eau de toilette. Tourists can reclaim the 14% VAT on purchases bought in South Africa whose total value exceeds R250. You can do this when departing, at the VAT reclaim desks at airports in Johannesburg, Cape Town and Durban or at border posts. For more information visit www.taxrefunds.co.za.

Electricity

Voltage 220/230 volts AC at 50 Hz. Most plugs and appliances are 3-point round-pin (1 10-mm and 2 8-mm prongs). Hotels usually have 2-pin sockets for razors and chargers.

Embassies and consulates

For embassies and consulates of South Africa, see embassy.goabroad.com.

Health

See your GP or travel clinic at least 6 weeks before departure for general advice on travel risks and vaccinations. Make sure you have sufficient medical travel insurance, get a dental check, know your own blood group and if you suffer a long-term condition such as diabetes, epilepsy or a serious allergy, obtain a Medic Alert bracelet/necklace (www.medicalert.co.uk). If you wear glasses, take a copy of your prescription.

Vaccinations
Confirm your primary courses and boosters are up to date. Courses or boosters usually advised: diphtheria; tetanus; poliomyelitis; hepatitis A. Vaccines sometimes advised: tuberculosis; hepatitis B; rabies; cholera; typhoid. The final decision on all vaccinations, however, should be based on a consultation with your doctor or travel clinic. A yellow fever certificate is required if over 1 year old and entering from an infected area. If you don't have one, you'll be required to get one at the airport before being permitted entry. Specialist advice should be taken on the best anti-malarials to use.

Health risks
Diarrhoea Diarrhoea can refer either to loose stools or an increased frequency of bowel movement, both of which can be a nuisance. Symptoms should be relatively short lived but if they persist beyond 2 weeks specialist medical attention should be sought. Adults can use an antidiarrhoeal medication to control

the symptoms but only for up to 24 hrs. In addition keep well hydrated by drinking plenty of fluids and eat bland foods. Oral rehydration sachets are a useful way to keep well hydrated. These should always be used when treating children and the elderly.

The standard advice to prevent problems is to be careful with water and ice for drinking. Be wary of salads (what were they washed in, who handled them), re-heated foods or food that has been left out in the sun having been cooked earlier in the day. On the positive side, very few people experience stomach problems in South Africa.

HIV/AIDS Southern Africa has the highest rates of HIV and AIDS in the world. Visitors should be aware of the dangers of infection and take the necessary precautions with sex, needles, medical treatment and in the case of a blood transfusion.

Malaria South Africa only has a very low seasonal risk of malaria in the extreme east of the country along the Mozambique border. This includes parts of the Kruger National Park where the risk period is between December and April. If you are travelling there during this time, consult your doctor or travel clinic about taking anti-malarials and ensure you finish the recommended course.

The best prevention is to try to avoid getting bitten. The most vulnerable times are between dusk and dawn; cover exposed skin with light clothing and insect repellents, and in

accommodation use mosquito nets or ensure netted screens are kept closed.

Sun Protect yourself adequately against the sun. Apply a high-factor sunscreen (greater than SPF15) and also make sure it screens against UVB. Prevent heat exhaustion and heatstroke by drinking enough fluids throughout the day.

If you get sick
There are plenty of private hospitals in South Africa, which have 24-hr emergency departments and pharmacies, run by **Medi-Clinic** (www. mediclinic.co.za) or **Netcare** (www. netcare.co.za). It is essential to have travel insurance as hospital bills need to be paid at the time of admittance, so keep all paperwork to make a claim. If you need to have a vaccination or buy malaria prophylactics in South Africa, visit one of the **Netcare Travel Clinics** in the major cities, www.travelclinic.co.za.

Holidays

South African school holidays are mid-Dec to mid-Jan; mid-Apr to early May; early Aug to early Sep. Exact dates can be found at www.schoolterms. co.za. Accommodation rates are often higher during school holidays in the parks and along the coast, but generally stay the same year-round in the cities. When a public holiday falls on a Sun, the following Mon becomes a holiday. Most businesses will close but shopping malls and large supermarkets in city centres remain open (public holidays are some of their busiest days – especially if a holiday weekend coincides with month-end pay day). All tourist attractions are open on public holidays.

1 Jan   New Year's Day
21 Mar   Human Rights' Day
Mar/Apr   Good Friday; Family Day (Mon following Easter Sun)
27 Apr   Freedom Day
1 May   Workers' Day
16 Jun   Youth Day
9 Aug   National Women's Day
24 Sep   Heritage Day
16 Dec   Day of Reconciliation
25 Dec   Christmas Day
26 Dec   Day of Goodwill

Money

→ *US$1 = R10.97; £1 = R17.58; €1 = R13.87 (Oct 2014).*
For up-to-the-minute exchange rates, visit **www.xe.com**.

Currency
The South African currency is the **rand** (R) which is divided into 100 **cents** (c). Notes are in 200, 100, 50, 20 and 10 rand, and coins are in 5, 2, 1 R and 50, 20, 10 and 5 cents. You can carry your funds in traveller's cheques (TCs), currency cards, credit and debit cards, or rand, US dollars, euros or pounds sterling cash.

Rand can easily be exchanged in all South Africa's neighbouring countries and in Lesotho, Swaziland, Namibia, Mozambique and Zimbabwe, it is used interchangeably alongside the local currency.

Changing money
South Africa's main banks are **ABSA**, **First National**, **Nedbank** and **Standard Bank**. All have foreign exchange services. You can also change money at **Bidvest**, www.bidvestbank.co.za, and **Master Currency**, www.mastercurrency.co.za, which both have branches at the main airports and large shopping malls. Larger hotels offer exchange facilities, but these often charge exorbitant fees.

Credit and debit cards
You can get all the way around South Africa with a credit or debit card. Not only are they a convenient method of covering major expenses but they offer some of the most competitive exchange rates when withdrawing cash from ATMs, and you can only hire a car with a credit (not debit) card. The chip and pin system is common, though not yet universal in South Africa. ATMs are everywhere; Plus, Cirrus Visa, MasterCard, American Express and Diners Club are all accepted. The amount you can withdraw varies between systems and cards, but you should be able to take out at least R2000 a day. Note that theft during or immediately after a withdrawal can be a problem, so never accept a stranger's help at an ATM, be aware of your surroundings and avoid using street-side ATMs. Instead, go into a bank or shopping mall, where guards are often on duty.

Lost or stolen cards American Express, T0800-110929; **Diners Club**, T0800-112017; **MasterCard**, T0800-990418; **Visa**, T0800-990475.

Currency cards

If you don't want to carry lots of cash, prepaid currency cards allow you to preload money from your bank account, fixed at the day's exchange rate. They look like a credit or debit card and are issued by specialist money changing companies, such as **Travelex** and **Caxton FX**, as well as the **Post Office**. You can top up and check your balance by phone, online and sometimes by text.

Opening hours

Banks Mon-Fri 0830-1530, Sat 0830-1130; bureaux de change in the airports and shopping malls are open longer hours 7 days a week. **Post offices** Mon-Fri 0830-1600, Sat 0800-1200. **Shops** Mon-Fri 0830-1700, Sat 0830-1300, Sun 0900-1300. Larger branches of the supermarkets stay open until late in the evening. Large shopping malls in the cities may stay open until 2100.

Safety

The most common crimes facing tourists are pickpocketing, purse-snatching and thefts from vehicles, and, on occasion, carjacking. Guns are prevalent and you should be aware that your assailant may well be armed and any form of resistance could be fatal. South Africa has had more than its fair share of well-publicized crime problems. But despite the statistics, much of the serious, violent crime is gang-based and occurs in areas that tourists are unlikely to visit (the inner-city ghettos of Hillbrow or Yoeville in Johannesburg for example). The crime rate in the districts where most of the hotels, restaurants and shops are located has dropped significantly in recent years, due mainly to an increase in security measures; you should experience few problems in these areas.

Nevertheless, listen to advice from locals about which areas to avoid, and the general common sense rules apply to prevent petty theft: don't exhibit anything valuable and keep wallets and purses out of sight, and avoid deserted areas and always take a taxi after dark. If you're driving, plan your route beforehand, avoid driving after dark, always keep car doors locked and windows wound up, and it's a good idea to bring (or hire) a mobile phone; useful in any case if you break down.

Telephone

→ *Country code: +27; international direct dialling code 00; directory enquires T1023; international enquires T1025.*
You must dial the full 3-digit regional code for every number in South Africa, even when you are calling from within that region.

The telephone service is very efficient. Card and coin phones are widespread and work well. Cards are available in supermarkets. Note that hotels usually double the rates and even a short international call can become very expensive.

Mobile phones
Overseas visitors should be able to use their mobiles on international

roaming. Alternatively, you can buy a local SIM card and start-up pack from any of the phone shops and at the 3 international airports, which also offer phone and SIM hire.

Time

South Africa has only 1 time zone: GMT +2 hrs (+1 during UK Summer Time Mar-Oct), 8 hrs ahead of USA Eastern Standard Time, 1 hr ahead of Europe; 8 hrs behind Australian Eastern Standard Time. There is no daylight saving.

Tipping

Waiters, hotel porters, stewards, chambermaids and tour guides should be tipped 10-15%, according to the service. It is common practice to tip petrol pump attendants, depending on their service – around R5 for a fill up, oil and water check and comprehensive windscreen clean. It is also customary to tip car guards R2-5 if parking on the street. On safari you are expected to tip guides.

Tourist information

South African Tourism (SATOUR), T011-895 3000, www.southafrica.net, has a very useful website with information on special interest travel, maps, latest travel news, airlines, accommodation and national parks. The website is published in 15 languages and each version provides specific information for people coming from each individual country. SATOUR also has offices around the world, which are useful for pre-travel information. Regional and local tourism authorities are some of the best sources of information once in the country; even the smallest town will have a tourist office with details of local sights and accommodation. Local tourist offices are listed under individual towns.

Visas and immigration

Most nationalities, including EU nationals and citizens from the USA, Canada, Australia and New Zealand, don't need visas to enter South Africa. On arrival, visitors from these countries are granted temporary **visitors' permits**, lasting up to 90 days. You must have a valid return ticket or voucher for onward travel and at least 1 completely empty page in your passport to get a permit; without these you maybe denied entry.

It is possible to apply for an extension to the permit at one of the offices of the **Department of Home Affairs**, Johannesburg, T011-836 3228; Pretoria, T012-395 4307, www.home-affairs.gov.za. Citizens of countries other than those listed above should consult the South African embassy or consulate in their country for information on visa requirements.

Weights and measures

The metric system is used in South Africa.

Contents

Johannesburg

Johannesburg, Joburg or Jozi is the largest financial, commercial and industrial centre in South Africa. With an estimated population of around four million spread over some 600 suburbs covering approximately 1600 sq km, the greater Johannesburg metropolitan area is the most densely populated region of the country and is considered Africa's fourth largest urban agglomeration. It began life in 1886 when the discovery of gold transformed this deserted heartland into one of the wealthiest cities in the world. The gold rush brought in settlers from far and wide creating a multiracial and cosmopolitan city, but Apartheid changed all that when forced relocations altered the fabric of Johannesburg, creating deep divisions in society.

But since the demise of Aparthied things have changed considerably. Soweto, once a vast, sprawling township of government housing and informal settlements, is now a city in its own right, with affluent suburbs, a fast-growing middle class and an excellent infrastructure. Meanwhile the notorious city centre, a condensed and impoverished area largely home to the urban black population, is undergoing extensive regeneration programmes drawing back a mixed community to live, work and play and once-high crime rates have dropped significantly.

For both residents and visitors alike, Johannesburg has an ever-increasing choice of attractions and entertainment. Places of interest include the many museums dedicated to old Johannesburg and the city's gold-mining past as well as the Apartheid struggle, and architecture ranges from the CBD's art deco buildings and tangle of skyscrapers to Sir Herbert Baker-designed mansions dotted around the city. The city also finds time to breathe and relax in the many beautiful open spaces and parks, which are very popular at the weekend, while the glitzy shopping malls, lively restaurant districts and sophisticated theatres and galleries add further dimensions to this vibrant city.

Arriving in Johannesburg → *Phone code: 011.*

Getting there

Johannesburg's **OR Tambo International Airport (JNB)** ① *Kempton Park, T011-921 6262, flight information T0867-277888, or check the Airports Company of South Africa (ACSA) website, www.acsa.co.za,* is 24 km from the city centre and 35 km from the northern suburbs on the R24, roughly halfway between Johannesburg and Pretoria. Outside rush hour, both city centres can be reached by car in around 45 minutes. Formerly Johannesburg International Airport, it was renamed in 2006 to honour late anti-Apartheid activist and former president of the ANC, Oliver Reginald Tambo. Today it handles more than 20 million passengers each year and is Africa's busiest airport, the third busiest in the Africa-Middle East region after Dubai and Doha, and the most important hub for air travel in the southern hemisphere. Note that sadly there has been an ongoing and unresolved problem with tampering by baggage handlers – make sure your bags and luggage are locked (or wrapped in plastic) and do not place valuables in unlocked, zipped side compartments.

The airport has a full range of facilities, and domestic and international arrivals and departures are linked by one long terminal. **Master Currency**, and **Bidvest** branches are open to meet all arriving flights and there are banks and ATMs throughout the airport. You can hire mobile phones and buy local SIM cards and top-up cards at **Vodacom** ① *www.vodacom.co.za,* or **MTN** ① *www.mtnsp.co.za,* open 0500-2400. Wi-Fi is available in all public areas and there are internet cafés in all terminals. In international arrivals, there is a post office, and a branch of **Postnet** on the shopping level of the domestic terminal. Porters with trolleys are available who wear ACSA permits and bright orange uniforms; a tip of R5 per bag is recommended. Opposite international arrivals is the **Parkade Centre**, a multi-storey car park and site of all car hire offices (see Transport, page 85). Picking up a car here is very straight forward, but the spaghetti-like freeway interchanges from the airport can be confusing. For those returning cars, there is an Engen petrol station on the way into the car rental drop-off zone but follow signs carefully so as not to miss the turnoff.

Behind the Parkade Centre is the bus and coach terminal. All the hotels located near the airport (see page 66) offer a free pickup (at quieter times of the day you may need to phone the hotel to tell them you are waiting). This is also the departure point for the shuttle bus companies that provide transfers to and from the major hotels in Johannesburg and Pretoria. They charge around R460 per person plus R50 for each additional person from the same group. Inside the Parkade Centre is a kiosk for **Magic Bus** ① *T011-394 6902, www.magicbus.co.za,* or you can pre-book a shuttle either though your hotel or directly with **Airport Link** ① *T011-794 8300, www.airportlink.co.za,* and **Airport Shuttle** ① *T012-348 8040, www.airportshuttle.co.za.* Metered taxis can be found outside the main terminal building but tend to be more expensive than the shuttle services and drivers often do not know the way without direction to the lesser-known hotels or guesthouses. Be sure to use an approved **ACSA** taxi with a logo on it and ignore the touts.

The station for the **Gautrain** ⓘ *call centre T0800-428 87246, www.gautrain. co.za*, is on the upper level between international and domestic arrivals. This is Gauteng's rapid rail network, and there is a line from the airport to Sandton, from where you can change to catch other trains to Johannesburg or Pretoria. Travel time to Sandton is around 25 minutes (see box, page 29).

Gauteng's second airport, **Lanseria International Airport** ⓘ *Randburg North, T011-367 0300, www.lanseriaairport-international.co.za*, is off the R512 from Randburg in Johannesburg's northern suburbs or the N14 from Pretoria, 40 km from Johannesburg's CBD, 45 km from Pretoria and roughly 65 km northwest of OR Tambo. Although fewer airlines fly to Lanseria than OR Tambo, it is closer to Sandton (a 20-minute drive), the Midrand region of Johannesburg and Pretoria. It is presently used by British Airways (operated by their subsidiary Comair), **Kulula**, **Mango and South African Airways (SAA)** on some of their daily flights between Johannesburg and Cape Town and Durban, as well as charter and executive jet services. The terminal building has shops and restaurants, free Wi-Fi, and outside there are a number of kiosks for the car hire companies. Taxis meet flights, and shuttle bus services can be pre-booked through the same companies as OR Tambo (see above), or through your hotel.

Johannesburg Park Station in the centre of the CBD bordered by Rissik, Wolmarans, Wanderers and Noord streets is a large integrated transport terminal and is where the railway station is for long-distance trains, the Gautrain and local Metrorail services; it is also the terminus for the mainline long-distance bus companies **Greyhound**, **Intercape** and **Translux** as well as local buses such as **Rea Vaya**. It has recently been revamped and there are plenty of cafés, ATMs and free Wi-Fi. Nevertheless it s a massive complex that is always thronging with people, so ensure you keep an eye on possessions at all times. ▸ *See Transport, page 82.*

Getting around

Although Johannesburg's public transport infrastructure has been greatly improved in recent years, and there are now a few options to get around efficiently and cost effectively, the city is a sprawling conurbation and the lack of direct and convenient public transport between the more spread-out sights can still be an obstacle for visitors. The best options to get to these places are guided day tours, hire cars and metered taxis. If you do hire a car, plan your route before setting out and always carry a map – the system of one-way streets and snaking highways can be utterly bewildering.

The Gautrain

The Gautrain, T0800-428 87246, www.gautrain.co.za, is an 80-km high-speed railway network linking Johannesburg with Pretoria with a branch line from Sandton to OR Tambo International Airport. It was built to relieve the chronic commuter traffic on the M1 and the N1 (which in the mornings and late afternoons resemble car parks), and was fully operational by 2012. From Park Station in Johannesburg's CBD, it goes north to Rosebank, Sandton (where it interchanges with the airport line), Marlboro, Midrand, Centurion, Pretoria CBD and Hatfield. The airport branch goes between Sandton Marlboro, Rhodesfield and OR Tambo International Airport. The trains can travel up to 160 kph and, while part of the lines in the built-up areas are underground (Park, Rosebank and Sandton stations are underground), many of the tracks are above ground including the section in Midrand which goes over an impressively long viaduct.

Trains run Monday-Friday 0530-0830 and 1600-1900 every 12 minutes; 0830-1600 and 1900-2030 every 20 minutes; Saturday and Sunday 0530-2030 every 30 minutes. It takes 15 minutes between Sandton and the airport, and it takes 40 minutes between Johannesburg's Park Station in the CBD and Pretoria. A **Gautrain Gold Card** can be bought at the stations by cash, credit or debit card and a one-off R13 registration fee is applicable. They can be loaded with a single or multiple journeys, and can be reloaded at anytime. Note: you must have at least R20 loaded on to the card to enter any gate. Children under three travel free. A short fare between two stations – Sandton and Rosebank or Hatfield and Pretoria, for example – costs R25, rising to R68 for journeys from one end of the line to the other. The fare between the airport and Sandton is R135; the additional extra fare to your final destination is calculated from Sandton.

There are also several 'feeder' buses from the Gautrain stations (for which you also use a Gold Card). If you use the Gautrain within an hour of using the bus, the fare is R6, otherwise it costs R20. Bus timetables match the train timetable and there are route maps and timetables at all Gautrain stations and bus stops as well as on the website. Useful Gautrain feeder bus routes for visitors in Johannesburg include: Park Station–CBD (north to Parktown); Park Station–CBD (south to Marshall and Anderson streets; Rosebank–Zoo Lake; Rosebank–Melrose Arch; Sandton–Montecasino; and Sandton–Rivonia, and in Pretoria: and Pretoria–CBD and Pretoria–Zoo (National Zoological Gardens of South Africa). All trains, stations and buses are wheelchair-accessible.

While improved security has recently attracted people back to Johannesburg's CBD and its neighbouring suburbs to live and work, for visitors, it's still sensible to take common sense precautions in terms of safety. While most of the sights in the CBD can now be explored on foot, remember that it is still a bustling, congested place and street crime may occur. Consider seeing the sights on a guided tour, which often includes a little of Johannesburg's chequered history (see page 82 for tour operators), or make use of the excellent new bus services by **City Sightseeing** and **Rea Vaya** (see box, page 84).

Orientation

Johannesburg is roughly ringed by a network of highways – the N1 loops around the western and northern sides and goes to both Pretoria and Cape Town; the N12 loops through the southern perimeters on its way between Nelspruit in the east and Kimberley in the west; while the N3 heads south from the eastern side of Johannesburg to the coast and Durban. Within this boundary are the 'M' roads; significantly the M1 that runs like a spine from the most northerly of the northern suburbs to south of the central business district (CBD).

The CBD is the oldest part of the city and now a hectic muddle of office blocks, congested streets and concrete flyovers. For many years it suffered considerable urban decay and associated high crime rates when a lot of businesses moved out to the safer northern suburbs, although recent regeneration projects are starting to draw back investment. A visit to the city centre is well worthwhile for an insight into how Johannesburg has developed over the decades. Johannesburg's affluent northern suburbs are clustered around the M1 in the hills to the north of the CBD. Of these, Sandton is effectively a city centre in its own right, with its own clutch of gleaming skyscrapers and is home to most of the city's tourist accommodation, restaurants and shopping malls.

The largest of Johannesburg's suburbs feels very different. The infamous former township of **Soweto** lies southwest of the city, named because of its location – South West Township. Soweto is linked to the city by a number of freeways that carry hundreds of thousands of commuters to the city centre and northern suburbs each day.

Tourist information

Gauteng Tourism ① *11th floor, 124 Main St, opposite the Carlton Centre, CBD, T011-085 2500, www.gauteng.net, Mon-Fri 0800-1700*, is responsible for information for the whole province. This is the head office in the CBD that also has a small selection of maps and brochures to pick up if you drop in, but the better place to collect information is their office at **OR Tambo International Airport** ① *T011-390 3614, daily 0600-2200*. **Joburg Tourism** ① *Grosvenor Corner, 195 Jan Smuts Av, Parktown, T011-214 0700, www.joburgtourism.co.za, Mon-Fri 0800-1700, Sat 0900-1300*, has limited information to pick up but an excellent website, while the **City Council** ⓘ *www.joburg.org.za*, also has tourist information on its comprehensive website, which covers every aspect of the city.

① Greater Johannesburg

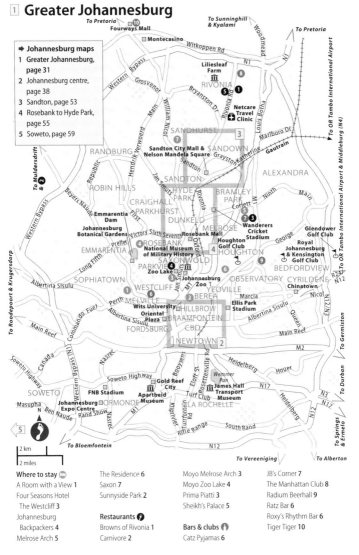

→ Johannesburg maps
1 Greater Johannesburg, page 31
2 Johannesburg centre, page 38
3 Sandton, page 53
4 Rosebank to Hyde Park, page 55
5 Soweto, page 59

Where to stay
A Room with a View 1
Four Seasons Hotel The Westcliff 3
Johannesburg Backpackers 4
Melrose Arch 5

The Residence 6
Saxon 7
Sunnyside Park 2

Restaurants
Browns of Rivonia 1
Carnivore 2

Moyo Melrose Arch 3
Moyo Zoo Lake 4
Prima Piatti 3
Sheikh's Palace 5

Bars & clubs
Catz Pyjamas 6

JB's Corner 7
The Manhattan Club 8
Radium Beerhall 9
Ratz Bar 6
Roxy's Rhythm Bar 6
Tiger Tiger 10

Background

The city of gold

The high plateau on which Johannesburg was built is known as the Witwatersrand; a 56-km-long scarp consisting of a hard, erosion-resistant quartzite sedimentary rock. Several north-flowing rivers form waterfalls, and Witwatersrand means the 'ridge of white waters' in Afrikaans. It was originally an arid place inhabited by a few Boer farmers grazing cattle and cultivating maize and wheat, but this harsh and isolated landscape was transformed after the discovery of gold in the 1880s. The credit for the discovery of the main gold reef on the Witwatersrand is attributed to George Harrison, whose findings on the farm Langlaagte were made in July 1886, either through accident or systematic prospecting. He travelled to Pretoria to register his claim, and within weeks hordes of prospectors and fortune hunters began to arrive and open-cast workings were being opened up along the full length of the main reef. The first miners' tents sprang up at Ferreira's Camp (now Ferreirasdorp), but by November 1886, officials of the Pretoria government had been sent to inspect the diggings and to lay out plans for a town. Johannesburg was named after two men; Johannes Meyer and Johannes Rissik, who both worked for the government in land surveying and mapping.

The gold rush attracted people from all over the world and capital poured into the new settlement. Johannesburg expanded at a phenomenal rate and within three years had become the largest town in the Transvaal; bigger even than Pretoria, the capital. Gambling dens, brothels and riotous canteens lined the streets and hundreds of ox-drawn wagons arrived daily to deliver food, drink and building supplies. By the end of the 19th century, the railways, electricity and telephones had all arrived. Confidence in Johannesburg's future was so great that traders in other regions of South Africa dismantled their wood and corrugated-iron buildings and transported them to reassemble them in the new boom town. One was the Star newspaper, which relocated to Johannesburg from Grahamstown and transported its printing press across the veld by ox wagon. Before long it became necessary to dig a lot deeper to reach the gold, even as much as a kilometre beneath the ground. New technologies had sunk deeper shafts by 1897 and Johannesburg quickly transformed from being a gold rush boom town to a large modern industrial city.

The northern suburbs

Meanwhile, the town's swirling dust storms and the interminable pounding of its stamp mills drove the more fastidious to move out, and the first residential suburbs to be developed were Doornfontein (1887), Bellevue (1889) and Yeoville (1891). The first definitive moves north over the Witwatersrand ridge were made in 1892 when H Eckstein & Co purchased some land beyond

Braamfontein for the purpose of establishing a plantation to supply timber to the mines. Local folklore has it that Florence Phillips, wife of Sir Lionel, who was a director of the company, went out riding in the area one day and discovered it to have sweeping views reaching to the Magaliesberg Mountains. She was so taken with the site that she persuaded her husband to build their home there and other families soon followed suit. The suburb was named Parktown in 1893, and become the preferred residence of Johannesburg's wealthier entrepreneurial, financial and upper management classes. The establishment of other 'northern suburbs' soon followed, including Auckland Park and Berea (1893), Rosebank (1894), Oaklands (1896) and Craighall (1902). By 1910, most of Johannesburg's northern suburbs had been proclaimed all the way to today's Illovo, and by the 1930s they had developed a distinct suburban character.

Migrant labour

In order to be profitable, the mines needed an ongoing supply of cheap labour. But most Africans were not willing to leave their fields to work underground, so the government and the mine owners worked together to guarantee the mines an ongoing supply of cheap labour by introducing systems of migrant labour. In rural areas 'hut' and 'poll' taxes were introduced forcing farmers to come into the towns to earn money to pay these taxes. They would go to the mines for specific lengths of time as short as three months or as long as two years while their wives and children stayed at home keeping the farms going. By 1895 almost 100,000 people lived in Johannesburg, of which more than 75,000 were African migrant workers. Over time, as gold flowed into the world's coffers and many more thousands flocked to Johannesburg to work, in a move to control a massive African labour force among an increasingly smaller white minority, the Natives (Urban Areas) Act was introduced in 1923. It deemed all black African men in urban areas to carry around permits called 'passes' at all times, and anyone found without a pass would be arrested immediately. Adding to this inequality, the wages of African miners and other industrial workers were kept pitifully low to ensure larger profits for the mine owners; by 1939 African workers earned about one-eighth of wages paid to whites.

The introduction of Apartheid

The National Party came to power in 1948 and began to implement a program of Apartheid ('being apart') – the legal system of political and social separation of the races – a policy intended to maintain and extend political and economic control of South Africa by the white minority. The first grand laws tightening any previous segregation regulations were the Prohibition of Mixed Marriages Act (1949), which prohibited marriage between persons of different races, and the Population Registration Act (1950), which formalized racial classification in 'pass books'. Then the thriving multiracial conurbation of Johannesburg was changed dramatically with the advent of the Group Areas Act (1950), which forcibly relocated the city's black population from the centre to specially built townships such as Soweto. Segregation of all amenities – such as transport, healthcare and education – was tightened and there became no areas of African life where the state did not intervene.

African opposition

The first significant opposition to racist policies was back in 1912 when a number of African political groups gathered at a meeting in Bloemfontein. This lead to the establishment of the South African Native National Congress, later renamed the African National Congress (ANC). Over the next few decades, however, despite the formation of a national opposition organization, African protest tended to be extremely moderate. But from the Second World War, there was opposition intensified as younger more militant leaders came to the forefront, including Nelson Mandela who had joined the ANC's Youth League in the 1940s. In 1952 the ANC launched the Defiance Campaign, a peaceful resistance to the new Apartheid legislations; in alliance with Indians, coloureds and a few radical whites, they took the lead in deliberately breaking racist laws and offering themselves up for arrest. These peaceful protests were often met with violence from the police and many ANC members were harshly treated after arrest.

In Johannesburg's Kliptown in 1955, the ANC adopted the Freedom Charter calling for 'rights for all' (see page 62), which later was the foundation of South Africa's 1996 post-Apartheid constitution. In response to this growing protest, the government put 156 ANC leaders on trial for treason, which lasted from 1956 to 1960, eventually resulting in their acquittal. But by the time the trial was over it had also been overtaken by other events. There was a massive anti-pass law campaign in 1960, and the idea was for people to leave their pass books at home and present themselves for arrest at the nearest police station. The belief was that the prison system would be swamped and the pass laws would have to be revoked. But on the morning of 21 March at Johannesburg's Shrapeville police station, protesters were attacked by police who suddenly opened fire on the crowd with machine guns – most of the 69 dead and 180 wounded were shot in the back as they fled. The Sharpville Massacre marked a turning point in the struggle against Apartheid, and around the country blacks rioted and went on strike. In response, the government cut off township food supplies to force people back to work, political parties (including the ANC) were banned, and police arrested thousands of activists from across the country and imprisoned them without charge.

The struggle

At the beginning of June 1961, and in response to the Sharpville Massacre, Mandela and other leaders of the ANC (by now in hiding or in exile) organized an armed wing named Umkhonto we Sizwe ('Spear of the Nation'). Later in his famous 1964 Rivonia Trial "it is an ideal for which I am prepared to die" speech, Mandela said: "I, and some colleagues, came to the conclusion that as violence in this country was inevitable, it would be unrealistic and wrong for African leaders to continue preaching peace and non-violence at a time when the government met our peaceful demands with force". During an 18-month period from December 1961 Umkhonto we Sizwe carried out a total of 200 sabotage attacks on post offices, government buildings, electricity sub-stations and railway lines, and although it was never their intention to harm anyone, there were causalities among both themselves and the police. The organization was effectively neutralized by police in July 1963 when its headquarters at Liliesleaf Farm in Rivonia (see page 57) was raided and the majority of its leadership, including Walter Sisulu and Govan Mbeki, was arrested. This was followed by the Rivonia Trial, in which 10 leaders of the ANC were tried for 221 acts of sabotage and sentenced to life imprisonment, including Mandela who had been arrested a few months before the Lilliesleaf Farm raid.

With organized opposition smashed for a time, the government set about fully implementing its Apartheid policies throughout the 1960s and 1970s. But the period was blighted by more strikes and an increasingly more vocal African student protest movement. The immediate issue for them was the new rules enforcing Afrikaans as the language used in schools. On the 16 June 1976 a Soweto school pupils' committee organized a peaceful mass march to deliver their complaints to the local authorities, but it ended in tragedy when the police opened fire and killed more than 170 students. The Soweto Uprising, as it became known, marked another important turning point; from 16 June 1976 onwards there was constant and violent unrest across South Africa. The ANC benefited greatly from this new generation of activists and again it was the spearhead of the anti-Apartheid struggle.

By the end of 1980s the South African government had more or less lost control of the townships and international sanctions were hitting the economy hard. These changes coincided with a change in leadership of the National Party and the replacement of PW Botha with FW de Klerk, who soon made it clear he was embarking on a bold new policy of reform. Mandela and others were released in 1990 and the process of negotiating a settlement got underway. South Africa's first democratic elections were held in 1994 and were overwhelmingly won by the ANC, with its leader, Mandela, duly elected president. A constitution with equality for all was passed by the Constitutional Assembly in 1996.

Urban decay and rejuvenation

Pass laws were banished in 1986, meaning the forced movement of Africans from the city centres to the townships was reversed. In Johannesburg this led to the rapid growth of the African population in the CBD and neighbouring suburbs in what were once white-only enclaves. The swelling population was also bolstered by the arrival of new immigrants as tens of thousands of Nigerians, Congolese, Zimbabweans and others flooded, often illegally, into South Africa in a period when the immigration and policing laws were yet to be consolidated under the transition of governments. This change in demographics in the CBD made it like any other burgeoning African city with a clamouring street life, but not without a new set of problems. In the 1990s the inner city suffered from much-documented urban decay and soaring crime rates, and it became an untidy and lawless place that was often dubbed the most dangerous city in the world. Consequently it witnessed a mass migration of businesses and offices (or 'capital flight') as they moved out to the northern suburbs. Most of the high-rise buildings in the CBD were abandoned, and after vandalism and theft, many became derelict and teetering on the edge of collapse. Other former office blocks were hijacked by slum landlords for use as informal housing; more often than not without basic services such as electricity, water or refuse removal where people lived in abject poverty.

But since then much has been done to reverse the trend. Massive raids on apartment blocks in Hillbrow have ousted thousands of illegal immigrants, an extensive network of CCTV cameras has been installed on every street corner, a Metro police force was established, and numerous regeneration projects have made the city centre far more attractive and considerably safer. The first of these regenerated areas was Newtown (see page 37), where from 2000 the streets were pedestrianized and Mary Fitzgerald Square upgraded and the area is now filled with restaurants and shops. This acted as a model for other parts of town, and there have been many more City Improvement Districts (CIDs) that have in turn attracted businesses back to the CBD. The benefit for residents and visitors alike is that many of these projects have not only rejuvenated areas in terms of visual enhancement and improving infrastructure, but much has been done to incorporate elements to celebrate and commemorate the history of Johannesburg – from the gold mining days to the struggle against Apartheid. A walk around the centre of Johannesburg would have been highly ill-advised just a few years ago, but today there are some wonderfully and innovatively designed sites and attractions.

Places in Johannesburg

Newtown → *For listings, see pages 66-86.*

ⓘ *www.newtown.co.za.*
Located to the west of the Central Business District (CBD), Newtown was one of Johannesburg's first City Improvement Districts (CIDs) and has been extensively and imaginatively rejuvenated from the early 2000s. It is roughly bordered by the elevated M1 highway and Quinn Street to the west, the marshalling yards and railway lines that lead into Park Station to the north, Ntemi Piliso Street in the east and President Street in the south. The Johannesburg Central Police Station visually forms the border between Newtown and Ferreirasdorp in the south (where the first gold prospectors camped), while Diagonal Street (see page 43) in the east has historically marked the border between Newtown and the original mining town (now the CBD).

Arriving in Newtown
The best way to approach Newtown by car is from Braamfontein in the north by the impressive Nelson Mandela Bridge. This 284-m steel-cable bridge with its distinctive white columns spans over 40 railway lines, and was opened in 2003 by Mandela as part of his 85th birthday celebrations. To get to Braamfontein from the northern suburbs, take the Jan Smuts turnoff from the M1 and then go along Jan Smuts Avenue, which then turns into Bertha Street, to the bridge. Once in Newtown there is a multi-storey car park on the southern side of Mary Fitzgerald Square, and more parking at the Market Theatre Complex. You'll also go over the bridge to and from Newtown as a part of many Johannesburg tours as well as on the City Sightseeing bus (see page 84).

Background
Newtown originally started out as a racially mixed working-class district where bricks were manufactured. In the late 1890s, the brickworks were removed to make way for the first railway marshalling yard in Johannesburg. Working-class people of all races continued to live in the area up until 1906 when the Johannesburg City Council forcibly removed the African and Indian residents. They were relocated to a camp south of Johannesburg near the sewerage works called Klipspruit, which was the first section of the township that was to become known as Soweto. This was the first forced removal to take place in Gauteng. From then until the 1960s, Newtown experienced a boom as a hub of commercial trade and industrial activities. It was the city's main gateway for goods and fresh produce, and three power stations, tram and

bus workshops, railway compounds and a major milling site were established. The Johannesburg Fresh Produce Market relocated from a few streets west in the congested city centre to Newtown in 1913 (the building now houses Museum Africa and the Market Theatre – see below), and in the early days, the municipality provided free tram rides for the city's housewives from the old to the new markets and a brass band entertained them on arrival.

However from the 1960s Newtown began its steady decline as expanding commercial activity moved out to larger premises in the suburbs. During the

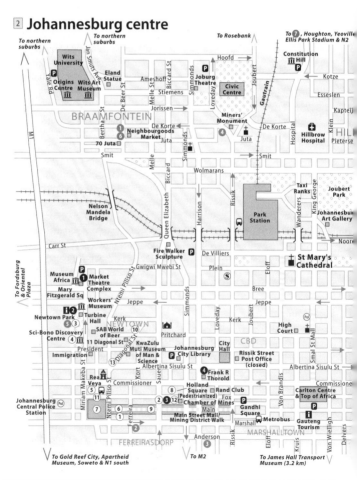

2 **Johannesburg centre**

1990s many key sites and buildings such as Turbine Hall (see below) were invaded by the homeless, while open areas next to the railway lines saw the rapid rise of informal settlements. Crime and grime became a problem in Newtown until 1997 when it was zoned as a CID and work began to rejuvenate the area.

Mary Fitzgerald Square

Today Newtown is dominated by Mary Fitzgerald Square, which was completely overhauled and reopened in 2000 and is hemmed in by Bree and Jeppe streets. It is a smart, landscaped, 11,000-sq-m piazza-style square lined with shops and cafés and a number of attractions. First known as Market Square, it was renamed in 1939 after Irish-born Mary Fitzgerald; the first female trade unionist in South Africa and the first woman to become a member of Johannesburg's city council in 1921. She was also a champion for women's rights, which led to the achievement of the women's right to vote in 1930. In 1911, Johannesburg saw its first major strike by white tram workers, and Mary Fitzgerald famously led a group of women to lie on the tram tracks and stop the trams. While she spoke at a protest meeting she held a pickhandle that had been dropped by mounted police to break up the strike. This became her trademark, and she is still referred to as 'Pickhandle Mary'. Since then numerous political and labour meetings have been held in the square, and today the space can accommodate up to 30,000 people for other special events including live music concerts and it was the principal fanpark during the 2010 FIFA World Cup™.

Market Theatre and Museum Africa

On the north side of the square along Bree Street is the block-long

➡ Johannesburg maps
1 Greater Johannesburg, page 31
2 **Johannesburg centre, page 38**
3 Sandton, page 53
4 Rosebank to Hyde Park, page 55
5 Soweto, page 59

N
200 metres
200 yards

Where to stay
Bannister **1**
Mapungubwe **2**
Reef **3**
Protea Parktonian All Suite **4**

Restaurants
City Perk Café **3**
Gramadoelas **1**
Guildhall Pub **4**
Sophiatown Bar Lounge **2**

Bars & clubs
Bassline **5**
Kitcheners **6**
Radium Beerhall **7**

Newtown sights ○
Anglo American Building **1**
BHP Billiton Headquarters **2**
Brenda Fassie Statue **3**
Bus Factory **4**
Chancellor House **5**
Impala Stampede Sculpture **6**
Johannesburg
  Magistrate's Court **7**
Mapungubwe Rhino Statue **8**
Mining Headgear Structure **9**
Old Johannesburg
  Stock Exchange **10**
Shadow Boxer Statue **11**
Stamp Mill **12**
Walter & Albertina Sisulu Statue **13**

BROW
Twist
Quartz
Kerk
Pritchard
President
Main St
Troye
Polly

Old Market Building, which was built in 1913, and now houses both Museum Africa (see below), and the **Market Theatre** complex. The Market Theatre is one of the best and most established in Gauteng (see also page 77), and was often known as South Africa's 'Theatre of the Struggle' as it was established by a troupe of dedicated anti-Apartheid actors in June 1976; coincidentally the same week that the Soweto Uprising began (see page 35). It was one of the only venues where blacks and whites performed on stage together for non-racial audiences, and today it remains at the forefront of South African theatre, showcasing local work. The complex also has a couple of popular restaurants and bars and stalls strung along the street selling African crafts.

Occupying most of the Old Market Building, **Museum Africa** ① *121 Bree St, T011-833 5624, Tue-Sun 0900-1700, free, café and shop*, is one of the city's major museums, and attempts to explain the black experience of living in Johannesburg. There are displays on the struggle for democracy and on life in the goldmines and the townships, with mock-ups of both a mine tunnel and an informal settlement. On the second floor is a gallery dedicated to San rock art and a gallery is called 'Tried for Treason', with some interesting original editions of newspapers dating from treason trials in the 1960s, although the displays pale in comparison next to those of the Apartheid Museum (see page 52).

Newtown Park and around

On the southern side of Mary Fitzgerald Square across Jeppe Street is the small but attractive **Newtown Park**, which is flanked by a number of interesting buildings; most of which have now been fully restored after many years of neglect. Possibly the most imposing and one of the finest examples of Johannesburg's industrial architecture is the enormous **Turbine Hall**, on the corner of Jeppe and Miriam Makeba streets. The original building was the coal-fired Jeppe Street Power Station, which was built in 1927 and extended in 1934 to keep pace with Johannesburg's growing electricity demand. It was the third of Newtown's power stations, but was decommissioned in the mid-1980s (when the Orlando Power Station in Soweto was built) after which it became derelict before being restored in 2005. Today it's a conference and event venue and headquarters for one of the mining companies.

At the north of the park is the **Workers' Museum** ① *52 Bree St, T011-833 5624, Tue-Sun 0900-1700, free*, which focuses on the hardships faced by migrant workers from the early 1900s to the 1970s. This U-shaped single-storey building was the Newtown Compound, which was built in 1913 to accommodate about 300 black electrical workers for the power station that is now the SAB World of Beer (see below). The men who lived here were recruited from the rural areas to work in the towns in the likes of power stations, mines and factories. Each night they returned to their dormitories where they slept side-by-side in concrete bunks. The compound manager exercised total control over their lives; there was no privacy, residents were not allowed visitors and no talking was permitted after 2200, and punishments included having buckets of ice water thrown at them. The north side of the compound is a row of houses that was built for the managers and skilled white workers with tiny quarters in the yards for black domestic workers. This sharp contrast between the living conditions for white and black workers demonstrates the racial segregation that characterized Apartheid.

Just south of the Workers' Museum is perhaps the most popular attraction in the park, **Bassline**, Johannesburg's premier venue for live jazz (see page 75). Even if not visiting the club, outside is a lovely statue of soulful barefooted legendary singer Brenda Fassie leaning into a microphone. You can sit on the seat next to her for a photo.

At the southern end of the park on the corner of Miriam Makeba and President streets is the **Sci-Bono Discovery Centre** ① *T011-839 8400, www. sci-bono.co.za, Mon-Fri 0900-1700, Sat-Sun 0930-1630 R35, children (3-16) R20, under 3s free*. This science and technology centre is housed in a building that was initially the First President Street Power Station, commissioned in 1906 to power the then new electric tram system. It was the shortest-lived of the three power stations built in Newtown owing to an explosion in the boiler house a few months later in 1907. The Second President Street Power Station was hurriedly opened on the site that is now the SAB World of Beer (below). The name comes from an abbreviation of 'Science' and 'Bono', the tshiVenda word for 'vision', and is a popular attraction for school groups and as such children will especially enjoy it. There are numerous interactive exhibits including a fully operational construction site with a 'site office' for children to get kitted out with hard hats before building walls of foam bricks, steel and cement, while Eskom (the South African electricity provider) has sponsored a display where they can play with circuits and currents. Even grownup children will enjoy the vast Lego pits and pressing the buttons to make the life-size dinosaurs move and roar.

To the west is another interesting building, the **Bus Factory**. The first electric buses were introduced to Johannesburg in 1931 and this vast industrial structure was built as a depot and repair workshop. When the Apartheid government passed the Separate Amenities Act in 1953, buses became racially segregated. Those that carried black people did not stop within the CBD as the government had designated it as a 'whites-only' area, and instead the bus stops for black passengers were located in Newtown. Later, the Bus Factory became a garage for double decker diesel buses when they replaced electric buses in the 1970s, which operated until the early 1990s. Today it's home to the offices of the Johannesburg Development Agency (JDA; www.jda.org.za), which has been responsible for many of the inner-city rejuvenation projects since its establishment in 2001.

On the eastern side of Newtown Park, the **SAB (South African Breweries') World of Beer** ① *15 President St, T011-836 4900, www.worldofbeer.co.za,*

Tue-Sat 1000-1800, R75, children (under 17) R20, including 1 complimentary beers (except for under 18s) and bar snacks, beer tasting available 1100-1500, will appeal to anyone who enjoys the golden nectar. SAB dominate the African beer industry and control many local breweries throughout southern and eastern Africa and now own Miller Lite in the US. Their flagship lager, Castle, was first brewed in Johannesburg in 1888 for thirsty miners and is probably now the most popular beer between Cape Town and Cairo. Exhibits cover the history of beer and the brewing process, and there's a greenhouse that nurtures ingredients, and a variety of mock-up bars from a township *shebeen* to a honky-tonk pub from Johannesburg's mining camps.

Central Business District (CBD)

ⓘ *www.joburg.org.za*

The CBD has one of the densest crops of skyscrapers in Africa, which are clearly visible from whatever approach you take to the city. Topping them all at 223-m-high is the Carlton Centre (see page 48), which, while construction of this tower was a lengthy process beginning in 1967 and ending in 1974, is still today Africa's tallest building. By contrast, Anderson Street is the southernmost street in the CBD that has any high-rise development. To the south of here, development is exclusively low rise, and the break between the two is dramatic and easily visible from both the M1 and M2 highways as you drive past the CBD. There is a very good reason for this: further south of Anderson Street are the historical underground mine workings that extend too close to the surface to allow the construction of foundations capable of supporting tall buildings. This is one of the very few planning restrictions that have been strictly enforced throughout Johannesburg's history.

Arriving in the CBD

If you drive in, there are two recommended and easily negotiated underground car parks – at the Library Gardens (entrance in Albertina Sisulu Street, just off the corner of Simmonds Street), or Gandhi Square (entrance in Joubert Street, just off the corner of Fox Street). You can also use the multi-storey car park opposite the Carlton Centre on Main Street. Alternatively make use of the excellent bus services by Rea Vaya and City Sightseeing, which both offer circular routes through the CBD (see page 84).

Background

The CBD has been the central area of Johannesburg since its inception on 20 September 1886, when President Paul Kruger declared the area open for public digging. It was the first part of the city to be built in a grid, which was designed by the Pretoria government's town planners around Commissioner Street. There is little evidence of the origin of Commissioner Street's name, although it is known that this street served as the major artery for the original mining town and was created in 1889 by dropping stones from an ox wagon up and down the existing dirt track from Ferreira's Camp to Jeppestown.

Since the capital flight and urban blight of the 1980-1990s, there have been significant moves to revive the area and increase security. Many banks, financial institutions, mining and corporate companies have reestablished or refurbished offices in the CBD, many of the previously neglected buildings are now up-market trendy apartment blocks, giving the city a lively vibe around the clock, and there are plenty of interesting things to see.

Diagonal Street

The first site of interest in the CBD if coming from Newtown is Diagonal Street, which is about 300 m or two blocks east of Mary Fitzgerald Square and runs from President Street in the south diagonally (as the name suggests) to Jeppe Street in the north. It was first established in the mid-1880s by Indian and Chinese settlers who set up businesses here to serve the original mining town. It had already settled on its current name by 1897, supposedly because it was the only street not to be on the rigid east–west north–south street grid system. Today a number of Victorian and Edwardian shops, with their balconies and filigree work remain and sell the likes of fabrics and hardware.

At 14 Diagonal Street, the **KwaZulu Muti Museum of Man and Science** ⓘ *T011-836 4470, Mon-Fri 0730-1700, Sat 0730-1300*, isn't actually a museum but a *muti* shop, which has been on this site since 1897. *Muti* is a form of witchcraft practiced exclusively by witch doctors, and this shop is crammed with products used in traditional herbal medicine and magic. The ingredients on sale include leaves, seeds and bark, as well as more specialized items such as monkey skulls, dried crocodiles and ostrich feet. It's worth poking your nose around, but be warned; the smells in the interior are quite pungent.

One of the more interesting modern buildings on the street is the 20-storey 80-m-high **11 Diagonal Street**. It was built as an office block for the mining corporate Anglo American in 1984 and designed by renowned German-American architect Helmut Jahn. It resembles a multi-faceted diamond, with massive glass sheets placed at varying angles reflecting different images of the CBD. Nearby at 17 Diagonal Street is another high-rise office building that is the **Old Johannesburg Stock Exchange**. It operated from here between 1978 and 2000 when inner city decay and increasing concerns about security caused it to relocate to its current premises in Sandton. Soon after gold was discovered, the first Johannesburg Stock Exchange was established in Donovan's livery stables on the corner of Sauer and Commissioner streets, and then three years later in 1888 it moved to a brick building on the corner of Commissioner and

Simmonds streets that had stained glass windows, tiled bathrooms, a bar, offices and a front porch. Then the trade in shares, land and property was so frantic that it went on late into the night and on Sundays too, and it was said that business overflowed 'between the chains' outside (the ends of Simmonds Street were blocked off by chains to accommodate the traders).

Also on Diagonal Street is an absolutely charming **statue of Walter and Albertina Sisulu**, which sits in a little wedge-shaped piece of ground at the junction of Ntemi Piliso Street and Albertina Sisulu Street (formerly Market Street and renamed after her death in 2011; eight years after her husband). The 2.3-m-high statue was unveiled in 2009 when the entire five blocks of Diagonal Street were also repaved. The figures sit opposite each other holding hands, and are in grey concrete, her dress and his jacket painted a gentle blue, and the sculpture sits at an angle, with Walter facing his old office in Master Mansions, on the corner of Ntemi Piliso and Commissioner streets. Although they don't receive as much publicity as the higher profile Mandelas, it is impossible to overstate the contribution that the Sisulus made to South Africa's liberation struggle. Walter held several influential positions in the ANC (including party secretary, and later, deputy President) and played an important role in determining the military strategy of the ANC's military wing, Umkhonto we Sizwe ('the spear of the nation'). He was one of the Rivonia treason trialists and – like Mandela – was sentenced to life imprisonment on Robben Island. Albertina was universally known as 'Ma Sisulu' as a mark of respect for her kind and motherly nature, and was a political activist in her own right. She was imprisoned many times and holds the dubious distinction of being the first woman imprisoned under the General Laws Amendment Act of 1963, which allowed the Apartheid government to hold prisoners in detention without being charged. There is a naive charm to the statue, which depicts these two titans of the anti-Apartheid struggle as a devoted elderly couple who delighted in each other's company. Around the concrete base of the statue are the words: 'Walter and Albertina Sisulu married in 1944. Through their enduring love and dedication they became parents to the nation'.

Johannesburg Magistrate's Court and around
A block west of the southern end of Diagonal Street where the statue is, it's a short walk of around 200 m down Ntemi Piliso Street, and crossing Commissioner Street to the **Johannesburg Magistrate's Court**. This is a vast building that takes up four blocks between Ntemi Piliso, Miriam Makeba, Marshall and Fox streets. Jan Smuts laid the foundation stone in 1936 in his capacity as Minister of Justice, and the impressive sandstone and granite building punctuated by grand columned entrances was completed in 1941. On the stairway from the Ntemi Piliso Street entrance are two large paintings painted in 1940. One depicts Captain Carl von Brandis, Johannesburg's first magistrate, settling a mine

digger's dispute, while the second, on the opposite wall, is of Voortrekker leader Louis Trichardt sitting in judgment over three boys on a Drakensberg farm in 1887. In its day the court was notorious as a place where as many as 500 blacks a day were tried for misdemeanors like not carrying their pass books, and if found guilty, were sent to jail (usually Number Four; now Constitution Hill, see page 50), without the option of a fine or suspended sentence; these options were offered to whites. It is also infamous for two car bombs deployed by the ANC's Umkhonto we Sizwe armed wing in 1987 that killed three policemen and injured many more. Unfortunately today, as the venue for high profile trials, it has been necessary to erect an unsightly security fence around it which makes it hard to appreciate the building's elegant façades to their full extent.

Opposite the court at 25 Fox Street at the corner of Gerard Sekoto Street is **Chancellor House**. In the 1950s, Nelson Mandela & Oliver Tambo Attorneys operated out of this humble three-storey building, which was restored in 2010. It is not open to the public, but has been designed as a pavement museum whereby documents, letters and previously unseen photographs are on display in the ground floor windows. The building was owned by the Essas, an Indian family, and at the time, it was a brave decision to lease their building to two black African lawyers since it was technically illegal to rent to Africans in what was an 'Indian area'. But between 1952 and 1956, Mandela and Tambo had a thriving law practice, trying to help others who were accused of crimes against the state and disobeying the draconian laws of the Apartheid government. Ironically, both were ultimately arrested for crimes for which many of their clients had been accused, and in 1956 were both put on trial for high treason in the infamous Treason Trials. The case dragged on for five years and they were acquitted in 1961, after which Tambo fled the country into exile, while Mandela continued his law practice for a few more years from 13 Kholvad House on nearby Market Street (now Albertina Sisulu Street). This was the flat of Ahmed Mohamed Kathrada; another anti-Apartheid activist who like Mandela, later spent a lengthy incarceration on Robben Island, and who Mandela considered as one of his greatest friends. Between Chancellor House and the Fox Street entrance to the court, look out for the **Shadow Boxer Statue** – a 6-m-tall painted steel cutout of Mandela that was inspired by a legendary photograph of Nelson Mandela sparring on a Johannesburg rooftop. An interesting feature is that its unique lighting allows the sculpture to cast a shadow onto the Johannesburg Magistrate's Court at night.

Main Street
A little to the east and opposite the Ntemi Piliso Street side of the court, is the start of the pedestrianized Main Street (or Main Street Mall), which continues for six blocks west all the way to Gandhi Square (see page 47) and is the hub of Johannesburg's modern-day corporate mining industry and home to South

African headquarters of several international mining companies. Walking down the street here is a great way to get a feel for the inner-city's rich mining past from the outdoor museum that has been created here; dubbed the **Mining District Walk** (it's a stop on the City Sightseeing route, see page 84). Dotted along the street, between trees, are various sculptures, water features and relics from the early gold-rush days and the plaques along the way make interesting reading. This is one of the city centre's most impressive rejuvenation projects thanks principally to the dogged determination of some major companies including Anglo American, BHP Billiton and Standard Bank who refused to vacate their traditional head offices and follow their peers to Sandton during the CBD's decline – instead of joining the exodus, these companies chose to participate in the upliftment of this area. On weekdays Main Street is filled with office-workers enjoying its many street cafés and with the mining companies requiring a high security presence the area is safe, clean and pleasant to explore at your own pace.

Heading east from Johannesburg Magistrate's Court, the first building of note is the impressive façades and sweeping entrance steps of the **Anglo American building** at 44 Main Street, which was built in 1937 and designed by the London-based firm of Sir John Burnet, Tait & Lorne. Anglo American was effectively founded in South Africa (as De Beers Consolidated Mines Ltd. in 1888 at the diamond mines in Kimberley) and has since used their South African assets as a springboard to develop an international portfolio in mining – today it is the world's largest producer of platinum, and is also a major producer of diamonds, copper, nickel and iron ore. Look out for the **Leaping Impala or Impala Stampede sculpture** along the brick walkway outside the building. It is a herd of 17 bronze antelope leaping in an elegant arc spanning 8.5 m over a fountain – the sense of grace and movement is quite extraordinary. The statue was commissioned and donated to the city by the mining magnate Oppenheimer family in 1960, and was initially installed in the Sir Ernest Oppenheimer Park behind the Rissik Street Post Office, but due to the inner-city decline in that area and vandalism in the 1990s, the sculpture was rebuffed and moved to its new home outside Anglo American in 2002.

A little further down Main Street Mall on the western side of the corner of Sauer and Main streets is a structure that is a '**mining headgear**' or a mine head frame. These structures are constructed over the entrance to a mine shaft, and allow the winching of men and materials between the surface and underground. This particular head frame was relocated from Langlaagte, a few kilometres west of the CBD, which was close to George Harrison's original gold find that triggered the start of the gold rush in 1886.

Hollard Square is at the centre of the Mining District Walk, and opens up among the buildings along Main Street Mall between Sauer and Simmonds streets and extends over to the northern side of Fox Street. Of interest here is the impressive Art Deco-style bas relief on the side of the **headquarters of BHP Billiton** (an Anglo-Australian multinational mining company), showing scenes of early miners working above and below ground, and the **stamp mill** on display in front of the **Chamber of Mines building**. A stamp mill is a steam-driven piece of equipment that was used to crush rock from the mines and was the first step in extracting gold. This technology was first used at the mines in 1886, and within the first five years after gold was discovered, an estimated 10,000 or so were being used in Johannesburg. This particular one was made in 1886 at the Robinson Mill at Langlaagte.

On the northern side of Hollard Square across Fox Street, is the lovely **Mapungubwe rhino statue**. This is a replica of arguably one of the most significant artifacts ever discovered in South Africa and the figure of a rhino was created by draping thinly beaten gold around a wooden frame and securing it using tiny nails. It was discovered in 1933 by archaeologists from the University of Pretoria at a royal burial site on Mapungubwe Hill (now the Mapungubwe World Heritage Site) in Limpopo Province close to the corner where South Africa, Botswana and Zimbabwe meet. The rhino is thought to have been made by the Mapungubwe people who lived in this region around the 13th century. One of their characteristics of this society was its sophisticated skills in mining and metalwork (both in gold and iron); hence the inclusion of the rhino replica in The Mining District Walk. It is made of fiberglass but treated to appear as though it is metallic, and at 1 m long is upscaled from the original which is only 12 cm long.

Further east at the end of the pedestrianized section of Main Street Mall and the Mining District Walk, and between Marshall and Commissioner streets, is **Gandhi Square**. Built in 1893 as Government Square, it was renamed after Mahatma Gandhi in 1999 and completely refurbished as a large piazza-style public space in 2002. Gandhi arrived in South Africa in 1893 and came to Johannesburg in 1902 and worked as a lawyer, and it was a corner of Rissik and Anderson streets to the south of the square that Gandhi once had his legal offices. But in time he became more active in resistance politics, and was tried in the Johannesburg Law Courts, which were the city's first law courts then in Government Square. He was convicted and sentenced to prison for pass law offences; among them the call to Indians and Chinese to burn their pass books in 1906. He left the country for India in 1914, after having shaped and established his policy of **Satyagraha** or passive resistance, which he continued to practice for the rest of his life. There are plaques around the square telling the history of his time in South Africa and a 2.5-m-high bronze statue of him in his lawyer's robes with a law book under his arm. Gandhi Square is also the main terminus for the Metrobus in the CBD (see Transport, page 85).

From Gandhi Square head another three blocks east along Main Street to get a feel for why locals call Johannesburg the Manhattan of Africa at the

Carlton Centre and Top of Africa ① *access is on the 2nd floor of the Carlton Centre shopping mall, Mon-Fri 0900-1800, Sat 0900-1700, Sun 0900-1400, R15, children (under 12) R10, café, curio shop.* The tallest building in Africa since it opened in 1974, the soaring 223-m-tall Carlton Centre is a popular stop-off for tours and the City Sightseeing bus stops here (see page 84). The lift whisks visitors up to the Top of Africa viewing deck on the 50th floor, from where a glass-fronted lookout deck is wrapped around the building. The views are astounding, and the glittering grid of skyscrapers tapers out to an endless urban sprawl, and on an exceptionally clear day you can see the Voortrekker Monument near Pretoria on the northern horizon. The complex was once also home to the five-star 30-storey **Carlton Hotel**, which was popular with the rich and famous (Henry Kissinger, François Mitterand, Hillary Clinton and Margaret Thatcher were all guests), but the urban decay of the 1990s took its toll on the hotel and it shut its doors in 1997 after nearly 25 years of operation. However the shopping mall at the tower's base is popular, if a little down-at-heel, and features a number of chain stores and fast-food outlets.

Towards Albertina Sisulu Street

There are a few other interesting buildings dotted around the CBD, although they are not linked by any corresponding walk. On Loveday Street between Fox and Commissioner streets is the historic **Rand Club** ① *33 Loveday St, T011-870 4260, www.randclub.co.za, open to non-members for lunch Mon-Sat 1000-1700, booking essential.* The first brick-and-thatch structure was established in 1887 and was the brainchild of the legendary British empire-builder Cecil John Rhodes. He allegedly walked to a point where the fledgling Commissioner Street meets the present-day Loveday Street and imperiously exclaimed, 'here we must have a club', and so one of Johannesburg's great institutions was born. The four-storey building that is the club today was built in 1904, and the interior has been lovingly refurbished in recent years. The imposing columns, a splendid stained glass dome ceiling, wood panelling, chandeliers, antiques, billiard rooms, library, dining rooms and possibly one of the longest bars in Africa capture the bygone era, and there are many original portraits on the walls of past members including Rhodes himself. Once only the domain of the male social elite, the club now a admits women, but non-members can only visit for lunch when you'll be able to look around the public areas and enjoy the elegant dining room and bar (only if suitably attired that is). Historically those scruffier citizens that were denied access at the Rand Club went around the block to the **Guildhall Pub** on the corner of Harrison and Market (now Albertina Sisulu) streets (see page 70).

On Albertina Sisulu Street between Simmonds and Sauer streets, the **Johannesburg City Library** ① *T011-870 1225, Mon-Fri 1000-1700, Sat 0900-1300, free,* has a fine Italian-style façade and was built in 1935 and extensively refurbished in 2012 thanks to a US$2 million grant from the Carnegie Corporation of New York. It's home to more than 700,000 books and the reference section has good collections of historic books on Africa. In the Library Gardens is a useful underground car park which provides easy access to Diagonal Street and around. **City Hall** takes up the block between Albertina Sisulu, Loveday, President and Rissik streets with its main entrance and an impressive flight of steps leading onto a small square on Rissik Street. It was built in 1915 in the distinctive, 19th-century, classic city hall style, with porticos and high-domed towers and today is the seat of the Gauteng Provincial Legislature. Across the road, the **Rissik Street Post Office**, a once beautiful building built in 1887, was almost destroyed by fire in 2005 and is awaiting restoration.

Johannesburg Art Gallery
ⓘ *King George St, T011-725 3130, Tue-Sun 1000-1700, free, bookshop, café, parking in front of the gallery*.
This treasure trove of valuable art, to the east of Park Station and in the south of Joubert Park, houses collections of 17th-century Dutch paintings, 18th- and 19th-century British and European art, 19th-century South African works, a large contemporary collection of 20th-century local and international art and a print cabinet containing works from the 15th century to the present. The initial collection was put together by Sir Hugh Lane and exhibited in London in 1910 before being brought to South Africa. With 15 exhibition halls and lovely sculpture gardens, the collection is larger than that of the National Gallery in Cape Town, and notable works include those by Rembrandt van Rijn, Pablo Picasso, Claude Monet and Henry Moore.

    Joubert Park itself is the city's oldest park, established in 1887 and named after a Boer military hero, Commandant-General PJ Joubert.

Braamfontein

ⓘ *www.braamfontein.org.za*.
With its mix of 1950s-style office buildings, student accommodation, fast-food restaurants and *spaza* (informal) shops, Braamfontein is the central Johannesburg suburb north of the railway lines. Colloquially known as 'Braamies', it is the seat of the City of Johannesburg's local government at the Civic Centre, the University of the Witwatersrand (Wits) and Constitution Hill.

Arriving in Braamfontein
Jan Smuts Avenue and Empire Road are the two major thoroughfares that run through the suburb, which in turn go northwards to Rosebank and the other northern suburbs, while the Nelson Mandela Bridge connects Braamfontein to

Newtown and the CBD. There is parking at Constitution Hill, and you can use the car park at Wits University accessed off Yale Road near the Origins Centre. Again Rea Vaya and City Sightseeing buses stop in Braamfontein (see page 84).

Background

The name meaning 'blackberry fountain' or the 'spring by the brambles' dates to back when a farm stood here in 1853 and it first became urbanized around 1888 as Johannesburg expanded. Like other parts of the city centre, it became clear that urban decay in Braamfontein desperately required attention, and the Braamfontein City Improvement District (CID) project has done much for rejuvenation in this area since its inception in 2004.

Statues and sculpture

Arriving in Braamfontein from the northern suburbs via Jan Smuts Avenue, the most notable sight is the concrete **Eland Statue** on the corner of Bertha and Ameshoff streets. Nearly 6 m high, it was erected as a public work of art in 2007. Another eye-catching public work of art installed in 2009 is the **Fire Walker sculpture** off of the Queen Elizabeth Bridge at the top of Sauer and Simmonds streets which roughly marks the boundary between Braamfontein and the CBD. It represents a woman carrying a brazier on her head in a nod to the activity that took place in this area in the 1980-1990s during the period of urban decay; congested informal traders and unauthorized minibus taxi ranks flourished around the railways lines here and ladies would prepare food on open fires to sell to passing trade. The 11m-tall sculpture is made of fragmented pieces of black and white steel to create the feeling of the figure disintegrating or becoming reassembled (depending on how you interpret it), hinting at the fragility of spaces and the people who pass through them.

Another older but equally striking statue is the **Miner's Monument** at the top of Rissik Street below the Civic Centre and Joburg Theatre (see page 76). The 3-m-high bronze statue on a 5-m-high plinth is of two black miners with muscular arms and legs and bare backs wearing gum boots and holding a giant drill, and a white supervisor wearing a vest, trousers and proper boots and holding a lantern (a typical underground team of the era). It was erected by the Chamber of Mines in 1964 to pay tribute to Johannesburg's mining origins, and the men face westwards towards Langlaagte, the place where gold was discovered.

Constitution Hill

ⓘ 11 Kotze St, T011-381 3100, www.constitutionhill.org.za, Mon-Fri 0900-1700, Sat-Sun 1000-1500, R50, children (under 16) R20, the complex is completely wheelchair accessible.

To the east of the Miners' Monument, the leading attraction in Braamfontein is **Constitution Hill,** the site of the notorious Old Fort Prison Complex known as Number Four. The original prison was built to house white male prisoners in 1892, and the Old Fort was built around it by Paul Kruger from 1896 to 1899 to protect the South African Republic from the threat of British invasion during the Anglo Boer War. It was later extended to include 'native' cells, called Section 4 and Section 5, and, in 1907, a women's section was added. Opened in 2004, this is another of Johannesburg's excellent contemporary museums and, in a similar way to the Apartheid Museum, it uses multimedia tools to display its exhibits. Number Four, which only closed in 1983s, held prisoners from rebellious British soldiers who fought with the Boers at the turn of the 20th century to striking mineworkers, Treason Trialists, and youths caught up in the Soweto Uprising. But its notoriety was because for decades during Apartheid thousands of blacks streamed through the complex's delousing chambers, were beaten and abused, and kept in appalling, dirty overcrowded conditions with the ever-present dread of spending time in the *Ekhulukhuthu* (the deep hole) isolation cells; these were ordinary people arrested in their droves every day for not carrying their pass books. Illustrious prisoners include Nelson Mandela, Mahatma Gandhi and many of the leading anti-Apartheid activists. You can wander around the complex yourself or there are regular tours, which include a film about Mandela's time here, a tour of the women's gaol (where the likes of Winnie Madikizela-Mandela and Albertina Sisulu were held), and a photo exhibition of ex-inmates and wardens. You can still see graffiti on the backs of the cell doors and the giant pots that prisoners ate simple porridge from. South Africa's Constitutional Court has been built here and some of the bricks from the old prison were used in the new court to demonstrate the injustice of the past being used towards justice in the future.

University of the Witwatersrand

The sprawling **Wits University** (www.wits.ac.za) occupies most of the western side of Braamfontein. The university has its roots in the mining industry and was founded in 1896 as the South African School of Mines in Kimberley before moving to Johannesburg in 1908. It is the third oldest university in South Africa after the University of Cape Town (1829) and Stellenbosch University (1866). Today the Wits campuses spread over 400 ha in Braamfontein and Parktown and more than 30,000 students enroll each year.

There are a couple of worthwhile attractions here. **Origins Centre** ⓘ *access from Yale Rd, T011-717 4700, www.origins.org.za, Mon-Sat 0900-1700, Sun 1000-1700, R60, children (under 12) R35, café and book/curio shop*, is another of Johannesburg's excellent contemporary museums. It is run by Wits's Rock Art Research Institute, which has over the last few decades been very much involved in the archaeological sites to the northwest of the city in the Cradle of Humankind (see page 64). The museum covers archaeological and genetic materials relating to the origins of humankind. There are displays of tools made by early man that show how they were made, as well as their spiritual significance. There are also examples of South Africa's ancient rock paintings and engravings, and their supposed meanings, with a large part of the display dedicated to the beliefs of the San (Bushmen). There's a film of the San retreating into their spiritual world through trance which is both vivid and a little disturbing. The final exhibit focuses on how genetic testing can contribute to understanding our ancestry and visitors can add their own DNA to a world database.

Wits Art Museum ⓘ *access from Jorissen St, T011-717 1365, www.wits.ac.za/wam, Wed-Sun 1000-1600, free, café,* is referred to as WAM, and was completely refurbished and reopened in 2012 and is now the city's leading museum of African art. The Wits University started its collection in the 1920s and in addition to unrivalled South African works, there are fascinating and important collections from West and Central Africa, plus several temporary exhibitions are held each year of contemporary pieces. There are masks and ceremonial ritual objects, paintings, textiles, beadwork, sculptures, etchings and drawings, and everything is displayed attractively in galleries with huge glass windows.

Neighbourgoods Market and 70 Juta

If you are in Braamfontein on a Saturday don't miss the **Neighbourgoods Market** ⓘ *73 Juta St, www.neighbourgoodsmarket.co.za, Sat 0900-1500,* which is located in a former office building and is the latest in Joburg's thriving food market scene offering two extensive floors of indoor stalls of food, craft beers and home-made gin, seasonal fruit and veggies as well as a smattering of decor items. Large wooden tables and benches stretch the length of the main hall, and on the second floor is a terrace bar with views over the CBD.

On the opposite corner across De Beer Street is the attractive **70 Juta** ⓘ *70 Juta St, Tue-Fri 1000-1700, Sat 0900-1500,* formerly an old army surplus store (the original gun safe is still on display in the cobbled courtyard), which is now a creative space for music and fashion boutiques, art galleries, a deli and coffee shop and a number of bars. The City Sightseeing bus (see page 84) drops off on Melle Street one block east of Juta Street.

Outside the city centre → *For listings, see pages 66-86.*

Apartheid Museum

ⓘ *Corner of Northern Parkway and Gold Reef Rd, Ormonde, take the M1 South past the CBD on your left and follow signs for Bloemfontein, then take the Booysens exit and follow signs, City Sightseeing (see page 84) also stops here, T011-390 4700, www.apartheidmuseum.org, Tue-Sun 1000-1700, entry R70, children (under 16) R55 (because of the graphic nature of some of the exhibits, not suitable for children under 11), café.*

This is the most critically acclaimed museum in the country and an excellent insight to what South Africa – past and present – is all about. This extraordinarily powerful museum was officially opened by Nelson Mandela in April 2002 and is the city's leading tourist attraction. It focuses on the notorious system of racial discrimination that became synonymous with South Africa from 1948 (when the white-minority National Party was voted into power) until 1994, the year in which the country held its first fully democratic elections. When paying your entry fee you are issued with a random white or non-white ticket that takes you through two different entry points to symbolize segregation. The building itself has an innovative design to reflect the cold subject of Apartheid – harsh concrete, raw brick, steel bars and barbed wire.

The 'spaces' inside are dedicated to the rise of nationalism in 1948, the Population Registration Act, which assigned every citizen to a racial category, the Group Areas Act, which enforced separate urban areas for each of the racial groups, forced removals, and limiting the freedom of movement for

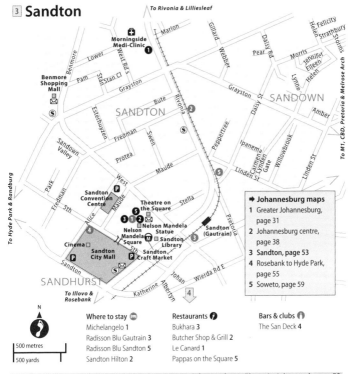

3 Sandton

→ **Johannesburg maps**

1 Greater Johannesburg, page 31
2 Johannesburg centre, page 38
3 Sandton, page 53
4 Rosebank to Hyde Park, page 55
5 Soweto, page 59

Where to stay 🛏
Michelangelo 1
Radisson Blu Gautrain 3
Radisson Blu Sandton 5
Sandton Hilton 2

Restaurants 🍴
Bukhara 3
Butcher Shop & Grill 2
Le Canard 1
Pappas on the Square 5

Bars & clubs 🍸
The San Deck 4

non-whites through curfews and pass books. From here, exhibits cover the first response from townships such as Sharpeville and Langa, the student uprisings in Soweto in 1976, the states of emergency in the 1980s, and political prisoners and executions.

The reforms during the 1980s and 1990s are well documented, including President FW DeKlerk's un-banning of political parties, Mandela's release, the 1994 election, sanction lifting, and the new constitution. One of the most interesting 'spaces' is the House of Bondage, named after a book of photographs published in 1967 by Ernest Cole and banned in South Africa at the time. A white photographer, he managed to class himself as coloured in order to go into the townships and take the pictures. The black and white photographs are both tragic and beautiful. The exhibitions effectively use multimedia, such as television screens, recorded interviews and news footage, all providing a startlingly clear picture of the harshness and tragedy of the Apartheid years. Allow at least two to three hours for a visit.

Next door to the Apartheid Museum is **Gold Reef City** ① *Northern Parkway, Ormonde, for directions see above, City Sightseeing (see page 84) also stops here, T011-248 6800, www.goldreefcity.co.za, Wed-Sun 0930-1700, Story of Jozi, 2-hr guided tours 0900, 1000, 1100, 1400 and 1500, R250, children (under 6) R130 (excludes mine tour), theme park rides, R165, children (under 1.3-m tall) R100, family combination tickets available, cafés and fast-food outlets*, is built on the site of one of Johannesburg's gold mining areas, but today has developed into a garish theme park with rides, amusement arcades and a gaudy casino. Of greater interest is the Story of Jozi tour, which takes you around the restored miners' cottages with staff dressed in period costume, and includes a gold-pouring demonstration and a tour of the gold mine. The tour drops to a depth of about 220 m, taking you down No 14 Shaft, which opened in 1897 and closed in 1971, and was one of the richest deposits of gold in its day.

James Hall Transport Museum
① *Across the road from the Turffontein Race Course, Rosettenville Rd, La Rochelle, 3.5 km south of the CBD, City Sightseeing (see page 84) also stops here, 011-435 9485/7, www.jhmt.org.za, Tue-Sun 0900-1700, free but donations are welcome, the Penny Farthing Tuck Shop sells snacks and drinks.*

This museum, in the south of the city, was founded in 1964 and houses an historical collection of various modes of vintage land transport used in South Africa. Quite astonishingly there are more than 2500 items on display and include early motorcycles, penny-farthings, trams and trains, electric and steam cars, Voortrekker ox-wagons, a travelling library and fire engines among many other contraptions. Of particular interest are the electric trams, which were used in Johannesburg until 1961, and the pre- and post-World War II classic cars. Exhibits in the massive halls are quite cleverly arranged according to power output – animal power, steam power and pedal power for example.

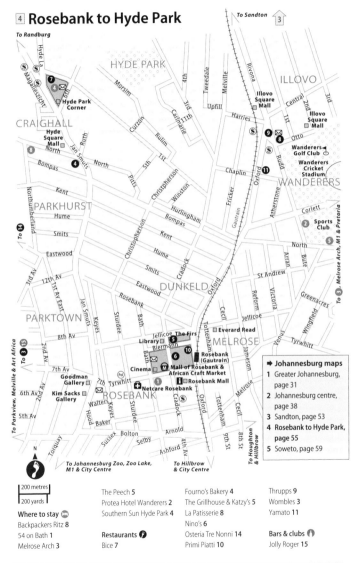

4 Rosebank to Hyde Park

To Randburg

To Sandton

HYDE PARK

ILLOVO

CRAIGHALL

PARKHURST

DUNKELD

WANDERERS

Wanderers Golf Club

Wanderers Cricket Stadium

Sports Club

MELROSE

Everard Read

The Firs

Jellicoe Library

Rosebank (Gautrain)

Cinema

Mall of Rosebank & African Craft Market

Rosebank Mall

Netcare Rosebank

Goodman Gallery

Kim Sacks Gallery

ROSEBANK

PARKTOWN

To Parkview, Melville & Art Africa

To Johannesburg Zoo, Zoo Lake, M1 & City Centre

To Hillbrow & City Centre

To Houghton & Hillbrow

To Melrose Arch, M1 & Pretoria

➡ **Johannesburg maps**
1 Greater Johannesburg, page 31
2 Johannesburg centre, page 38
3 Sandton, page 53
4 Rosebank to Hyde Park, page 55
5 Soweto, page 59

200 metres
200 yards

Where to stay
Backpackers Ritz 8
54 on Bath 1
Melrose Arch 3
The Peech 5
Protea Hotel Wanderers 2
Southern Sun Hyde Park 4

Restaurants
Bice 7
Fourno's Bakery 4
The Grillhouse & Katzy's 5
La Patisserie 8
Nino's 6
Osteria Tre Nonni 14
Primi Piatti 10
Thrupps 9
Wombles 3
Yamato 11

Bars & clubs
Jolly Roger 15

Johannesburg Zoo and around

Johannesburg Zoo ① *corner Jan Smuts Av and Upper Park Dr, Parkview, T011-646 2000, www.jhbzoo.org.za, open 0830-1730, last ticket 1600, R65, children (3-12) R40, golf carts can be hired, café and snack kiosks*, was established in 1904 and covers 54 ha of parkland with spacious vegetated enclosures surrounded by moats and trees. The zoo is home to over 2000 animals from 355 species. Among other animals, there are the big cats, elephants, gorillas, chimpanzees and the only polar bears in Africa. The ponds attract free-ranging aquatic birds, which come here to breed. There is also a petting farm for children and the pre-booked night tours to see the nocturnal animals are fun, ending with marshmallows and hot chocolate around a bonfire.

Across Jan Smuts Avenue from the zoo, **Zoo Lake** ① *corner Jan Smuts Av and West World St, Parkview, open sunrise-sunset, swimming pool, 011-646 8495, 1000-1800, R6, children R3; rowing boats T011-646 5803, Tue-Sun 0930-1630, 6 per boat, R8 per person*, is a large, lovely well-established park with manicured lawns and lots of trees. It was first laid out 1904, and during Apartheid the park and the zoo remained open to all races. The lake's Coronation Fountain was built in 1937 to commemorate the coronation of King George VI, and in 1956, as part of Johannesburg's 70th birthday celebrations, Margot Fonteyn danced Swan Lake in front of the lake. It's popular for picnics, jogging, dog-walking and duck-feeding; the Muslim community come here each year to celebrate Eid at the end of Ramadan, and it is the venue for the annual Carols by Candlelight in December. Rowing boats are for hire, there's a large open-air swimming pool, a tea garden and a couple of restaurants including **Moyo**, see page 72.

Near the zoo is the **South African National Museum of Military History** ① *20 Erlswold Way, Saxonwold, T011-646 5513, www.ditsong.org.za, 0900-1630, R30, children (under 16) R25*, which has exhibits on the role South African forces played in the Second World War, including artillery, aircraft and tanks. There is a more up-to-date section illustrating the war in Angola with displays of modern armaments, including captured Soviet tanks and French Mirage fighter planes. In the section on Umkhonto we Sizwe (the ANC's armed wing), *CASSPIRS*, the formidable armoured personnel carriers used by security forces in the townships during black uprisings against Apartheid, are on display.

Johannesburg Botanical Gardens

① *Olifants Rd, just off Beyers Naude Dr, Emmarentia, T011-782 7064, ww.jhbcityparks.com. Daily sunrise-sunset, free, café 0900-1700.*

Just 6 km northwest of Johannesburg's city centre, this 81 ha park is popular for jogging, cycling and dog walking along the well-marked tracks through the gardens' evergreen, acacia and podocarpus forests. Specialist areas include the Shakespeare Garden planted with herbs referred to by the bard in his plays, and a quote accompanies each one, and the Herb Garden that

Joburg's parks

Johannesburg is a city full of trees and there are an estimated six million on pavements, in parks and private residences. The city resembles a rainforest on pictures taken from satellites, making it one of the greenest urban areas in the world. When the Voortrekkers arrived, the highveld was savannah grassland, and it was these early farmers who planted the first seeds that they'd brought up from the Cape. When Johannesburg began to grow, the mining companies planted trees such as blue gum to be used as mining props below ground and the miners were paid a penny to plant a sapling. Meanwhile, residents also planted oaks, jacarandas and plane trees in their gardens, especially in the northern suburbs which were established as middle- and upper-classes areas with spacious homes on large plots of land. The trees attract a large number of birds, and more than 300 species are present in Gauteng – 134 of which are endemic or near-endemic. The first public park to be laid out was Joubert Park in 1904 (where the **Johannesburg Art Gallery** is; see page 49), and over the years many more were established in just about every neighbourhood. Today there are a staggering 2300 parks in the greater metropolitan area, and one of the loveliest and most popular is **Zoo Lake** in Parkview near the Zoo (see page 56). Visit **Johannesburg City Parks** at www.jhbcityparks.com.

features culinary, cosmetic, oil-yielding and African medicinal herbs. The Arboretum has a variety of indigenous and exotic trees, including Californian redwoods, silver birches and English oaks. In the northeast of the garden the 7.5 ha Emmarentia Dam is popular for canoeing and sailing, and birdwatchers can see geese, dabchicks, moorhens and other waterfowl. The land was once part of the Braamfontein (meaning 'blackberry fountain' or the 'spring by the brambles') farm that was established here in 1853 and owned by the Geldenhuys family. They contracted landless Boers to build the dam after the Anglo-Boer War which was named after Louw Geldenhys's wife, Emmarentia.

Liliesleaf Farm
ⓘ *7 George Av, Rivonia, 8 km north of Sandton, follow Rivonia Rd north, T011-803 7882, www.liliesleaf.co.za, Mon-Fri 0830-1700, Sat-Sun 0900-1600, R60, children (8-17) R30, under 8s free, 45-min tours are available R110/70, café.*
Now a museum, in the 1960s this is where the most prominent leaders of South Africa's struggle from the then-banned ANC and Communist Party sought shelter and attended meetings. These included Nelson Mandela, Govan Mbeki and Walter Sisulu, among many others. Although today it's surrounded by Johannesburg's northern suburbs, it was once an isolated rural

spot and the farm was fronted by 'white owners', Arthur Goldreich, a member of the Communist Party, and his family. Nelson Mandela himself lived here for a while posing as a cook-cum-gardener under the name of David Motsamayi. On 11 July 1963, a meeting was held by Umkhonto we Sizwe or the MK (meaning 'spear of the nation' and the ANC's armed wing) to discuss Operation Mayibuye, a plot to overthrow the Apartheid government. However, the police had been tipped off that Walter Sisulu was at the farm and it was raided. Sisulu and just about the entire leadership of the MK were arrested (Mandela had been arrested six months earlier in KwaZulu-Natal). This led to what became known as the Rivonia Trials in late 1963, and the subsequent imprisonment of the ANC's leaders. Today you can walk around the farm – there are exhibits in the main house and outbuildings – and watch a short film.

Soweto → *For listings, see pages 66-86.*

The most popular excursion in Johannesburg is to the (in)famous former township of Soweto, lying roughly 13 km southwest of the city centre. Soweto was, from the start, a product of segregationist planning, but today is no longer referred to a 'township' as such, as it has mushroomed into, and given the status of, a Johannesburg suburb in its own right; albeit still a predominantly black one. It covers 135 sq km and is home to around 1.3 million people; about a third of the greater Johannesburg metropolitan area's total population.

Background
Short for South West Township, it was created to house mainly black labourers, who worked in mines and other industries and people first moved here in 1904 from Sophiatown where there was an outbreak of plague. The township increased in size dramatically in the 1950s and 1960s when black people were forced to relocate into designated areas outside the city centre which the Apartheid government then reserved for whites. Soweto's growth was phenomenal, but largely unplanned, as despite the government's attempts to curb the influx of black workers to the cities, waves of migrant workers moved from the countryside and neighboring countries to look for employment; hence large sprawling areas of 'informal settlements' (rudimentary home-built shacks) spread out around the peripheral of the formal housing (pockets of which still exist today). By the 1980s and the breakdown of Apartheid people could of course live where they wanted to, but the majority of Soweto residents stayed where they were as the township by now represented a real home where generations of families had grown up.

Despite the perennial problems since its inception included poor housing, overcrowding, high unemployment and poor infrastructure, and its former reputation as a hotbed for crime and chaos, Soweto feels remarkably ordinary today. Large areas are given over to tidy rows of affluent suburban houses with well-tended gardens and satellite dishes, and as in any other South African city, there are districts with amenities such as shopping centres, banks, schools and transport terminuses. Meanwhile there is a steady stream of commuter minibus taxis, Metrorail trains and the newer Rea Vaya buses taking commuters to Johannesburg's CBD and other areas every day. The changing socio-demographics of the suburb are more than evident and it is now home to one of Johannesburg's largest shopping malls, **Maponya Mall**, on Chris Hani (Old Potchefstroom) Road, while there are gourmet restaurants, a golf course, and car dealerships for BMW and Mercedes. The flip-side, however, much like any other city in the country, is that there are also still areas of squatter camps and informal housing, where unemployment is high and people have to share amenities like taps and toilets. The government is constantly trying to improve the situation by building houses to replace the shacks, but efforts are hampered by the thousands of people who flood into Soweto every month, fleeing rural poverty and desperate for jobs.

Those visitors who know very little else about South Africa are often familiar with the word Soweto as being significant in the struggle against Apartheid. It

5 Soweto

➡ **Johannesburg maps**
1 Greater Johannesburg, page 31
2 Johannesburg centre, page 38
3 Sandton, page 53
4 Rosebank to Hyde Park, page 55
5 Soweto, page 59

Where to stay 😴
Soweto Backpackers 1
Soweto Hotel 2

Restaurants 🍴
Nambitha 1
Wandie's 2

has a rich political history and many protest campaigns germinated in Soweto before spreading to the rest of the country. These events – and the people involved including Nelson Mandela – are commemorated and celebrated in a number of museums, landmarks and historic sites that are well worth dedicating some time to understand the past, while enjoying the cheerful energy and bustle of activity that is today's Soweto.

Arrving in Soweto

These days it is quite feasible to visit Soweto independently. For drivers, although the seemingly endless identical streets of small houses can appear bewildering, the roads are clearly marked and the museums and significant sights are well signposted and have safe parking, especially those in Orlando West, such as the Hector Pieterson Museum and the nearby Mandela Family Museum. The Maponya Mall and Orlando Cooling Towers are easily accessed off the Chris Hani (Old Potchefstroom) Road, and are a short drive from its intersection with the N1. The Rea Vaya bus (see page 84) from the east of the CBD to Soweto takes only 40 minutes, even in rush hour traffic as the bus follows dedicated bus lanes. Nevertheless, a guided tour is still the most convenient and productive way to visit Soweto, and most take in a handful of important historical sites, with perhaps a visit to an informal settlement and a township shebeen for lunch, with the added benefit of having a guide to talk you through the stories. ▸▸ *For tour operators, see What to do, page 82. City Sightseeing offers the option of adding in a two-hour tour by minibus to Soweto from the Gold Reef City stop, page 84.*

Places in Soweto

Hector Pieterson Museum ⓘ *Khumalo and Pela streets, Orlando West, T011-536 0611, daily 1000-1700, free.* This remarkable (and free) modern museum, which opened in 2002, stands two blocks away from where 13-year-old Hector Pierterson was shot dead by riot police during a school demonstration on 16 June 1976. The children had been demonstrating about the use of Afrikaans as the dominant language in education, before the police opened fire and killed more than 170 students. This event, captured on camera by a photojournalist in an image that shocked the world, sparked the final 10-year battle against Apartheid causing townships across the country to rise up in bitter revolt. (The incident is now known as the Soweto Uprising and the 16 June, Youth Day, is a public holiday.) Outside the museum is a memorial to Hector, marked by the iconic photograph of his body being carried by a friend with Hector's wailing 17-year-old sister running alongside. The inscription on the memorial reads: "To honour the youth who gave their lives in the struggle for democracy and freedom".

This incredibly moving and powerful museum is similar to the Apartheid Museum in that it uses multimedia exhibits, films, newspapers, personal accounts and photographs to piece together what happened on and around that date. The exhibit route follows a loop around a central courtyard where the names of all the children who died are inscribed on a granite bed. Strategically placed windows allow visitors to look out on buildings and streets where the events of the day unfolded, including Orlando Stadium where the ill-fated demonstration was supposed to, but never did, finish. There is an excellent museum bookshop with dozens of interesting books on South Africa, and from the museum it is a short walk along a tree-lined avenue to Vilikazi Street below.

Mandela Family Museum ① *8115 Vilakazi St, Orlando West, T011-936 7754, www.mandelahouse.co.za, daily 0900-1645, R60, children (6-16) R20, under 6s free, tour guides are available at no extra charge, allow 40 mins for the tour.* A short walk from the Hector Pieterson Museum (and often referred to as the Mandela House Museum), this is where Nelson Mandela lived before he was incarcerated. He moved into the diminutive four-roomed house in 1946 with his first wife, Evelyn Mase, and in 1958 brought his second wife, Winnie, to live with him. He was, however, to spend little time here in the ensuing years, as his role in struggle activities became all-consuming and he was forced underground in 1961 until his arrest and imprisonment in 1962. Winnie Madikizela-Mandela, herself imprisoned several times, lived in the house with her daughters while Nelson Mandela was in jail, until her own exile to Brandfort in 1977, where she remained under house arrest until 1986. Mandela said of the house in his autobiography, *Long Walk to Freedom*: "It was the opposite of grand, but it was my first true home of my own and I was mightily proud. A man is not a man until he has a house of his own." Mandela insisted on moving back to the house on his release from prison in 1990, and again in *Long Walk to Freedom* he wrote: "That night I returned with Winnie to No 8115 in Orlando West. It was only then that I knew in my heart I had left prison. For me No 8115 was the centre point of my world, the place marked with an X in my mental geography". But sadly after only 11 days, its small size and the difficulty of keeping it secure put too much of a strain on him. He was moved from one secret location to the next until he settled in a larger house in Houghton where he lived with his third wife, Graca Machel (who he married on his 80th birthday in 1998) until his death in 2013.

Mandela separated from Winnie in 1992 and the couple divorced in 1996, and the house was opened as a museum by Winnie herself in 1997 and for many years it displayed an odd collection of Mandela's personal effects and (now-famously) sold bottles of 'Mandela garden soil'. It's now in the hands of the Soweto Heritage Trust who refurbished it in 2008 to what it looked like in the 1950s, with bare concrete floors and a corrugated-tin roof – it only accommodates about 20 people at a time so you may have to wait. There are displays about his time in the house and an assortment of memorabilia, paintings and photographs of the Mandela family, as well as a collection of honorary doctorates bestowed on Mandela by universities and institutions around the world. Further down the street is the house where Archbishop Desmond Tutu lived during much of the liberation struggle. Hidden behind high walls, he still often stays there when he visits Johannesburg, and **Vilakazi Street** is also famous for being the only street in the world to have been home to two Nobel Peace Prize winners, Nelson Mandela and Desmond Tutu.

Regina Mundi Roman Catholic Church ① *1149 Khumalo St, T011-986 2546, www.reginamundichurch.co.za, 0800-1700, R20 per person.* To the southwest, off Chris Hani (Old Potchesfstroom) Road, this church, an ordinary 1960s-built construction, is the largest church in Soweto and is famous for opening its doors and providing shelter to activists during the anti-Apartheid struggle. The most significant event was when during the 1976 Soweto Uprising, protesting students fled to Regina Mundi from Orlando Stadium to escape the police's bullets and teargas canisters. The police followed the students into the church, firing live ammunition and damaging the marble altar and crucifix – you can still see bullet holes in the ceiling. The church's garden has been transformed into a striking park with a plaque recording the history.

Walter Sisulu Square ① *corner Klipspruit Valley and Union roads, Kliptown, T011-945 2200, www.waltersisulusquare.co.za, Mon-Sat 1000-1700, Sun 1000-1630, free.* This is where the Freedom Charter, calling for equality for all, was presented by the ANC to a mass gathering of people in 1955. The square, which used to be called Freedom Square, was renamed after one of the delegates, Walter Sisulu, when he died in 2003. The authorities broke up the illegal gathering but the charter was adopted as a guiding document, and it remains the cornerstone of ANC policy to this day; it is seen by many as the foundation of South Africa's 1996 Constitution. Back in 1955 it was just a dusty patch of land, but in 2003 was redeveloped into an attractive paved square housing a number of monuments. These include the 10 Pillars of the Freedom Charter: 10 giant slabs of concrete representing the clauses of the Freedom Charter, and the red-brick conical Freedom Charter Monument. Additionally, there are a few market stalls, shops and restaurants lining the square and the **Soweto Hotel** (see Where to stay, page 69).

Orlando cooling towers Finally, Soweto's boldest attraction are the two 100-m-high cooling towers on Dynamo Street, on the north side of Chris Hani (Old Potchefstroom) Road in Orlando West. They have long been a landmark and are part of a now-disused power station that was built in the 1950s to provide central Johannesburg with electricity (even though Soweto didn't get electricity until 1986). The power station closed in 1998, long after its intended lifespan and, in 2003, the First National Bank (FNB) sponsored the painting of the towers. One is painted with an elaborate version of the FNB's logo, while the second tower is painted with a fantastic vivid mural of life in Soweto, with cartoon characters of musicians, children playing, a woman selling her wares on a stall, minibus taxis, a Metrorail train, a football stadium, Baragwanath Hospital, a Madonna and child which represents the Regina Mundi Roman Catholic Church, and of course a figure of a smiling and waving Nelson Mandela in one of his trademark African print shirts. The largest hand-painted murals in South Africa, they took six months to create, and the 100-m-high scaffolding around the tower was dropped into place by helicopter. The murals have become iconic, not only to Soweto but to Johannesburg as a whole.

Apart from admiring the murals, the other reason to come to the cooling towers is the **Orlando Towers Adventure Centre** ⓘ *T011-312 0450, www. orlandotowers.co.za, Fri-Sun 1000-sunset, bungee jump R480, power swing R360, internal swing R360, abseil R260, viewing platform only R60*. Opened in 2008, there is a 100-m lift on one of the towers, and a number of bungee jumps and power swings inside and out. The less adventurous can go up to the viewing platform at the top. This is not for the faint-hearted – the lift is open air and the last 3 m to the top is by a sort of suspended stairway as the top of the tower curves outwards. Nevertheless the views of Soweto are unbeatable.

Around Johannesburg → *For listings, see pages 66-86.*

There are a number of attractions to the northwest of Johannesburg that are within 40 minutes' drive from the northern suburbs and offer an alternative to the urban sights. They are also en route from Johannesburg to the Magaliesberg Mountains (see page 107) in the North West Province. These can just as easily be visited from Pretoria on a day trip.

Lion Park ⓘ *on the R512, 17 km northwest of Randburg and 9 km south of Lanseria Airport, T011-691 9905, www.lion-park.com, Mon-Fri 0830-1700, Sat-Sun 0830-1800, self-drive R160, children (4-12) R80, under 4s free, guided game drives R270/160, family discounts available, cub interaction (when available) R30 per person, cheetah walk (pre-booking essential) R500 (no under 16s), restaurant and curio shop*. En route to Lesedi (see below), it is worth stopping here for the excellent photo opportunities. There are over 85 lions in the park, including many cubs and a rare pride of white lions. Although they are bred in captivity, they are well cared for and have ample room in the drive-through enclosures. The lions are accustomed to vehicles and don't think twice about strolling right up to a car. Keep windows at least half closed. Other animals include hyenas, cheetah and a variety of antelope. Walks and close encounters with cubs are on offer if they are in residence, as are one-hour walks with a couple of tame cheetahs, and you can climb a tower to feed giraffes.

Lesedi Cultural Village ⓘ *on the R512, 12 km north of Lanseria Airport, T012-205 1394, www.lesedi.com, tours at 1130 and 1630, R400 per person including lunch or dinner, or R250 excluding lunch or dinner, children (6-12) half-price (under 5s) free.* Four African villages have been recreated from the Xhosa, Zulu, Pedi and Sotho tribes. The three-hour tours include an audio-visual presentation on all aspects of tribal life of the 11 ethnic groups that live in South Africa, as well as music, singing and traditional dancing from over 60 performers around a large fire in an amphitheatre. The morning tour concludes with lunch, and the afternoon tour finishes with dinner of game meat such as impala or crocodile. Lesedi is the Sotho word for 'light'. For those who wish to extend the experience, there is mid-range accommodation in traditional bomas or rondavels decorated with Ndebele crafts.

Walter Sisulu National Botanical Gardens ⓘ *Malcolm Rd, Roodepoort, take the M47 northwest out of Johannesburg, T086-100 1278, www.sanbi.org/gardens/walter-sisulu, R35, children (6-16) R12, under 6s free, daily 0800-1700, restaurant.* Formerly known as the Witwatersrand National Botanical Gardens, about 30 km northwest of the city centre, many walks and trails meander through 300 ha of lush gardens and green lawns. They will particularly appeal to bird-watchers for the 226 bird species that have been recorded. Take the 1-km loop trail to the top of the lovely Witpoortjie Waterfall and hopefully you'll catch a glimpse of Johannesburg's only nesting pair of Verreaux's (black) eagles. Of the 600 plant species look out for the vast collection of lithops (small succulents that look like small stones), which are indigenous to southern Africa, while the Cycad Garden and the Succulent Rockery are also worth exploring. Naturally the best time to visit is in spring and summer when the flowering shrubs are in bloom. Guided walks are on offer, the Eagles Fare restaurant has outside tables under the arms of a huge white stinkwood tree, and the gardens hold occasional classical and jazz concerts.

Cradle of Humankind ⓘ *www.cradleofhumankind.co.za.* Some 40 km to the northwest of Johannesburg, this region is dubbed the 'Cradle of Humankind' thanks to thousands of humanoid and animal fossils being unearthed over recent decades. It holds some of the world's most important archaeological sites, revealing over 40% of all hominid fossils ever discovered and rivals Tanzania's Olduvai Gorge in significance. The 470-sq-km area was declared a UNESCO World Heritage Site in 1999. The two significant tourist attractions are Maropeng and the Sterkfontein Caves, which are 10 km apart and both well-signposted off the R563 towards Hekpoort.

Maropeng ⓘ *Hekpoort Rd, Sterkfontein, take the N14/R563 north out of Johannesburg past Roodepoort and Krugersdorp and turn left on to the R400, T014-*

577 9000, www.maropeng.co.za, 0900-1700, last boat ride 1600, R145, children (4-14) R82, under 4s free, combination tickets with Sterkfontein Caves R215/R115 (available until 1300 to allow visitors to get to both sites), restaurant and café. Maropeng means 'returning to the place of origin' in the Setswana language, and is an interactive museum that tells the story of the creation of our world and the evolution of man over a four billion-year period; another of Johannesburg's excellent cutting-edge museums that uses computer wizardry and multimedia displays. The entrance has been built as a grassy burial mound, while the exit is a sleek structure of modern glass and concrete and the journey from one to the other takes the visitor from the birth of planet earth to where we are today. The first experience is a boat ride through a tunnel of erupting volcanoes, icebergs, an eye of a storm and swirling gases that made up the planet. It's rather magical and the sounds and temperatures are lifelike, but be warned that it may frighten very small children. Once off the boat the series of exhibits start from how the earth was formed, early life forms and the emergence of man, and go through to cover topics on how man has changed the environment, such as population explosion, use of the earth's resources and global appetite. Towards the end is a large display of photographs of people's faces from all over the world and a mesmerizing series of images of man's achievements are flashed on a giant screen, covering everything from man inventing the wheel to landing on the moon. Allow at least two to three hours for the absorbing experience.

Sterkfontein Caves ⓘ *Koomtrai Rd, Sterkfontein, Take the N14/R563 north out of Johannesburg past Roodepoort and Krugersdorp but turn right off the R563 9 km before Maropeng, T014-577 9000, www.maropeng.co.za, 0900-1700, guided tours run every 30 mins, last tour 1600, R150, children (4-14) R88, under 4s free, combination tickets with Maropeng R215/R115 (available until 1300 to allow visitors to get to both sites), restaurant.* Although the dolomite hill holding the caves was discovered in the late 19th century, it was not until 1936 that the most important find was made; the first adult skull of the ape man *Australopithecus africanus* – 'Mrs Ples' for short. The skull is estimated to be over 2.6 million years old, and was found by Dr Robert Broom. Even older hominid remains have been found here since. The caves consist of six chambers connected by passages. Tours begin in the impressive multimedia visitor centre, which includes comprehensive exhibitions on our ancestors, with displays of life-sized hominid replicas and a large amphitheatre. Tours then pass through the six caves, taking in the archaeological sites. **Note** Wear comfortable shoes and be prepared for a lot of stairs.

Rhino and Lion Nature Reserve ⓘ *T011-957 0349, www.rhinolion.co.za, Mon-Fri 0800-1700, Sat-Sun 0800-1800, lion feeding Sat-Sun 1300, R140, children (3-12) R100, under 3s free, Wonder Cave R90/70, combo ticket R210/130, restaurant, off* *the R563, 7 km to the northeast of Sterkfontein Caves, or off the R512, 2 km north of Lanseria Airport, turn left at the Kromdraai sign for 13 km.* This private 1600-ha game park which opened in 1985 with just two white rhinos is today home to more than 600 animals including buffalo, lion, white rhino, wild dog, cheetah, hippo, crocodile and more than 20 species of antelope. Around 200 species of bird occur here naturally. The predators are kept in separate enclosures and visitors can watch them being fed, there's a snake and reptile park and 'vulture restaurant', and like the Lion Park, you can pet some lion cubs if any are in residence in the 'crèche'. Game drives in the reserve's open-topped vehicles depart from reception throughout the day. A family-orientated setup, there are *braai* areas, a curio shop, swimming pool, children's play park, the Crocodile Pub from where visitors can watch the crocodiles, and some self-catering log cabins (**$$**). Also on the property is the **Wonder Cave**, a natural limestone cavern discovered by gold prospectors in the late 1890s. It measures 125 m long, 54 m wide and 60 m deep, and the stalagmites and stalactites are weirdly impressive. Reasonable fitness is required however as 88 steps lead down into the cave.

◉ Johannesburg listings

For hotel and restaurant price codes and other relevant information, see pages 13-18.

◉ Where to stay

Johannesburg has an enormous selection of hotels, mostly in the northern suburbs, which are convenient for shopping and eating out. There's an excellent choice of luxury hotels, many of which have facilities that are open to non-guests, but few in the lower price bracket other than the odd backpackers. Good mid-range options in modern, functional blocks with comfortable rooms, DSTV and Wi-Fi, are from the City Lodge Group, and there are dozens of **City Lodges**, **Road Lodges** and **Town Lodges** all over Johannesburg and Pretoria. Check the website for locations; www.citylodge. co.za. The other mid-range chains

with hotels across Gauteng include **Protea**, www.proteahotels.com, and **Tsogo Sun Garden Court**, www.tsogosunhotels.com.

Near the airport

There are several hotels within a few kilometres of OR Tambo International Airport, all providing free shuttle services. **$$$$ Intercontinental OR Tambo Airport**, T011-961 5400, www. tsogosunhotels.com. Smart 4-star hotel located directly opposite the terminal building; you can push your trolley into your room. 138 rooms, restaurant, bar, indoor and outdoor pools, 24-hr gym and spa is available for passengers on long waits between flights. **Tsogo Sun** also has the **$$$ Southern Sun OR Tambo Airport**, T011-977 3600, 500 m from the airport, with 366 rooms, restaurant with reasonable Mediterranean-style menu, 24-hr bar, pool and gym, and there's the cheaper **$$ Garden Court OR Tambo International Airport**, 2 Hulley Rd, Kempton Park, T011-392 1062, 2 km from the airport.

$$$ City Lodge, 5th floor, Parkade, T011-552 7600, www.citylodge.co.za. Above the airport's car park and an easy walk to the Gautrain, uses the airport's facilities, plus rooftop pool with deck, and gym. There's another **$$ City Lodge**, Sandvale Rd, Edenvale, T011-392 1750, 4 km from the airport, plus a **$$ Town Lodge**, T011-974 5202, and **$$ Road Lodge**, T011-392 2268, are both within striking distance of the airport in Germiston.

$$-$ Africa Centre, 65 Sunny Rd, Lakefield-Benoni, T011-894 4857, www.africacentrelodge.co.za. Upmarket backpacker set-up only 15 mins' drive from the airport with modern double, single and family/ group triple or quad rooms, shared kitchen, meals available, garden with pool, sauna, jacuzzi and Wi-Fi. Good travel centre and free airport pickup (must be pre-booked).

City centre *p37, map p38*
$$$-$$ Mapungubwe Hotel, 50-54 Marshall St, corner of Ferreira St, Marshalltown, T011-429 2600, www.mapungubwehotel.co.za. Stylishly-decorated and fun setup handy for the **Mining District Walk** (see page 46) with 98 apartments with kitchenettes, but choose the inward facing rooms as some overlooking Marshall St may be noisy. Twist restaurant, bar in an old bank vault in the basement (with original copper safety deposit boxes), swimming pool, undercover parking.

$$$-$$ Protea Parktonian All Suite, 120 De Korte St, Braamfontein, T011-403 5740, www.parktonian.co.za. Close to the Civic Centre and Jo-burg Theatre, 300 rooms in one of Braamfontein's highest blocks with 300 plain but well-equipped rooms with DSTV, Wi-Fi, kitchenettes, and all with balconies for great city views (book the higher floors). Restaurant, bar and swimming pool on the roof, parking and free shuttle from Park Station.

$$ Reef Hotel, 58 Anderson St, Marshalltown, CBD, T011-689 1000, www.reefhotels.co.za. A well-run option and close to Gandhi Square (see page 47) with 120 modern rooms in a tower block with rooftop bar on the 16th floor with great views, the Gold **Mine Café** and **Reef Grill Room** restaurant, and an underground car park.

$ Bannister Hotel, 120 9 De Beer St, T011-403 6888, www.bannisterhotel.co.za. A cross between a backpackers and a budget hotel with 31 tiny but bright and fashionable rooms from around R500 in a 1960s converted office block. Restaurant, bar, and parking is available (R40) but a little tricky in a 'tandem' arrangement about 100 m away. The **Saturday Neighbourgoods Market** is across the road (see page 52).

Outside the city centre *p52, maps p31, p53 and p55*
$$$$ Four Seasons Hotel, The Westcliff, 67 Jan Smuts Av, Westcliff, T011-481 6000, www.fourseasons.com/

johannesburg. Recently taken over by acclaimed **Four Seasons**, the iconic **Westcliff** is a Mediterranean-style hillside village on a 3-ha estate, with 117 super-luxurious rooms and suites, 2 heated pools, floodlit tennis courts, gym, spa, 5 restaurants and bars, great views of the northern suburbs and Johannesburg Zoo.

$$$$ Melrose Arch, 1 Melrose Sq, Melrose Arch, Corlett Dr, Melrose North, T011-679 2994, www.africanpride hotels.com. Hip hotel with 117 stylish rooms, lots of chrome, bare-brick walls, mood-enhancing lighting, designer furniture. Smart bar and superb **March Restaurant** for gourmet food, unusual pool with underwater music. Great location overlooking the piazza in Melrose Arch.

$$$$ The Michelangelo, 135 West St, Sandton, T011-282 7000, www.legacyhotels.co.za. One of the best luxury options of Sandton, with 242 super-luxury rooms, including a variety of giant suites, residents' lounge, restaurants, bar, heated pool, gym. Built around a Renaissance-style central atrium and makes up one side of the lovely Nelson Mandela Sq.

$$$$ Saxon, 36 Saxon Rd, Sandhurst, T011-292 6000, www.thesaxon.com. Voted the 'World's Leading Boutique Hotel' every year since it opened in 2000, with 26 suites including one named after Nelson Mandela, who spent 7 months here working on his book *Long Walk to Freedom*. Beautifully decorated with African objets d'art, set in 2 ha of beautifully tended grounds, gigantic heated swimming pools, state-of-the-art gym, spa, restaurant, 2 wine cellars.

$$$ 54 on Bath, 54 Bath Av, Rosebank, T011-344 8500, www.tsogosunhotels.com. Right next to **Rosebank Mall** with 74 large rooms, some with great city views, restaurant, popular cocktail bar, stunning pool and terrace garden on the 4th floor, good extras such as a 'pillow menu' and afternoon tea (see page 73).

$$$ The Peech, 61 North St, Melrose, T011-537 9797, www.thepeech.co.za. Stylish boutique hotel with 16 rooms set in an acre of gardens with pool, some with peaceful private patios, eco-friendly features like solar power and water recycling, and has an organic menu in the bistro-style restaurant with walk-in wine cellar.

$$$ Protea Hotel Wanderers, corner of Corlett Dr and Rudd Rd, Illovo, T011-770 5500, www.proteahotels.com. Quality modern Protea hotel directly opposite Wanderers Cricket Stadium and handy for Melrose Arch. 230 rooms, restaurant, 24-hr bar and coffee shop serving snacks, pleasant pool area except for the traffic noise from the busy road below.

$$$ Radisson Blu Gautrain, corner Rivonia Rd and West St, Sandton, T011-286 1000. Next to the Gautrain station and Sandton City, with 216 rooms.

$$$ Radisson Blu Sandton, corner Rivonia Rd and Daisy St, Sandton, T011-245 8000, www.radissonblu.com. Stylish hotel with 290 rooms and 11 penthouses in a commanding block with outstanding views of Sandton's high-rises. Good facilities with the Vivance, an Italian restaurant with open-plan kitchen, wine bar, spa. Pool and deck is on the 8th floor.

$$$ The Residence, 17 4th Av, Houghton, T011-853 2480, www.theresidence.co.za. Joburg's most popular luxury boutique hotel and deservedly so with just 11 rooms, beautiful opulent decor, terraced gardens, 2 swimming pools, tennis courts, spa, piano bar, gourmet restaurant, and 'sky lounge' on the top floor. Has both a Rolls Royce and Mercedes Benz Viano for shuttles.

$$$ Sandton Hilton, 138 Rivonia Rd, Sandton, T011-322 1888, www3.hilton.com. Big business hotel set in a landscaped garden with 329 luxury rooms, bar, 2 restaurants, a sushi bar, spa, tennis court, very large pool, and a free shuttle to Sandton City. Not as contemporary as some, but good Hilton standards.

$$$-$$ Sunnyside Park, Prince of Wales Terr, Parktown, T011-640 0400, www.legacyhotels.co.za. In a converted Victorian mansion declared a national monument, with new annexes and set in picturesque gardens close to the CBD. 154 rooms, country-style decor and pleasant old-fashioned atmosphere, restaurant, pub with a miners' theme and swimming pool.

$$ A Room with a View, 1 Tolip St, corner of 4th Av, Melville, T011-482 5435, www.aroomwithaview.co.za. As the name suggests, beautiful views over leafy Melville from this delightful guesthouse, 14 rooms with DSTV and Wi-Fi, some with balconies and fireplaces, set in 2 buildings; one is built like an Italian villa with bare-brick walls and soaring ceilings. Legendary breakfasts, pleasant pool and friendly service.

$ Backpackers Ritz, 1A North Rd, Dunkeld West, T011-325 7125, www.backpackers-ritz.co.za. Johannesburg's longest-established backpackers set in a large house in a leafy neighbourhood. Dorms and doubles, internet, meals available, garden and pool. The travel desk can arrange all tours. Close to shops and entertainment at Hyde Park and Rosebank.

$ Johannesburg Backpackers, 14 Umgwezi Rd, Emmarentia, T011-888 4742, www.joburgbackpackers.com. A little out of the way (5 km west of Rosebank) but close to the Johannesburg Botanical Gardens (see page 56) and a 5-min walk to Greenside for restaurants and bars. Neat dorms, doubles and family rooms, spacious garden with pool, bar, Wi-Fi, parking, travel desk and all Joburg tours can pick up from here.

Soweto *p58, map p59*

$$$-$$ Soweto Hotel, Walter Sisulu Sq, corner Union Av and Main Rd, Kliptown, T011-527 7300, www.sowetohotel.co.za. Soweto's only 4-star hotel and part of the Walter Sisulu Sq development. 46 neat rooms with DSTV and Wi-Fi, contemporary decor with historical touches like black and white photographs of Soweto's struggle heroes, the **Jazz Maniacs** restaurant, bar, underground car park, tours to the local sights, or walk around Kliptown.

$ Soweto Backpackers, 10823A Pooe St, Orlando West, T011-936 3444, www.sowetobackpackers.com. Also referred to as **Lebo's** after its charismatic owner, this is an excellent way to experience township life, especially if combined with one of their Soweto guided bike tours, and it's walking distance from the Hector Pieterson Museum and Vilakazi St. Dorms, doubles, camping in the garden, lively bar with great music, Wi-Fi, kitchen, home-cooked meals, free pickup from Rea Vaya buses.

⊘ Restaurants

Like New York, Johannesburg is a city that has culturally evolved from immigration, which means that almost every international cuisine features in the multitude of restaurants. Many are in the top-class hotels or are within the confines of a shopping mall but, thanks to good architecture, in the most part you will not be aware that you are eating in a mall. This is especially true of the 14 restaurants lining **Nelson Mandela Sq** (see Shopping, page 80), which is an atmospheric place to eat out with twinkly lights in the trees and a 6-m-tall bronze statue of a smiling Mandela looking over the outside tables. Other mall hotspots include the cobbled piazza at **Melrose Arch** (see Shopping, page 79), and the tree-lined avenues at **Rosebank Mall** (see Shopping, page 79). For a lively streetside scene, head to the corner of 7th St and 3rd Av in **Parktown North**, which is dubbed Parktown Quarter, or 4th Av in **Parkhurst**, where numerous sidewalk cafés and restaurants compete with antique and flower shops.

City centre *p37, map p38*
$$-$ Sophiatown Bar Lounge, corner of Jeppe and Henry Nxumalo streets, Newtown, T011-836 5999, www.sophiatownbarlounge.co.za. Mon-Thu 1030-2200, Fri-Sat 1030-0100, Sun 1030-2000. In Mary Fitzgerald Sq (see page 39), with a jazz-themed decor including photos of legends like Miriam Makeba. Mixed menu of township food like oxtail or chops served with pap, plus kudu and ostrich steaks, poultry and seafood, and good salads and wraps during the day. Live jazz on Wed and Sat nights.
$ City Perk Café, 70 Fox St, entrance on Main St next to FNB bank, T011-838 9755, www.cityperkcafe.co.za. Mon-Fri 0630-1600. Popular with office workers and with outside tables on Hollard Sq, this buzzing café is an ideal stop on the Mining District Walk (see page 46). Great coffees, breakfasts, sandwiches, salads, cakes and muffins, and more elaborate Greek and Mediterranean grills and sushi.
$ Guildhall Pub, corner Harrison St and Albertina Sisulu St, T011-833 1770. Daily 1100-2400. Established in 1888 this is considered the oldest pub in Johannesburg and retains the theme with its mining claim maps on the menus and historic photography on the walls. Portuguese-style pub grub includes peri-peri chicken and prego (steak) rolls and there are good views of the City Hall from the upstairs balcony.

Outside the city centre
p52, maps p31, p53 and p55
$$$ Bice, part of the **Southern Sun Hyde Park Hotel**, First Rd, Hyde Park,

Joburg's Chinatown

Johannesburg has had a sizeable and vibrant Chinese community since the first Chinese settlers were brought over as cheap labour to work in the mines. The first Chinatown settled along Commissioner Street in the early 20th century, but nowadays Chinese Joburgers have spread across the city, particularly to the new Chinatown, east of the city centre in Cyrildene, just east of Observatory and south of Houghton. Here on Derrick Avenue, where a pair of elaborate Chinese arches mark each end, you'll find a vibey strip of neon-lit massage parlours, acupuncturists, supermarkets, greengrocers, dumpling shops, teashops and of course restaurants. It's a great place to eat and most feature formica-top tables, plastic chairs, fluorescent lights, unbelievably kitsch decorations on the walls, and sometimes dead ducklings hanging in the window. Regional dishes include Szechuan, Shanghai, Hong Kong and Taiwanese; and there's sushi, Mongolian and Korean for good measure. The food is delicious and you won't get more authentic Chinese dishes anywhere else in South Africa. Few menus are written in English, and it's best to order a selection of dishes to share, or alternatively randomly pop into one restaurant, try something small then pop into the next one. Only cash is accepted and it's ridiculously cheap, and you can drink Chinese beer or tea, or bring your own wine. If you're here for Chinese New Year (late January/early February), Derrick Avenue is closed to traffic on the last day of the festival for a street party with fireworks, when patrons sit at long tables for a set meal, and a colourful dragon formed by several puppeteers blesses all the shops and restaurants.

T011-341 8080, www.tsogosunhotels. com. Mon-Fri 1200-1430, 1830-2230, Sat-Sun 1230-1500, 1900-2300. The African branch of the legendary Milan restaurant established in 1926 (others are in New York, Dubai and Tokyo). Chic and modern with monochrome decor and panoramic views of the leafy northern suburbs, superb Italian menu; think gnocchi with gorgonzola and walnuts, lamb shank with saffron and parmesan risotto, or classic tiramisu.
$$$ Browns of Rivonia, 21 Wessels St, Rivonia, T011-803 7533, www. browns.co.za. Sun-Fri 1200-1500, Mon-Sat 1800-2230. Pleasant setting in the courtyard of an old farm house, the extensive menu includes roast lamb, salmon timbale, mustard sirloin and crêpes and you can choose your own cheese from the cheese room. Impressive wine list with some 30,000 bottles in the cellar.
$$$ Bukhara, Nelson Mandela Sq, Sandton City, T011-883 5555, www. bukhara.com. Open 1200-1500, 1800-2300. Inarguably the best Indian food in South Africa, this elegant restaurant

at the entrance of the **Michelangelo Hotel** has a broad range of aromatic and flavoursome North Indian dishes, and you can watch the chefs in the glass-fronted kitchen.

$$$ Butcher Shop & Grill, Nelson Mandela Sq, Sandton City, T011-784 8676, www.thebutchershop.co.za. Mon-Sat 1200-2245, Sun 1200-2145. Justifiably famous for its aged steaks served with a variety of sauces and you can choose your cut of meat from the butcher. Also seafood, vegetarian options, and a good range of starters and desserts. There are other outlets around the country, but this is the original and gets through around 5 tons of steak each week.

$$$ The Grillhouse, The Firs, Oxford Rd, Rosebank, T011-880 3945, www.thegrillhouse.co.za. Open 1200-1500, 1830-2300, no lunch on Sat. Popular for its melt-in-the-mouth fillets and succulent sauces. Exposed brick and green leather furniture, excellent service and a lively atmosphere. Opposite and under the same ownership is **Katzy's**, Mon-Sat 1200-0100, a late-night piano bar and cigar lounge, with a vast selection of cognacs and malt whiskies and live music most nights.

$$$ Moyo Melrose Arch, Melrose Sq, Melrose Arch, Corlett Dr, Melrose North, T011-684 1477, www.moyo.co.za. Daily 1100-2300. The original branch of the popular chain of upmarket African-themed restaurants appearing around South Africa. This outlet is in chi-chi Melrose Arch, and is spread over 3 floors, with rustic, candlelit ethno-fashionable decor, and pan-African cuisine, including superb Mozambique seafood, Moroccan tagines and South African game dishes. Live music in the evenings. There's another branch in Zoo Lake Park near the zoo, (1 Prince of Wales Dr, Parkview, T011 646 0058, daily 1100-2200), which has some magical outdoor spaces.

$$$-$$ Le Canard, 163 Rivonia Rd, Morningside, Sandton, T011-884 4597. Daily 1200-1400, 1900-2200. French restaurant in a number of antique-filled dining rooms decorated with fresh flowers, and while it's not renowned for its good service, has a tasty traditional menu of frogs legs and snails with garlic parsley butter, duck a l'orange, flambéed crepes and some fine French wines.

$$$-$$ Osteria Tre Nonni, 9 Grafton Av, Craighall, T011-327 0095, www.osteriatrenonni.co.za. Tue-Sun 1200-1500, Tue-Sat 1800-2200. Sophisticated north Italian cuisine, home-made pasta, fresh seafood, best tiger prawns in the city, rich creamy sauces, an excellent selection of French and Italian wines and predictably good tiramisu for dessert.

$$ Pappas on the Square, Nelson Mandela Sq, Sandton City, T011-884 9991, www.pappasrestaurant.co.za. Daily 1200-2230. Authentic Greek-themed restaurant with plate breaking, Greek wine and a fun atmosphere, the chef once cooked for Christina Onassis. Share a mezze or try the *kleftiko* (lamb shank). One of the many restaurants overlooking the square.

$$ Sheikh's Palace, corner of 9th Av and Rivonia Rd, Sandton, T011-807 4119, www.sheikhspalace.co.za. Open

Jozi's top 3 high teas

Piano Lounge at the Saxon (see page 68), Thu-Sat 1000-1600, R395. This sophisticated 5-star hotel offers a pricy but delicately-presented buffet of sandwiches and scones and non-traditional items like sushi, bite-sized chocolate ganache tarts decorated with gold-leaf, and 'cake pops' (cakes on sticks). Teas range from black, green and herbal, to South African rooibos and fynbos varieties.

Il Ritrovo Lounge at The Michelangelo (see page 68), daily 1400-1700, R175. High tea at this iconic hotel on Nelson Mandela Square includes fruit skewers with chocolate dipping sauce, dainty finger sandwiches, miniature desserts and tartlets, and scones with cream and jam. As well as tea, there's Lindt hot chocolate or milkshakes with unusual flavours such as gingerbread, crème brûlée or lemon meringue.

The Lobby at 54 on Bath (see page 68), daily 1530-1700, R165, R245 with a glass of champagne. This art deco hotel offers traditional afternoon tea in its opulent lobby in the old-fashioned way – on stands with sandwiches at the bottom, scones in the middle, and desserts on top. There's a variety of Dilmah teas and a choice of flavour enhancements including star aniseed, mint and lemongrass.

1100-2300. Very authentic Lebanese restaurant with belly dancers in the evening and hubbly bubbly pipes, serving great lamb dishes and mixed grills, plus interesting and varied mezze selections which are ideal to share.

$$ Wombles, 17 3rd St, Parktown North, T011-880 2470, www.wombles. co.za. Mon-Fri 1200-1500, Mon-Sat 1830-2200. Established in Zimbabwe in 1984 and now in Johannesburg, has an excellent reputation for its choice cut matured steaks and delicious sauces. The setting is attractive colonial style, with dark wood tables, high-backed chairs and white linen tablecloths.

$$ Yamato, 198 Oxford Rd, Illovo, T011-268 0511, www.yamato.co.za. Daily 1200-1500, 1800-2200. Top-notch Japanese restaurant, very authentic and has much more than just sushi and sashimi, try the *cha soba* (buckwheat noodles with green tea powder) or *yamato nabe* (seafood hotpot). Elegant red, black and bamboo decor.

$$-$ Primi Piatti, The Zone, Rosebank Mall, T011-447 0300; 10 High St, Melrose Arch, Corlett Dr, Melrose North, T011-684 1648, www. primi-world.com. Daily 0900-2300. Stylish chain found in 9 locations, though the hippest are at Rosebank and Melrose Arch, with colourful, industrial-style decor and lively music. Huge portions of imaginative pasta, excellent wood-fired pizzas and big salads, and well known for its cocktails

Cafés

Fourno's Bakery, corner Jan Smuts Av and Bompas Rd, Dunkeld, Jan Smuts

Av, T011-325 2110, www.fournos. co.za. Mon-Fri 0600-1800, Sat-Sun 0700-1500. A legendary northern suburbs bakery now with a number of branches around the city including a 24-hr branch at the airport. The bakers work through the night to provide a huge range of fresh pastries, cakes, croissants, quiches and pies. Big breakfasts, coffee, simple lunches, very popular at the weekend.

La Patisserie, Rudd Rd Post Office Centre, Rudd Rd, Illovo, T011-268 0044. Mon-Fri 0800-1730, Sat 0800-1430. Parisian-style café with pink and white decor and a beautiful antique French chandelier, serving macaroons, petit fours, iced fancies, and cakes and gateaux so good they have been served at London's **Berkeley Hotel**.

Nino's, 23 Cradock Av, Rosebank Mall, Rosebank, T011-447 4758, www.ninos. co.za. Daily 0700-2000. Popular café with a large, open, street-side eating area, gourmet coffees, build-your-own panini sandwich bar, and a good place to start the day with a fat 3-egg omelette.

Thrupps, corner Oxford and Rudd roads, Illovo, T011-268 0298, www.thrupps. co.za. Mon-Fri 0745-1800, Sat 0800-1400, Sun 0800-1300. Once located on President St in the CBD, Johannesburg's 'Grocers of Distinction' has been going strong since 1892 when it imported items for English immigrants – it still sells Gentleman's Relish, along with pâtés, pheasant, caviar, quail, goose, imported cheese and Scottish smoked salmon. The café does excellent breakfasts and freshly baked treats. Also does takeaway picnics.

Soweto *p58, map p59*
$$ Wandie's, 618 Makhalamele St, Dube, Soweto, T011-982 2796, www.wandies.co.za. Daily 1100-2200. The affable Wandie Ndala significantly contributed to tourism in Soweto when he opened this restaurant in 1991 and today more than 100 tourists visit a day as part of Soweto tours. Traditional township food like chicken, oxtail and mutton stews, pap (mealie porridge), rice and dumplings is served buffet style and sociable eating is at long tables.

$ Nambitha, 6877 Vilakazi St, Orlando West, T011-936 9128, www. nambitharestaurant.co.za. Daily 1200-2300. Meaning 'to taste' in isiXhosa, this *shebeen* cum restaurant is a short walk from the Mandela Family Museum. The menu features Sowetan staples like *mogodu* (tripe), boiled chicken or mutton curry, served with peanut-butter spinach, pap or rice, plus good burgers, ribs and mixed grills. Great vibe and music and popular with both tourists and locals.

Around Johannesburg *p63*
$$$ Carnivore, at the Misty Hills Country Hotel, 69 Drift Blvd, Muldersdrift, 30 mins' drive (about 30 km) from the CBD on the N14, T011-950 6000, www.carnivore.co.za. Daily 1200-1600, 1800-2400. A franchise of the world-renowned **Carnivore** restaurant in Nairobi, is the ultimate 'African' eating experience. The standard meal is eat-as-much-as-you-can meat including ostrich, crocodile and warthog as well as beef and pork, which is carved off

Masai spears onto cast-iron plates. If vegetarians can bear it, they actually have a good choice, including *aviyal*, a mix of vegetables cooked in spicy coconut sauce.

🔾 Bars and clubs

Johannesburg *p37, maps p31, p38, p53, p55 and p59*
The best resource for Johannesburg's nightlife is *Johannesburg Live*, www.jhblive.com.
Bassline, 10 Henry Nxumalo St, Newtown, T011-838 9145, www. bassline.co.za. Established South African jazz venue set in Newtown's old red-brick Music Hall. Has a capacity of 1000 and regularly hosts South Africa's top jazz, hip-hop and *kwaito* artists. Tickets through **Computicket**, www.computicket.com.
Catz Pyjamas, corner of 3rd Av and Main Rd, Melville, T011-726 8596, www. catzpyjamas.co.za. Joburg's original 24-hr bistro and cocktail bar, with a funky shabby-chic atmosphere and 2nd floor balcony, reliably good food, and occasional live music and comedy.
JB's Corner, 1 High St, Melrose Arch, Corlett Dr, Melrose North, T011-684 2999. Daily 0700-1230. Glitzy Melrose Arch street café-cum-cocktail bar, with high industrial ceilings, long bar, tables on the piazza, and an impressive choice of drinks. Open early for breakfast, and has a varied menu of burgers, pasta and Tex-Mex.
Jolly Roger, 10, 4th Av, Parkhurst, T011-4423954. Daily 1200-late. Landmark pub in popular Parkhurst, with an excellent balcony perfect for

watching the area's stylish locals swan up and down 4th Av. Good draught beer and pizza specials, plus live music at weekends.
Kitcheners, corner Juta and De Beer streets, Braamfontein, T011-403 0166, www.kitcheners.co.za. Mon-Wed and Sun 1000-2100, Thu 1000-0200, Fri-Sat 1000-0400. Another historic bar (established in 1906 as the **Milner Hotel**) near the Neighbourgoods Market (see page 52). A pub by day that livens up in the evening with DJs and dancing when there's a cover charge. Music is fairly 'progressive' – indie and trance for example.
The Manhattan Club, 19 Wessels Rd, Rivonia, T011-803 7085, www. manhattanclub.co.za. Wed-Sat 2000-late. Popular northern suburbs club, predictable but danceable music, several bars and dance floors with different DJs, basic food such as pizzas and burgers.
Tiger Tiger, Fourways Mall, corner Witkoppen Rd and Fourways Blvd, Fourways, T082-370 2088, www.tiger tiger.co.za. Thu-Sat 2000-late. Mainstream club spread over 2 levels, with 8 bars including 1 for cocktails and another for shooters, VIP lounges, capacity for 1500 people, young affluent northern suburbs crowd, over 23s.
Radium Beerhall, 282 Louis Botha Av, Orange Grove, T011-728 3866, www. theradium.co.za. Daily 1000-2400. Opened in 1929, and the one of the oldest pubs in Johannesburg and not in the most salubrious part of town, but can be reached from the northern suburbs via Houghton. Hugely atmospheric, the wooden

bar comes from Johannesburg's first hotel, the **Ferreirastown Hotel**, and memorabilia and old photographs document the early mining days. Portuguese-inspired pub grub, including their famous Mozambique prawns, and regular live jazz.

Ratz Bar, 11 7th St, Mellville, T011-482 9965, www.ratzbar.co.za. Daily 1600-0200. Another lively spot in popular Melville with daily cocktail specials and music from old 80s pop to current hits. This section of 7th St is lined with many other bars and restaurants.

Roxy's Rhythm Bar, 20 Main Rd, Melville, T011-726 6019. Mon-Sat 2000-late. Melville's most established club has been in existence for more than 20 years, live music most nights and this is where many of South Africa rock groups got their first break, including *The Springbok Nude Girls* and *Just Jinger*.

The San Deck at the Sandton Sun Hotel, part of Sandton City at the corner of 5th and Alice rds, Sandton, T011-461 9744, www.tsogosunhotels.com. Daily 1000-2400. On the 26th floor of this lavish hotel (**$$$**), this Sandton premier drinking spot has an outdoor deck with three large fire pits, a number of luxurious couches and live music at weekends. Pricey cocktails but more than worth it for the best sunset views over Sandton's high-rises and the northern suburbs.

⏣ Entertainment

All tickets for live performances can be purchased online from **Computicket**, T011-340 8000,
www.computicket.com, or at their kiosks in the larger malls, as well as in **Checkers** and **Shoprite** supermarkets.

Cinema

All the latest Hollywood, European and home-grown releases can be seen at multi-screen cinemas in the shopping malls and casinos. The 2 major cinema groups are **Nu Metro**, www.numetro.co.za, and **Ster-Kinekor**, www.sterkinekor.com. New films are released on Fri. Newspapers have full listings. Rosebank Mall also has a separate **Cinema Nouveau**, which screens international and art-house films (information and bookings also at Ster-Kinekor).

Theatre

Emperor's Palace, 64 Jones St, Kempton Park, T011-928 1000, www.emperorspalace.com. Adjacent to OR Tambo International Airport, this glitzy casino and entertainment complex has 2 auditoriums showing cabaret, comedy, and local and international live bands.

Gold Reef City, Northern Parkway, Ormonde, T011-248 5168, www.goldreefcity.co.za. The 300-seat **Globe Theatre** shows cabaret and comedy, while the much larger 1100-seat **Lyric Theatre** shows musicals, pop concerts and tribute band acts.

Joburg Theatre, Loveday St, Braamfontein, T011-877 6800, www.joburgtheatre.com. Formerly the Civic Theatre, a modern complex with 3 auditoriums, frequent performances of South African plays, visiting international musicals, pantomimes, classical orchestras and home to the South African Ballet.

Market Theatre, 56 Margaret Mcingana St, Newtown, T011-832 1614, www.markettheatre.co.za. Opened in 1976, this was famous for its community theatre and controversial political plays during Apartheid. Today the 3 auditoriums show a mixture of locally written plays, Shakespeare and comedy.

Montecasino, corner of William Nicol Dr and Witkoppen Rd, Fourways, T011-511 1818, www.montecasinotheatre.co.za. Designed to resemble a Tuscan village, this casino and entertainment complex has 2 theatres, one of which was specifically built to stage South Africa's version of the **Lion King** musical and can seat over 1800.

Theatre on the Square, Nelson Mandela Sq, Sandton City, off Rivonia Rd, T011-883 8606, www.theatre onthesquare.co.za. Drama, comedy and on Fri at 1230 a lunchtime classical concert.

⊗ Festivals

Easter Rand Show, Johannesburg Expo Centre, corner of Rand Show and Nasrec Rds, Nasrec, www.rand show.co.za. First held in 1894 by the Witwatersrand Agricultural Society, and opened by Paul Kruger, today this 10-day show over Easter attracts more than 400,000 for shopping and food stalls, a fairground, and entertainment including motor and air displays, live music and a carnival.

Aug Dance Umbrella, www.dance forumsouthafrica.co.za. A festival of contemporary choreography and dance from community-based dance troupes to international companies; at various venues including the Joburg and Market theatres.

FNB Joburg Art Fair, Sandton Convention Centre, Maude St, Sandton, www.fnbjoburgartfair.co.za. A showcase for contemporary art from leading South African artists, galleries and collectors.

Standard Bank Joy of Jazz, www.joy ofjazz.co.za. Joburg's biggest annual jazz festival with over 200 local and international performers at different venues across the city, with the main events at Sandton Convention Centre adjacent to Sandton City.

Sep Arts Alive, www.arts-alive. co.za. A 4-day festival with over 600 performances in dance, visual art, poetry and music at venues across Johannesburg including the Joburg Theatre and Montecasino.

Soweto Wine Festival, University of Johannesburg, Soweto Campus, Chris Hani Rd, Soweto, www.sowetowine festival.co.za. Held over 3 evenings, sociable festival with more than 900 exhibitors for wine, food and lifestyle.

Taste of Johannesburg, Montecasino, corner of William Nicol Dr and Witkoppen Rd, Fourways, www.taste ofjoburg.com. Some of the city's top gourmet restaurants showcase their food; buy a book of coupons and a wine glass for tastings.

Oct Bierfest, Montecasino, corner of William Nicol Dr and Witkoppen Rd, Fourways, www.bierfest.co.za. Closely resembling the Oktoberfest in Munich, this Bavarian-themed festival has German food, oompah bands and plenty of beer.

O Shopping

Arts, crafts and curios

Art Africa, 62 Tyrone Av, Parkview, T011-486 2052. Mon-Fri 0900-1800, Sat 0900-1600. Located on a charming Parkview street lined with cafés, sells ceramics, carvings, jewellery, beadwork and items made from recycled drink cans, bottle tops or telephone wire. The back section is aimed at collectors for authentic African artefacts including Luba headrests, Ghanaian kente cloth, Yoruba figurines and Xhosa pipes.

Everard Read, 6 Jellicoe Av, Rosebank, T011-788 4805, www.everard-read. co.za. Mon-Fri 0900-1800, Sat 0900-1300. Founded in 1913 when the art seller exhibited on Joburg's dusty streets, Everard Read has become one of South Africa's most respected dealers in fine and contemporary art, now displayed in bright white galleries in a landmark postmodern building in Rosebank. There's another branch in Cape Town.

Goodman Gallery, 163 Jan Smuts Av, Parkwood, T011-788 1113, www. goodman-gallery.com. Tue-Fri 0930-1730, Sat 0930-1600. Established in 1966, and one of Johannesburg's best venues for showcasing local and international contemporary artists, also publishes quality art and photography books.

Kim Sacks Gallery, 153 Jan Smuts Av, Parkwood, T011-447 5804, www. kimsacksgallery.com. Mon-Fri 0900-1700, Sat 0900-1600. A selection of quality ethnic art housed in a lovely old home and regarded as one of the top galleries in the city. There is a good range of contemporary South African pieces, including prints, sculptures, beadwork and ceramics, and some genuinely rare antiques from across Africa.

Sandton Craft Market, Nelson Mandela Sq, Sandton City, corner of Sandton Dr and Rivonia Rd, T011-880 2906, www.craft.co.za. Daily 0900-1800. On the square flanked by several terrace cafés with over 70 stalls selling curios from all over Africa. Credit cards are accepted and shipping can be arranged. Touristy but lively with street performers and musicians.

Books and maps

Exclusive Books, www.exclusivebooks. co.za. National bookshop chain, the best branches are at Hyde Park Corner and Sandton City (see shopping malls below), which also have cafés. Particularly good for maps, guide books and coffee-table books on Africa and carry a full range of international magazines and newspapers.

Frank R Thorold, Meischke's Building, 42 Harrison St, CBD, T011-838 5903 www.thorolds.com. Mon-Fri 0900-1700, Sat 0900-1200. Established in 1904 and the city's oldest bookshop, specializing in antiquated books especially Africana, and it's a good place to pick up books on the early explorers or on the history of South Africa. The shop's original Latin logo, *ex Africa semper aliquid novi*, means 'always something new coming out of Africa'.

Camping and hiking equipment

Cape Union Mart, Hyde Park Corner, Jan Smuts Av, T011-325 5038, www.capeunionmart.co.za. Mon-Sat 0900-1800, Sun 1000-1400. Excellent shop selling outdoor equipment, clothing, backpacks, mosquito nets, and a great range of walking shoes. 14 other branches in Johannesburg's various shopping malls, plus one at the airport.

Gold

Scoin Shop, in the banking mall at Sandton City (see Shopping malls, below), T011-784 8525, www.sagoldcoin.com. Mon-Fri 0830-1630. Krugerrands, South Africa's famous gold coins, can be bought here as an investment or souvenir. It also produces collector's coins such as the Mandela Medallion. There are other Scoin shops at other shopping malls and at the airport.

Shopping malls

Johannesburg has more than 25 vast, modern shopping malls filled with shops, restaurants, cinemas and bars, some of which are so enormous and extravagant that they are worth visiting in their own right. Shop opening hours are listed; the restaurants and cinemas stay open later, until 2200 or 2300.

Hyde Park Corner, Jan Smuts Av, Hyde Park, T011-325 4340, www.hydeparkshopping.co.za. Mon-Sat 0900-1800, Sun 1000-1400. Luxury shopping aimed at ladies who lunch. The excellent **Exclusive Books** has its flagship outlet here, which often hosts book launches and literary events, and there are cinemas and the 132-room **Southern Sun Hyde Park Hotel ($$$)**, T011-341 8080, www.tsogosunhotels.com.

Rosebank Mall, Bath Av, Rosebank, T011-788 5530, www.rosebankmall.co.za. Mon-Fri 0900-1800, Sat 0900-1700, Sun 1000-1700. One of the more pleasant malls with a large open-air plaza lined with cafés and 12 cinema screens. **The Zone@Rosebank** features stylish boutiques and music shops aimed at young people. The Gautrain is located opposite the mall in Oxford Rd.

Maponya Mall, Chris Hani (Old Potchefstroom) Rd, Klipspruit, Soweto, T011-938 4448, www.maponyamall.co.za. Mon-Thu 0900-1900, Fri-Sat 0900-2000, Sun 0900-1700. Soweto's premier mall with all the usual chain stores, plus specialist shops and large supermarkets. It attracts 1 million shoppers a month. To commemorate the 1976 Soweto Uprising, there's a striking statue at the entrance of the famous photograph that grabbed the world's attention of Hector Pieterson's body being carried by a friend with Hector's wailing 17-year-old sister running alongside (see page 60 for the Hector Pieterson Museum).

Melrose Arch, Corlett Dr, Melrose North, T011-684 0002, www.melrosearch.co.za. Mon-Sat 0900-1800, Sun 0900-1600. Glitzy mall featuring a triple-storey branch of **Woolworths** and the country's largest branch of **Edgars** department store, plus a variety of upmarket shops featuring international brands not found elsewhere in South Africa and specialist boutiques sell couture clothing and accessories from Paris and Milan. Also well known for its restaurants lining the attractive piazza. **Oriental Plaza**, Bree St and Margaret Mcingana St, Fordsburg, T011-838 6752, www.orientalplaza.co.za. Mon-Fri 0830-1700 (closed Fri 1200-1400), Sat 0830-1500. A vast complex a couple of blocks west of Newtown in the CBD, offering 360 closely packed shops and stalls selling everything imaginable from India, China and other manufacturing countries in Asia. Household items, fabrics, spices, clothes and shoes, and if you're prepared to rummage, the odd designer label can be found. The highlight here is browsing while listening to Bollywood music and eating Indian snacks.

Sandton City and Nelson Mandela Square, corner of Sandton Dr and Rivonia Rd (attached by a walkway and sky bridge), T011-217 6000, www. sandton-city.co.za; T011-217 6000, www.nelsonmandelasquare.com. Mon-Thu 0900-1900, Fri 0900-2000, Sat-Sun 0900-1800. Massive triple-storey mall featuring all of South Africa's chain stores, cinemas, African art galleries and hyper-markets. The opulent Nelson Mandela Sq has international exclusive stores and fashionable restaurants around an attractive piazza-style square, which is home to a formidable 6-m bronze statue of the great man himself. His shoes are 1 m across and children can sit on them. The Sandton Gautrain station is a 5-min walk from Sandton City.

⏻ What to do

Bungee jumping
Orlando Towers Adventure Centre, Dynamo St, on the north side of Chris Hani (Old Potchefstroom) Rd, Orlando West, Soweto, T011-312 0450, www. orlandotowers.co.za. See page 63.

Cricket
Wanderers' Stadium, Corlett Dr, Illovo, information T011-340 1500, www.wanderers.co.za, book tickets online through **Computicket**, T011-340 8000, www.computicket.com, or at their kiosks in **Checkers** and **Shoprite** supermarkets. This is one of South Africa's premier cricket grounds and regular international matches are played in season.

Football
FNB Stadium, Nasvec Rd, Ormonde, book tickets online through **Computicket**, T011-340 8000, www. computicket.com, or at their kiosks in **Checkers** and **Shoprite** supermarkets. More popularly called **Soccer City**, and also **The Calabash** because of its resemblance to an African pot, this is the largest of Johannesburg's stadiums (and the largest in Africa) and home of the South African Football Association. This was the venue of the opening ceremony, the opening match and the final of the 2010 FIFA World Cup™ and the whole of Soweto was euphoric that these were played on their doorstep. The stadium seats 94,700 and now regularly hosts Soweto-based Premier Soccer League clubs, the Orlando Pirates and Kaizer

Chiefs. A derby between the two is not to be missed. In 2011, it broke a concert-going record for rock band U2 when it accommodated 98,000 on their 360° Tour.

Golf
There are over 40 golf courses around Johannesburg including several of South Africa's top courses. The high altitude means golfers are able to strike the ball further than they might be used to.

Glendower Golf Club, Marais Rd, Bedfordview, T011-453 1013, www. glendower.co.za. Beautiful location in a bird sanctuary, tough course with 85 bunkers, 20 mins from the city centre.

Houghton Golf Club, 2nd Av, Lower Houghton, T011-792 2349, www. houghton.co.za. First established in 1926, the present layout has been designed by Jack Nicklaus.

Royal Johannesburg and Kensington Golf Club, 1 Fairway Av, Linksfield North, T011-640 3021, www. royaljk.za.com. Established in 1909, 2 18-hole courses and a frequent venue for the South African Open.

Wanderers Golf Club, Rudd Rd, Illovo, T011-447 3311, www. wanderersgolfclub.co.za. One of the oldest courses in South Africa, quite challenging, hosts the South African PGA Championship, next to the cricket ground, just north of Rosebank.

Helicopter flights
Like any massive city, seeing Johannesburg from the air puts a different perspective on its sheer size and varied geography.

Fly Jozi, Grand Central Airport, New Rd, Midrand, T083-721 8393, www. flyjozi.co.za. Operates 1-hr scenic flights which take in Sandton, Alexandra, the CBD, Soweto and the Cradle of Mankind. Also has 1-hr flights over Hartbeespoort Dam and the Magaliesburg Mountains (see page 107). Prices start from R5500 for 2 people, and come down to around R1800 per person for 4; includes transfers from hotels to the airport.

Rugby
Ellis Park, Staib St, Doornfontein, information T011-402 8644, book tickets online through **Computicket**, T011-340 8000, www.computicket. com, or at their kiosks in **Checkers** and **Shoprite** supermarkets. South Africa's premier rugby venue and matches are played regularly during the season. The stadium seats 62,000 spectators and it can be a rowdy day out, with fans bringing their *braais* and beers with them. It's also home to Orlando Pirates soccer club, and was a venue for the 2010 FIFA World Cup™. It was first constructed in 1928 and named after a city councilor, Mr JD Ellis, who authorized the land for the stadium – hence the name. More significantly, it was where the South African team, the Springboks, defeated New Zealand's All Blacks 15-12 in the 1995 Rugby World Cup. The event became an international news story as images of then-president Mandela and Springbok captain Francois Pienaar holding up the trophy were published worldwide. It was a poignant moment in South Africa's history that

demonstrated that all races had a common cause for celebration, and the story was made into the movie *Invictus* by Clint Eastwood in 2009.

Tour operators

There are dozens of tour operators in Johannesburg that offer a range of ½- and full-day tours. These use minibuses, have registered guides and pick up from hotels, and some offer walking tours of the CBD. The standard day tours are to Soweto, city tours of both Johannesburg and Pretoria, Gold Reef City and the Apartheid Museum, Maropeng and Sterkfontein Caves, Lesedi Cultural Village and the Lion Park. Expect to pay in the region of R500-600 for a ½-day tour and R700-900 for a full-day tour. They also arrange tours further afield, including comprehensive 2- to 4-day tours to the Kruger National Park, and to Sun City and Pilanesberg Game Reserve. This is far from an exhaustive list; hotels can make recommendations and **Johannesburg Tourism**, has a full list of tour operators on their website, www.joburgtourism.com.

A Taste of Africa, T011-482 8114, www.tasteofafrica.co.za.
African Time Out, T011-477 4612, www.africantimeout.com.
Big Six Safaris, T0832-730632, www.bigsixtoursafaris.com.
Hylton Ross, T012-653 3695, www.hyltonross.com.
Joburg Places, T082 8-945216, www.joburgplaces.com.
Lords Travel & Tours, T011-791 0746, www.lordstravel.co.za.

Main Street Walks (CBD), T0728-80 9583, www.mainstreetwalks.co.za.
Past Experiences, T011-678 3905, www.pastexperiences.co.za.
Spurwing, T0788-02 7777, www.spurwingtourism.com.
Vhupo Tours, T011-936 0411, www.vhupo-tours.com.

⊖ Transport

From Johannesburg it is 540 km to the **Zimbabwe border** (Beitbridge), 403 km to **Bloemfontein**, 1400 km to **Cape Town**, 589 km to **Durban**, 961 km to **East London**, 1117 km to **Harare** (Zimbabwe), 480 km to **Kimberley**, 1141 km to **Knysna**, 560 km to **Maputo** (Mozambique), 356 km to **Nelspruit**, and 1080 km to **Port Elizabeth**.

Air

For information on airports, see Getting there, page 27, and for details of the international airlines serving Johannesburg, see Planning your trip, page 6. **OR Tambo International Airport** has numerous daily flights to/ from all South Africa's major cities, as well as regional destinations. Increasingly, **Lanseria International Airport** is also being used by some domestic airlines. By booking early online, good deals can be found with all the airlines, and you can either book directly or through **Computicket**, T011-915 8000, www.computicket.com, or in South Africa, at any of their kiosks in the shopping malls or any branch of **Checkers** and **Shoprite** supermarkets.

South African Airways (SAA) has countless daily flights run in conjunction with its subsidiaries SA Airlink, and SA Express, www.flysaa.com, covering the entire country and regional cities. British Airways Comair, T011-441 8600, www.britishairways.com, has daily flights between Johannesburg, Cape Town, Durban, Nelspruit and Port Elizabeth, as well as regional flights between Johannesburg and Mauritius, Windhoek, Livingstone, Victoria Falls and Harare.

Kulula, T0861-585 852 (in South Africa), T011-921 0111 (from overseas), www.kulula.com, also owned by British Airways, is a no-frills airline with daily services between Johannesburg, Cape Town, Durban, Port Elizabeth, Nelspruit, East London and George.

Mango, T0861-162 646 (in South Africa), T011-359 1222 (from overseas), www.flymango.com, another no-frills operator owned by SAA, has daily flights between Johannesburg, Cape Town, Durban, George and Bloemfontein.

Bus
Local For details of Johannesburg's public buses, see box, page 84. Additionally to the formal bus companies, minibus taxis also serve all areas of the city on fixed routes but with no timetables or formal stops and are flagged down on the street. They are generally fine to use for a short journey along a main road, but are best avoided on longer journeys as they are generally driven rather recklessly and there is often no way of knowing where they're heading – in Johannesburg there is a confusing unwritten system of hand-signals used to indicate where the taxi is going (cupping hands into an 'O' indicates a passenger wants to go to Orlando, for example). Most trips cost around R6, and they stop running at about 1900.

Long distance Greyhound, www.greyhound.co.za, Intercape, www.intercape.co.za, and Translux, www.translux.co.za, cover routes from Johannesburg across the country and to neighbouring countries. Full timetables can be found on the websites, and tickets can be booked online through Computicket, T011-915 8000, www.computicket.com, or in South Africa, at any of their kiosks in the shopping malls or any branch of Checkers and Shoprite supermarkets. For more information, see Getting around, page 28.

These and other smaller bus companies depart and arrive at **Park Station** on Rissik St in the CBD, which is also the railway station (see below) and the terminus for the **Gautrain** (see box, page 29). While Park Station is a perfectly safe, modern and efficient transport terminal inside, with shops, restaurants and ATMs, the surrounding area has long had a bad reputation for petty theft. Although crime levels have dropped in the area, be extra vigilant in and around the terminal and don't go wandering outside with

Johannesburg by bus

City Sightseeing, T021-511 6000, www.citysightseeing.co.za, is a red, double-decker, open-top, hop-on hop-off bus that follows a two-hour circular route around the city centre. The first bus departs from Park Station at 0900 and the last bus arrives back there at roughly 1730; timetables are on the website. The circular route has 12 stops and a bus comes by every 40 minutes (Monday-Friday), and every 30 minutes (Saturday-Sunday). Audio-commentary is available in 16 languages and there's a special kids' channel. The stops are Park Station (for the Gautrain and other transport); Gandhi Square; Carlton Centre; James Hall Transport Museum; Gold Reef City; Apartheid Museum; a stop on the corner of Fox and Ferreira streets for what is referred to as the Mining District Walk (see page 46); Newtown; the Origins Centre and Wits University; Braamfontein; Constitution Hill; and it completes its loop back at the Gautrain at Park Station. From the Gold Reef City stop there is the additional option of adding in a two-hour tour by minibus to Soweto taking in drive-bys of the Soccer City stadium, Baragwanath Hospital and taxi rank, and Orlando,

and stops at the Hector Pieterson Museum, Vilakazi Street and the Mandela Family Museum, and Kliptown. There are ticket offices at the Gautrain Park Station and Gold Reef City stops, and you can also buy tickets on the bus or online (for a discount) and join anywhere on the routes. A one-day ticket costs R170, children (5-15) R80, under 5s free, and a two-day ticket is R270/R170. With Soweto, the one-day ticket is R420/200, and the two-day ticket R500/280.

Rea Vaya, T0860-562 874, www.reavaya.org.za, is a new rapid bus transport system, with (in the most part) dedicated bus lanes and stations. Buses run roughly every 10-20 minutes from roughly 0600 to 1900 (depending on the route). It presently operates routes between Ellis Park in the east of the CBD and Soweto; Braamfontein and Soweto; and Parktown and Soweto. More usefully, there is also a circular route (the C3) in the CBD, which goes from Chancellor House (see page 45) in Fox Street, north via Rissik or Harrison streets to Park Station, past Wits University, the Joburg Theatre and Civic Centre complex and Constitution Hill in Braamfontein,

luggage. Many of the buses and trains depart and arrive late at night or early in the morning, so make sure you have pre-arranged a pickup with your hotel or take a metered taxi.

The **Baz Bus**, reservations Cape Town T021-422 5202, www.bazbus.com, is the best option for backpackers. See Planning your trip, page 10, for full details of the service.

then south to the Johannesburg Art Gallery and Joubert Park on Twist Street, and back east along Albertina Sisulu or Commissioner streets to the Carlton Centre and then completes the loop again at Chancellor House. Also useful for visitors is the T1 route, which runs from Ellis Park and passes through the CBD stopping at the Johannesburg Art Gallery, the Carlton Centre, Chancellor House, and west past the FNB Stadium into Soweto where it stops in Orlando and at the Regina Mundi Roman Catholic Church (see Soweto page 62 for details of the sights here). Fares start from R5.50 for a short journey under 5 km and fares are 10% less during off-peak times (Monday-Friday 0830-1500 and all day Saturday-Sunday). Cash is not accepted and passengers need a Rea Vaya Smartcard loaded with money. The initial fee for a card is R20 and they can be bought at any Rea Vaya main station. Cards are 'tapped' in and out on the bus so the fare is calculated; route maps and timetables are published on the website. Rea Vaya means 'we are going' in *Scamto* (a slang developed in the townships and frequently spoken by young people in Soweto today).

Metrobus, T011-833 5918, www. mbus.co.za, are single and double-decker buses that run along 330 routes on the main roads around the greater Johannesburg metropolitan area, (0600-1900), and bus stops are clearly marked. Tickets run on zones; the central zone starts from the bus terminus in Gandhi Square (see page 47) at the corner of Main and Rissik streets where there is an information office. There are also information offices at Park Station and Rosebank Mall. The most useful routes are those that follow the main roads from the CBD to the northern suburbs of Rosebank, Sandton and Randburg. Short single fares are R8.70 and routes and timetables are published on the website.

The final bus option is to use the **Gautrain feeder buses** from the Gautrain stations. Many of the routes go to and past the major sites of interest; for example there are feeder routes from Park Station through Braamfontein to Parktown, from the Sandton station to Melrose Arch, and from Rosebank to Zoo Lake past Johannesburg Zoo. For details of these see the Gautrain box, page 29.

Car hire

The following are at **OR Tambo International Airport**. Check the websites for other branches in the city including those at **Lanseria**

International Airport. **Avis**, T011-923 3730, www.avis.co.za; **Budget**, T011-390 1924, www.budget.co.za; **Europcar**, T011-574 1000, www. europcar.co.za; **First Car Rental**, T011-

230 9999, www.firstcarrental.co.za; **Hertz**, T011-390 2066, www.hertz. co.za; **Tempest**, T011-394 8626, www. tempestcarhice.co.za; Thrifty, T011-230 5201, www.thrifty.co.za.

Train
Local **Metrorail**, enquiries T011-773 5878, www.metrorail.co.za, operates suburban commuter trains across the Johannesburg metropolitan region as far as Soweto and Randfontein in the west, Springs in the east, and Pretoria in the north. However, few routes are useful for tourists and while these trains are fine to use in rush hour (0700-0800 and 1600-1800), are best avoided at quieter times due to the possibility of petty crime. But in saying that, CCTV cameras have been installed at larger stations to monitor activities on the platforms and there are visible security guards on trains, making the service safer than it was in the past. They generally operate 0400-2100 and run about every 20 mins in peak periods. Short single fares start from R8, and routes and timetables are published on the website.

For details of the **Gautrain**, between Johannesburg and **Pretoria** and the service between Sandton and the airport, see box, page 29.

Long distance The railway station is at Park Station. Passenger trains are run by **Shosholoza Meyl**, T086-000 888 (in South Africa), T011-774 4555 (from overseas), www.shosholozameyl.co.za. **Shosholoza Meyl** also operates a more upmarket service, the **Premier Classe**, T011-774 5247, www.premierclasse. co.za, between Johannesburg and **Cape Town**, **Durban** and **Port Elizabeth**. It has a dedicated lounge for boarding passengers at Park Station. For more information on all rail services, see Transport, page 10.

❶ Directory

Immigration Dept of Home **Affairs**, President St, T011-836 3228, www.home-affairs.gov.za, Mon-Fri 0730-1600. Visa extensions take 10 working days. You will need to produce an onward ticket and proof of funds. **Medical services** Netcare **Rosebank Hospital**, 14 Sturdee Av, Rosebank, T011-328 0500, and there are more than 30 other private Netcare hospitals in Gauteng; for 24-hr medical services and ambulances T082-911, to locate a hospital T011-301 0000, www.netcare.co.za. **Netcare Travel Clinic**, Morningside Close, 1 Michelle St, off Rivonia Rd, Morningside, Sandton, T011-802 0059, www.travelclinic.co.za, Mon-Fri 0730-1800, Sat 0830-1300, useful stop to update vaccinations and pick up anti-malarials. **Morningside Medi-Clinic** (private), corner of Rivonia and Hill roads, Morningside, Sandton, T011-282 5000, 24-hr emergency, T011-282 5126, www.mediclinic.co.za.

Contents

Footprint features

Pretoria & North West Province

Pretoria

Pretoria is one of the South Africa's three capital cities, serving as the executive (administrative) capital; the other two being Cape Town (the legislative capital) and Bloemfontein (the judicial capital). The name Pretoria was given to the new settlement by Marthinus Wessel Pretorius, in memory of his father, Andries Pretorius, who had led the Voortrekkers in the bloody massacre of the Zulus at Blood River. Today it is home to government departments and ministries, foreign embassies and diplomatic missions, and with a population of around 1.5 million is the fourth largest city in the country. Despite being almost joined to Johannesburg 56 km to the south by a band of green-belt towns, the atmosphere of each city couldn't be more different. While Johannesburg was built on gold and industry, Pretoria's was founded during the Voortrekker period of South Africa's turbulent past and retains a rather stern, bureaucratic atmosphere – albeit softened by a large student population thanks to it being home to the University of South Africa and the University of Pretoria among other educational institutions.

Arriving in Pretoria → *Phone code: 012. Altitude: 1363 m.*

Getting there

The centre of Pretoria is 45 km from Johannesburg's **OR Tambo International Airport** and 45 km from **Lanseria Airport**. For details of arriving by air, see page 27. You can travel to/from the airport by using an airport shuttle bus service, or by the **Gautrain** (see box, page 29), which links both Pretoria and Johannesburg and the airport via Sandton. The Pretoria Gautrain station is in the CBD adjacent to the main railway station on the corner of Scheiding and Paul Kruger streets, and Hatfield Station is on the corner of Grosvenor Road and Arcadia Street. Metrorail suburban trains run between Pretoria and Johannesburg but high crime levels means you should generally avoid it (see Transport, page 86). The central Metrorail station, as well as the terminal for the long-distance buses (**Intercape**, **Greyhound** and **Translux**) are at the main railway station on the corner of Scheiding and Paul Kruger streets in the city centre. ▸ *See Transport, page 105.*

Getting around

Most of Pretoria's sights are in the city centre or lie in the surrounding hills and can easily be seen in a day. While there is a good local metropolitan bus service connecting the city centre and suburbs, as well as some Gautrain feeder bus routes (see box, page 29), buses do not go to the various monuments, so the easiest way to get to these is either to hire a car or go on a guided tour.

Orientation

Church Street is Pretoria's main through road, running from east to west and, at 26 km long, is considered to be one of the world's longest streets. From the city centre it leads east to the suburbs of **Arcadia**, where many of the embassies and the Union Buildings are located, and to **Hatfield** and **Brooklyn**, a few kilometres further east. The city's colleges, universities and sports stadiums are located in this area, as well as the majority of the hotels and restaurants. Both are attractive suburbs, dotted with parks and gardens, and streets lined with Pretoria's distinctive jacaranda trees (see box, page 94). Church Street however has recently and confusingly gone through one of those complicated name changes that have been rolled out in many South African cities to replace old-fashioned colonial and possibly offensive Apartheid names, with more contemporary ones celebrating modern heroes or personalities. To the east of the city centre, Church Street has become Stanza Bopape Street (after a black anti-Apartheid activist who died in police custody in 1988); from Nelson Mandela Drive to Church Square in the city centre it is now Helen Joseph Street (a white anti-Apartheid activist who in 1955 was one of the leaders who read out the clauses of the Freedom Charter and consequently was a defendant at the 1956 Treason Trail); from Church Square to the R511 it is WF Nkomo Street (a former Trustee of the Bantu Welfare Trust, which aimed to improve the lot of urban Africans from the 1940s until the 1970s); and from the R511 west it is Elias Motsoaledi Street (a black anti-apartheid activist, who along with Nelson Mandela, was one of the eight men sentenced to life imprisonment at the 1964 Rivonia Trial). Many other street names in Pretoria have been changed, but while most are now signposted, not all are reflected on maps or in literature.

Tourist information

Tshwane Tourism ⓘ *Old Nederlandsche Bank Building, Church Sq, T012-358 1430, Mon-Fri 0800-1700, Sat 0900-1300,* doesn't have the usual desk and helpful staff found in most local tourist offices, but it does produce a couple of useful maps, highlighting the major sights. The Pretoria office of **South Africa National Parks (SANParks)** ⓘ *643 Leyds St, Groenkloof, T012-428 9111, www. sanparks.org, Mon-Fri 0730-1535, telephone reservations also Sat 0800-1300,* is the head office and handles all bookings for accommodation and special long-distance hikes such as the Wilderness Trails in the Kruger National Park.

Background

The area was originally occupied by Ndebele people in the early 1600s, but it wasn't until 1840, when the first Afrikaans settlers arrived, that the area was established as a permanent settlement led by Voortrekker leader Andries Pretorius. In 1854, work began on building a church right by today's Church Square, and by the 1860s, as the city was steadily growing, Marthinus Pretorius (Andries's son), who had been made president of the republic, tried to unite the Orange Free State with the Transvaal. He failed, resigned as president and was replaced by the Reverand Thomas François Burgers in 1870. Under Burgers, the city developed and schools and parks were built, but the problems of administering the region remained unresolved. The British eventually annexed the Transvaal in April 1877, and their first action was to establish a garrison which attracted a large number of immigrants. New buildings were erected and the fortunes of the city began to look more promising. However, during the Transvaal War of Independence, the British withdrew and the city was taken over by the Paul Kruger who was to cause countless problems once gold had been discovered.

At the end of the Anglo-Boer War, Pretoria was named as the capital of the British colony, and as such it continued to prosper so that when the Union of South Africa was created in 1910, Pretoria was made the administrative capital of the new state. Shortly afterwards, the Union Buildings were constructed to

1 Greater Pretoria

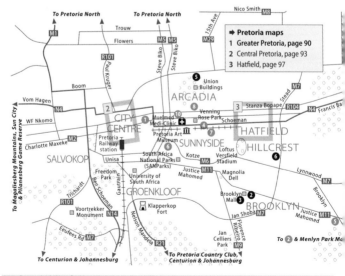

Name change

From 2005, Pretoria has been under-going a name change of sorts to Tshwane, the Setswana name of the Apies River, which flows through the city. Since then it has been often marketed as the 'City of Tshwane', which is reflected on some local maps and signposts. However, while Tshwane has been adopted successfully for the wider metropolitan municipality that forms the local government of northern Gauteng, to date the name Tswhane has confusingly not come into common usage for the central business district (CBD) of Pretoria itself. This proposed name change remains a controversial issue among both residents and administrative bodies, although recently many of Pretoria's street names have been changed successfully to commemorate anti-Apartheid struggle heroes or cultural icons.

house the new government. The growth of the town was now closely related to the expanding civil service and its status was assured and in 1931, Pretoria gained status as a city and in 1961 was named as the capital of the Republic of South Africa.

Pretoria previously had a rather sinister image as 'the capital of Apartheid South Africa' given that all the Apartheid government policies were made there, but its political reputation was changed significantly with the inauguration of Nelson Mandela as the country's first black president at the Union Buildings on 10 May 1994. Like Johannesburg, Pretoria has large townships to the northwest and northeast of the city, and after the creation of new municipal structures across South Africa in 2000, the metropolitan council reorganized itself to unite the previously segregated areas under one administration. The greater area is now called Tshwane, generally believed to be the Setswana name of the Apies River, which flows through the city. The municipality covers around 6300 sq km of northern Gauteng south to the borders with the greater Johannesburg metropolitan area around Midrand, midway between the two cities.

N

1 km
1 mile

Where to stay
224 **1**
Bohemian House **2**
Casa Toscana Lodge **3**
Court Classique **4**
Elegant Lodge **5**
Illyria House **6**
Pretoria Backpackers **7**
Sheraton Pretoria **8**
Southern Sun
Pretoria **10**

Restaurants
Bistro Boer'geoisie **1**
Cynthia's Indigo
Moon **3**
Just Cuban **6**
Kream **2**
La Madeleine **4**
La Pentola **5**

To Bela-Bela &
Limpopo Province

To Nelspruit & Kruger National Park

Pretoria
National
Botanical
Garden

N1

M6

To

To Johannesburg & OR Tambo
International Airport

City centre

The oldest buildings in Pretoria are clustered around Church Square in the heart of the city centre, once a Voortrekker marketplace where farmers would gather to observe Holy Communion. A rather unattractive statue of a grim-faced, grizzled Paul Kruger stands in the middle surrounded by the statues of four anonymous Voortrekkers, which was commissioned by Jewish industrialist Sammy Marks in the late 1890s to express his gratitude for being allowed to build the town's first synagogue. Today it is surrounded by fluttering flocks of pigeons and flanked by important late 19th-century banks and government offices. The most interesting of these is the **Palace of Justice**, where Nelson Mandela and other leaders of the ANC were tried during the notorious Treason Trials of 1963-1964. On the southwest side is the Raadsall, or parliament, and the Old Netherlands (Nederlandsche) Bank building, which now houses the tourist office.

Two blocks west of Church Square, the **Kruger Museum** ① *60 WF Nkomo St, T012-326 9172, www.ditsong.org.za, daily 0830-1700, R35, children (under 16) R15*, is where President Kruger lived between 1884-1901 when he was president of the **Zuid-Afrikaansche Republiek**. It is now a museum that displays a fairly diverting collection of his possessions, as well as objects relating to the Anglo-Boer War. At the back of the house are the state coach and his private railway carriage.

South of Church Square, the **National Museum of Natural History** (formerly the **Transvaal Museum**) ① *432 Paul Kruger St, T012-322 7632, www.ditsong. org.za, daily 0800-1600, R25, children (3-13) R10*, is a typically dusty natural history museum that was founded in 1892 and moved into its current premises in 1912. The museum serves as a research and documentation centre for the fauna of southern Africa, and is one of the leading centres for zoological research in the country. The displays, focusing on geology and stuffed animals, are spread over a series of halls, including the Austin Roberts Bird Hall, which showcases the varied birdlife of southern Africa, and a collection of semi-precious stones. More interesting, perhaps, is the fact that the world-renowned hominid fossil, 'Mrs Ples' (*Australopithecus africanus transvaalensis*), is kept here, although sadly the public doesn't have access to her. Opposite the museum is **City Hall**, dating from 1935, a grand building in a semi-Italian classical style with 32 tower bells, donated by George Heys, owner of Melrose House (below). It is fronted by broad square, with a fountain and three statues; Andries Pretorius on horseback, his son Marthinus Pretorius who officially founded the city in 1855 and named it after his father, and a newer 6-m-tall bronze statue of Chief Tshwane that was unveiled in 2006. The latter is controversial as although he was a local leader in the 1600s, said to have

② Central Pretoria

➡ **Pretoria maps**
1 Greater Pretoria, page 90
2 Central Pretoria, page 93
3 Hatfield, page 97

Where to stay 🛏
StayEasy Pretoria **3**

Restaurants 🍴
Café Riche **1**
Oriental Palace **2**

Jacaranda City

During an eight-week period over October and November, Pretoria is transformed into a glowing purple mass when the magnificent jacaranda trees (*Jacaranda mimosifolia*) are in bloom and carpet the streets and parks with their blossoms. It is estimated that there are between 40,000-70,000 jacarandas in Pretoria, but the trees are not indigenous to South Africa. Their history starts as early as 1888 when two trees were imported from Argentina and planted at a school in Arcadia, and their popularity as an ornamental tree soon took off. Jacarandas have become such a large part of Pretoria's culture that the most popular local radio station is called Jacaranda FM, and a legend among Pretoria's university students is that if a jacaranda blossom lands on your head, you will pass all your year-end exams. However today, since the jacaranda tree is exotic, it is considered to be an invader plant and prevents growth of native species by consuming a lot of water. While laws allow existing jacarandas to be kept, new trees may not replace them when they die.

inspired the naming of the Tshwane municipality, it is also claimed that the renaming (from 2000) was after the Setswana name of the Apies River.

The **Treaty of Vereeniging** ending the Anglo-Boer War (1899-1902) was signed in **Melrose House** ⓘ *275 Jeff Masemola St, T012-322 2805, www. melrosehouse.co.za, Tue-Sun 1000-1700, R20, children (under 16) R10, small café in the converted stables*, on 31 May 1902, between the British High Command and Boer Republican Forces. The house was originally built in 1880 for George Heys, who made his fortune in the diamond rush in Kimberley and established a stagecoach service to the Transvaal. With his newfound wealth he commissioned British architects to design him a house, and it was named after Melrose Abbey in Scotland, where Heys and his wife had visited on honeymoon. It is regarded as one of the finest examples of Victorian domestic architecture in South Africa; marble columns, stained-glass windows, turrets, Dutch gables and mosaic floors all help create a feeling of serene style and wealth. Across the road is the attractive Burgers Park (see box, opposite).

Follow Paul Kruger Street north of Church Square for about 900 m to the **National Zoological Gardens of South Africa** ⓘ *corner of Paul Kruger and Boom streets, entrance on Boom St, T012-328 3265, www.nzg.ac.za, daily 0800-1730, R75, children (2-15) R50, last ticket 1630, night tours Wed, Fri and Sat 1830-2030, R100/85, café and the Zoovenir Shop*, formerly Pretoria Zoo, which was established in 1899 and now covers 85 ha and houses over 8000 animals, reptiles, fish and birds. Heavily involved in research and conservation, it is South Africa's largest and best-designed zoo and many of the enclosures

Pretoria's parks

Like Johannesburg, Pretoria is well known for its public parks and the city takes much pride in its magnificent open spaces, which are enjoyed by many residents. Opposite Melrose House (see page 94), the oldest and most central is **Burgers Park** between Lilian Ngoyi and Thabo Sehume Streets. It was named after the second president of the Transvaal, Thomas Francois Burgers, and George Heys, owner of Melrose House, was responsible for the final layout along with government botanists. It was completed in 1892, and is a fine example of a Victorian-style park, with its irregular, curved paths, a large fish pond and a cast-iron bandstand. The 'florarium' houses a collection of exotic plants in contrasting environments, from subtropical flowers to succulents from the Karoo and Kalahari regions. The park also has a statue of remembrance for the officers of the South African Scottish Regiment who were killed during the First World War.

The 3-ha **Springbok Park** is between Francis Baard and Grosvenor Streets in Hatfield. Previously known as Grosvenor Park, it was first planted in 1905 during planning for the suburb and in commemoration of Hugh Richard Arthur Grosvenor, Duke of Westminster, who was closely associated with South Africa. A stream flows through it and there are some fine trees from different regions of the country,

as well as a branch of the popular family restaurant chain Dros on its northeastern corner.

Established and named after a director of the city's parks in the 1940s, the neatly laid out **Venning Rose Park** is between Francis Baard and Eastwood Streets in Arcadia. It's known for its immaculate rose beds featuring more than 30 rose species including one called the 'City of Pretoria'. An avenue of palm trees ends beside a pleasant tea garden, and as the park is close to the diplomatic enclave many international families come here at weekends.

Jan Celliers Park, on the corner of Wenning and Broderick streets, west of Florence Ribeiro Avenue in Groenkloof, is named after the Afrikaans poet who wrote during the Anglo-Boer War and is also known as Protea Park. On a natural slope with good city views, it features rock gardens, indigenous trees and a water garden, where two ponds are linked by a series of 14 small waterfalls.

Magnolia Dell on the corner of Florence Ribeiro Avenue and University Road in Muckleneuk is one of Pretoria's most beautiful parks, especially when the magnolia trees bloom in spring. It's ideal for picnics next to the willow-lined stream, while Huckleberrys is the tea garden and licenced restaurant. The Art-in-the-Park art and crafts market is held on the last Sunday of the month.

resemble the natural environments of the animals as much as possible. There's also a large aquarium, reptile park, and a walk-through aviary. Golf carts are available to get around the 6 km of walkways and there's an aerial cableway and tractor rides for kids. On some nights there are guided tours to see the nocturnal animals, which ends with a *braai* (bring your own meat and drinks). If you have a tent, it's also possible to camp at the zoo.

Outside the city centre → *See map, page 90. For listings, see pages 100-106.*

The Pretoria Art Museum ① *667 Francis Baard St, on the corner of Wessels St, Arcadia, T021-344 1807, Tue-Sun 1000-1700, www.pretoriaartmuseum.co.za, R20, children (under 16) R5*, takes up a whole block and originally held the City Council of Pretoria's art collection which had been built up since the 1930s, although the rather ugly long, flat glass and concrete structure as it stands today was built in 1962. It houses a fine collection of South African art as well as a selection of run-of-the-mill 17th-century Dutch paintings. The collection includes works of the country's 'Old Masters', such as Henk Pierneef, Frans Oerder and Anton van Wouw, and interesting temporary exhibitions.

The magnificent red sandstone complex of the **Union Buildings** ① *Government Av, Arcadia, T012-300 5200*, sits proudly on top of Meintjeskop, the highest point in the city centre. This is the official seat of government, most famous for being the site of Nelson Mandela's speech after his inauguration as president on 10 May 1994, when the grounds in front of the building where packed with thousands of well-wishers. The building was completed in 1913 to house the entire civil service of the Union of South Africa, and was then the largest building in the country. It was designed by Herbert Baker, who was strongly in favour of Meintjeskop, which was within a mile of the centre of Pretoria and reminded him strongly of some of the acropolises of Greece where he had studied Mediterranean architecture. He also designed St George's Cathedral and Rhodes Memorial in Cape Town, as well as some fine homes in Parktown in Johannesburg and went on to help the planning of New Delhi, India. Baker gave the 275-m-long Union Buildings a typically English monumental elegant design and it has two curved wings which at the time represented the English and Afrikaans sections of the population. While the interior is not open to the public, the formal gardens below the buildings are pleasant to walk around, and enjoy the city views, and look out for the statues of South Africa's famous generals: Botha, on horseback, Hertzog and Smuts. But the best reason for coming here is to see the inspiring new statue of Mandela, which was unveiled on 16 December 2013 (the Day of Reconciliation) just shortly after his death. It was in fact initially commissioned in June 2013 by the National Heritage Council as part of the celebrations to mark the centenary of the Union Buildings, but it was unveiled in a ceremony on 16 December to mark the close of the official 10-day mourning period for much loved Mandela, who died at his Johannesburg home on 5 December. The astonishingly nine-metre tall bronze sculpture has him smiling broadly with one leg slightly in front of the other to demonstrate a nation on the move, and his arms are outstretched as if embracing the whole country.

South of the city is the looming granite hulk of the **Voortrekker Monument** ⓘ *Eeufees Rd (M7), Groenkloof, T012-326 6770, www.voortrekkermon.org.za, May-Aug 0800-1700, Apr-Sep 0800-1800, R55, children (under 16) R30, family of 4 R110, restaurant and tea garden*, a controversial Afrikaner memorial. The monument, a 40-m cube, was completed in 1949 after 11 years of work. It is a sombre and unattractive structure, a windowless block dominating the landscape, but one of particular significance to Afrikaners. It was built to commemorate the Great Trek of the 1830s, when the Afrikaners struck inland from the Cape with just their ox wagons and little idea of the trials that lay ahead of them. Inside is the cavernous Hall of Heroes, where around the walls

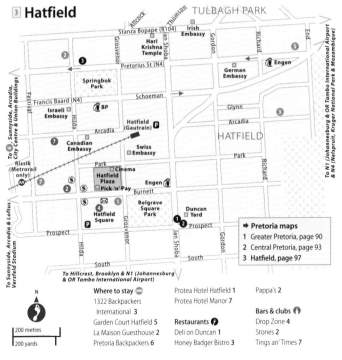

3 Hatfield

Where to stay 🛏
1322 Backpackers
  International **3**
Garden Court Hatfield **5**
La Maison Guesthouse **2**
Pretoria Backpackers **6**

Protea Hotel Hatfield **1**
Protea Hotel Manor **7**

Restaurants 🍴
Deli on Duncan **1**
Honey Badger Bistro **3**

Pappa's **2**

Bars & clubs 🍸
Drop Zone **4**
Stones **2**
Tings an' Times **7**

➡ **Pretoria maps**
1 Greater Pretoria, page 90
2 Central Pretoria, page 93
3 Hatfield, page 97

27 marble friezes depict both the trek and scenes from the Zulu wars, including a seriously suspect portrayal of the Battle of Blood River, where the Afrikaners are shown as brave soldiers and the Zulus as cowardly savages. The monument used to be the site of a huge annual celebration on 16 December, the date of the battle (known as the Day of the Covenant). At exactly midday on this date a ray of sunlight falls onto a large slab of stone in the centre of the basement (rather like a tomb), spotlighting the carved words: "Ons Vir Jou, Suid Afrika" (We are for you, South Africa). The fact that this date celebrated the bloody massacre of Zulus proved, unsurprisingly, hugely controversial, and after the end of Apartheid, this national holiday was renamed the Day of Reconciliation. Today, the celebrations for this event are held at Freedom Park (see below). For impressive views of the surrounding countryside and the city, take the lift to the viewing area on the roof.

You can walk around the battlements and enjoy more of the excellent city views from **Fort Klapperkop** ① *off Nelson Mandela Dr (R21) on Johan Rissik Dr, Groenkloof, T012-346 7703, Tue-Sun 1000-1700, R20, children (under 16) R10.* It was one of three forts erected in Pretoria before the outbreak of the Anglo-Boer War (1899-1902) to guard the southern entrance to the town, but no resistance was put up when the British entered Pretoria in May 1900. Today it's a museum of South Africa's military history, with Anglo-Boer War objects and furniture. It also has a stable complex, an old steam locomotive which was used during the war, the last tram used in Pretoria and a commemorative war statue.

Freedom Park ① *corner Koch and 7th avenues, Salvokop, across from the Central Prison, T012-336 4000, www.freedompark.co.za, daily 0800-1630, R90, children (5-12), under5s free, R70, maps are available for self-guided tours or tours can be arranged for groups, no restaurant but vending machines are at the entrance,* is purposefully and significantly located on a hill opposite the Voortrekker Monument. A 52-ha open-air museum, and one of the most ambitious heritage projects in South Africa, it opened in 2007 to commemorate the country's political history and to celebrate its cultural heritage. Its mission is to be a testament to the truth and reconciliation process that occurred at the end of Apartheid. The impressive sleek design and architecture uses lots of slate and granite, with neat pathways and tranquil ornamental water features linking the several components. Like the Voortrekker Monument, there are tremendous views over the city from here.

There are several significant elements to the complex. The Khoi word for dream, //hapo is an interpretative museum that tells the story of South Africa in several parts from the first civilizations and the colonialists to Apartheid and democracy. **Isivivane** is the symbolic resting place of those who died in the struggle against Apartheid, and is represented by a circle of 11 giant boulders – one from each of South Africa's nine provinces, and two more representing the national government and international community.

Cullinan Diamond Mine

About 40 km east of Pretoria on the R513, the small town of Cullinan is home to the Cullinan Diamond Mine, the third richest diamond producer in South Africa, that to date has yielded more than 120 million carats. Its functioning open pit is four times larger than the well known Big Hole in Kimberley. In 1905, the largest rough diamond in history was found at the mine and was named the Cullinan Diamond after the mine owner at the time. The Transvaal government presented it to King Edward VII for his 66th birthday (quite remarkably it was sent to England by ordinary parcel post). It was fashioned into nine cut stones, the largest of which was the Great Star of Africa, a pear-shaped diamond of 530.20 carats, which was set in the sceptre of the British crown jewels; today it can be seen in the Tower of London. This was the largest polished diamond in the world until it was superseded in 1985 by the Golden Jubilee Diamond (545.67 carats), also from the Cullinan Mine, which was named after the 50th-anniversary ascent of Thailand's royal couple, King Bhumibol and Queen Sirakit, and is now part of Thailand's crown jewels and on display at the Royal Museum in Bangkok. Another famous Cullinan diamond is the Taylor-Burton Diamond (69.42 carats), which was found in 1966 and sent to New York to be polished into two pieces. In 1972 Richard Burton bought the larger one to be put into a diamond necklace for the 40th birthday of his wife Elizabeth Taylor.

Surface tours of the mine are on offer, and are run by **Premier Diamond Tours**, Bank St, Cullinan, T012-734 0081 www.diamondtourscullinan.co.za. 1½- to two-hour tours Mon-Fri 1030 and 1400, Sat-Sun 1030 and 1200, R100, no children under 10, advance bookings essential. They include a 15-minute DVD about how diamonds are formed, replicas of the famous diamonds, a mock-up of an underground tunnel, and a lookout to see the top of the shafts and big hole. They end in the cutting and polishing facility where the skill and mastery required to transform a diamond from a rough stone into a sparkling faceted gem is demonstrated, and you can buy stones in the jewellery shop.

Sikhumbuto is the largest element, where the massive 697-m-long Wall of Names has tens of thousands of names inscribed of those who lost their lives in the eight conflicts that have shaped the history of South Africa. These include the slave trade period, the Boer wars, world wars and the struggle against Apartheid. This element also includes the eternal flame and the 2000-seat amphitheatre which is used for ceremonial purposes including the gathering of government dignitaries on Reconciliation Day (16 December).

The most impressive component is the structure at the summit of the park built to resemble a graceful spiral of reeds symbolizing the re-growth of South Africa. With almost 200 reeds, the tallest measuring 32 m, this is a spectacular sight and can be seen from across Pretoria; especially at night when they are dramatically lit up.

Established in 1946, the **Pretoria National Botanical Garden** ① *2 Cussonia Av, Brummeria, T012-843 5172, www.sanbi.org, daily 0800-1800, last entry 1600 except on concert days, R26, children (6-16) R12, under 6s free, restaurant and craft and garden shops,* are to the east of the city and to the northeast of the junction with the N1 and N14. The 76-ha gardens are cleverly laid out on either side of a 35-m-high quartzite outcrop, which divides a cooler south-facing section with a north-facing, warmer section presenting two different environments (and hence vegetation). The formally laid out sections are planted with oaks, cherry trees and indigenous plants including cycads and aloes and some 50% of South Africa's tree species. The ponds attract around 200 species of bird, including yellow-billed ducks, Egyptian geese and crested grebes, while lucky visitors may spot the diminutive grey duiker.

◉ Pretoria listings

For hotel and restaurant price codes and other relevant information, see pages 13-18.

◉ Where to stay

Pretoria *p88, maps p90, p93 and p97*
Pretoria has far fewer luxurious or contemporary hotels than Johannesburg, but it does have a better choice of smaller guesthouse-type accommodation, most of which are in the suburbs.

$$$$ Illyria House, 337 Bourke St, Muckleneuk, T012-344 5193, www.illyria.co.zawww.illyria.co.za. Colonial whitewashed manor house with old-world charm, French antiques and valuable 17th-century tapestries on the walls. 14 elegant rooms with Victorian baths, gourmet food, pool in peaceful grounds, spa, special touches include gloved butlers and pre-dinner classical or jazz piano recitals in the drawing room.

$$$ Bohemian House, 389 Eridanus St, Waterkloof Ridge, T012-460 1219, www.bohemianhouse.co.za. Upmarket guesthouse in lovely terracotta-tiled villa in a peaceful and leafy suburb, 10 individually themed rooms – colonial, Egyptian, Moroccan, for example – with a/c and DSTV, pool surrounded by tropical gardens, high tea is served on the terrace, excellent food in the romantic candlelit dining room.

$$$ Court Classique, corner of Francis Baard and Beckett streets, Arcadia, T012-344 4420, www.courtclassique.co.za. Practical option in the diplomatic area with 58 spacious suites with kitchenettes,

DSTV, Wi-Fi and contemporary black and red decor, landscaped patios with water features, swimming pool, good restaurant, wine and cocktail bar.

$$$ Sheraton Pretoria Hotel, corner Stanza Bopape and Wessels streets, Arcadia, T012-429 9999, www.sheratonpretoria.com. A diplomats' haunt and 5-star Sheraton standards, 175 a/c rooms with Italian marble bathrooms, DSTV and Wi-Fi, palatial lobby, heated pool, gym, restaurant, and the terrace at **Tiffins Bar** has uninterrupted views of the Union Buildings.

$$$ Southern Sun Pretoria, corner Steve Biko and Pretorius streets, Arcadia, T012-444 5500, www.tsogo sunhotels.com. Good standards and facilities in this modern block, short walk to the CBD, 242 rooms, gym, pool, restaurant and bar.

$$ Casa Toscana Lodge, 5 Darlington Rd, Lynnwood, T012-348 8820, www.casatoscana.co.za. Elaborately designed Tuscan-style lodge in large gardens to the east of the city with easy access from the N1. 20 individually decorated rooms with DSTV and Wi-Fi, pool, **Lé-Si**, is a well-regarded continental restaurant with wine cellar and outside tables in a garden gazebo.

$$ Elegant Lodge, 83 Atterbury Rd, Menlo Park, T012-346 6460, www.elegantlodge.co.za. Attractive guesthouse with mock Cape Dutch architecture, easy access to the N1 and Menlyn Park Mall, 16 a/c rooms, comfortable furnishings, DSTV, Wi-Fi, small reasonable restaurant, 24-hr bar, and pretty courtyards.

$$ Garden Court Hatfield, corner End and Pretorius streets, Hatfield, T012-432 9600. 157 rooms, a pool and restaurant.

$$ La Maison Guesthouse, 235 Hilda St, Hatfield, T012-430 4341, www.lamaison.co.za. A grand white mansion built in 1922 close to many diplomatic missions and the Gautrain. 6 large rooms with DSTV, lush gardens, swimming pool, roof-top terrace, the **Catemba**, restaurant is popular and specializes in Portuguese food and wine.

$$ Protea Hotel Hatfield, 1141 Burnett St, Hatfield, T012-364 0300, www.proteahotels.com. A quality Protea offering, with 119 a/c small but modern rooms with DSTV and Wi-Fi, pleasant contemporary decor, splash pool, restaurant and bar.

$$ Protea Hotel Manor, 1050 Burnett St (entrance in Festival St), Hatfield, T012-362 7077/8. 29 a/c 1- or 2-bed good sized suites with kitchenettes, and another 16 standard rooms. Both in a great location near Hatfield Plaza and a short walk to the Gautrain.

$ 1322 Backpackers International, 1322 Arcadia St, Hatfield, T012-362 3905, www.1322backpackers.com. Neat and well managed set up in a quiet street in Hatfield but just 500 m from the Gautrain, with dorms, and doubles in garden huts, TV lounge, pool and thatched garden bar/*braai* area with open fire-pit, kitchen, basic breakfast and suppers available or can order in takeaways. There's secure parking, Wi-Fi, bike hire and a travel desk.

$ Hotel 224, corner of Francis Baard and Leyds St, T012-440 5281, www.hotel224.com. Huge concrete block built in the 1980s with 224 very small rooms but cheap, recently upgraded with DSTV and Wi-Fi, buffet restaurant, pub, secure parking, and great city views from the upper floors, including the Union Buildings.

$ Pretoria Backpackers, 425 Farenden Rd, Clydesdale, T012-343 9754, www.pretoriabackpackers.net. The most established backpackers in town, in 2 houses around the corner from each other, within walking distance of Loftus Stadium. Dorms, doubles and family rooms, stylishly decorated with a guesthouse feel, lovely tropical gardens with fishponds and gazebos, swimming pool, internet, good breakfasts, and travel desk for booking local tours, plus Sun City/Pilanesberg or Kruger.

$ StayEasy Pretoria, 632 Lilian Ngoyi St, T012-407 0600. 136 simple but good value rooms, a pool and breakfast room and is handy for the railway station and Gautrain.

---

❷ Restaurants

Pretoria *p88, maps p90, p93 and p97*
In a city as spread out as Pretoria, restaurants tend to be found in or near the large shopping malls (see page 104), or head to **Hatfield** or **Brooklyn**.

$$$ Cynthia's Indigo Moon, 283 Dey St, Brooklyn, T012-346 8926, www.cynthiasindigomoon.co.za. Mon-Fri 1200-2200, Sat 1800-2200. Upmarket restaurant spread over a series of classy rooms with sophisticated glass and wood decor with art and mirrors

on the walls. Traditional meat dishes such as fillets with gourmet toppings and chateaubriand, some seafood and game. Extensive wine list.

$$$ La Madeleine, 122 Priory Rd, Lynnwood Ridge, T012-361 3667, www.lamadeleine.co.za. Tue-Sat 1900-2200. Long-standing top restaurant in a suburb on the eastern side of the N1, running for over 30 years, with a pleasant, airy setting, classical French cuisine, and award-winning wine list. Dishes include fois gras mousse, Provençal lamb and confit of duck.

$$$-$$ Kream, Brooklyn Bridge, 579 Fehrsen Rd, Brooklyn, T012-346 4642, www.kream.co.za. Mon-Sat 1200-2300. Stylish all-cream, marble and glass interior, a separate lounge/bar, a rare whisky menu, long wine list, varied menu with good seafood and game meat and specials like frogs legs, scallops, crayfish or crocodile.

$$ Bistro Boer'geoisie, Greenlyn Village, 13th St, Menlo Park, T012-460 0264, www.bistrotboergeoisie.co.za. Mon-Fri 1200-1500, 1800-2200, Sat 1100-2200. Great place to try traditional Afrikaner food in a recreated old general store with corrugated-iron roof, wooden floors and stoep and decorated with South African memorabilia from ox-wagon parts to photos of Mandela. Try lamb *potjieko* with dumplings, venison pie with mampoer jelly, *skilpadjies* (lambs liver) or *waterblommetjie bredie* (stew with flowers).

$$ Just Cuban, 129 Duxbury Rd, Hillcrest, T012-362 1800, www.justcuban.co.za. Open 0900-late. Located in a converted old post office, and more like a gentlemen's club with formal dining rooms, a whisky and cognac bar furnished with 18th-century antiques, and an upstairs cigar lounge. Cuban fare such as espetadas, plus seafood platters and gourmet steaks.

$$ La Pentola, 5 Well St, Riveria, T012-329 4028, www.lapentola. co.za. Mon-Fri 1200-1500, 1800-2230, Sat 1800-2230. To the north of the Union Buildings with arty interior, Mediterranean menu with good use of local produce and fresh herbs, plus some game dishes like crocodile and warthog, award-winning wine list.

$ Oriental Palace, Colosseum Hotel, 410 Francis Baard St, Arcadia, T012-322 2195. Daily 1100-2100. A bare dining room on the ground floor of a cheap apartment-style hotel, but very popular for its authentic and cheap Indian food with chefs from Pakistan and north India, genuine curries, good tikka and tandoori, delicious dhal and tandoori breads. No alcohol but try the lassis.

$ Pappa's, corner of Duncan and Prospect streets, Hatfield, T012-362 2224. Mon-Sat 0800-2230, Sun 0800-1400. In a converted historical building, Duncan Yard, with its quirky shops, art galleries and cobbled alleyways, offers gourmets burgers, Mediterranean fare and decadent desserts, and has occasional live music in the pub.

Cafés and delis
Café Riche, 2 Church Sq (southwest corner), CBD, T012-328 3173. Daily 0600-1800. The oldest café in town which first opened in 1905, feels like a Parisian café, great views over the square, serves breakfasts, light meals and is well known for its pastries, croissants and baguettes.

The Deli on Duncan, corner of Duncan and Prospect streets, Hatfield, T012-362 4054, Mon-Fri 0900-1700, Sat 0900-1500, Sun 1000-1400. Quaint, old-fashioned deli serving generous breakfasts, and light lunches such as quiche or pies and salad and delicious home-baked cheesecake and cupcakes.

Honey Badger Bistro, 1100 Pretorius St, Hatfield, T0731-70 9347. Mon-Fri 0830-1600, Sat 0900-1500. Near Springbok Park (see page 95), this café cum daytime bistro offers a preservative-free and seasonal menu with some interesting and creative combinations for the sandwiches, salads and pastas.

◑ Bars and clubs

Pretoria *p88, maps p90, p93 and p97*
Drop Zone, Hatfield Sq, Burnett St, T012-362 6528, www.clubdropzone. co.za. Mon-Sat 2000-0400. Over 21s, more popular with young professionals than the usual student crowd, happy hour daily 2000-2100.

Stones, 1081 Burnett St, Hatfield, T012-362 3022, www.stones.co.za. Daily 1200-late. Popular pub among the local university students, good choice of imported beers, pool tables and a snack menu, at the weekend has DJs and stays open until 0400.

Tings an' Times, 1065 Arcadia St, Hatfield, T012-430 3176, www.tings. co.za. Mon-Sat 1200-0130. Venue for live music, can get very crowded, best to arrive mid-evening to secure a table. Great cocktails, Middle Eastern and vegetarian meals, including filled pittas.

⦿ Entertainment

Pretoria *p88, maps p90, p93 and p97*
Cinema
All the latest Hollywood, European and home-grown releases can be seen at multi-screen cinemas in the shopping malls. The 2 major cinema groups are **Nu Metro**, www.numetro.co.za, and **Ster-Kinekor**, www.sterkinekor. com. New films are released on Fri. Newspapers have full listings. Brooklyn Mall also has a separate **Cinema Nouveau**, which screens international and art-house films (information and bookings also at Ster-Kinekor).

Theatre
State Theatre, Lilian Ngoyi Sq, corner Church and Prinsloo streets, T012-392 4000, www.statetheatre.co.za, tickets booked through **Computicket**, T011-915 8000, www.computicket. com, or in South Africa, at any of their kiosks in the shopping malls or any branch of **Checkers** and **Shoprite** supermarkets. The city's main theatre with 5 auditoriums hosts opera, ballet, musicals, drama, cabaret and children's theatre.

⦿ Shopping

Pretoria *p88, maps p90, p93 and p97*
Pretoria has numerous large shopping malls. Shop opening hours are listed; the restaurants and cinemas stay open later until 2200 or 2300. These are the best:
Brooklyn Mall, corner Fehrsen and Lange streets, New Muckleneuk, T012-346 1063, www.brooklynmall. co.za. Mon-Fri 0900-1800, Sat 0900-1700, Sun 0900-1400. 170 shops, a 14-screen **Ster-Kinekor** cinema, plus a **Cinema Nouveau**.
Hatfield Plaza, 1122 Burnett St, Hatfield, T012-362 5842, www. hatfieldplaza.com. Mon-Fri 0900-1730, Sat 0900-1500, Sun 0900-1300. 70 shops, an 8-screen **Nu Metro** cinema, and on Sun 0900-1700 there is a good outdoor market with over 200 stalls for crafts, decor, clothes, jewellery, antiques and collectables, and an excellent food section.
Menlyn Park, Atterbury Rd, Menlo Park, clearly seen from the N1, T012-348 8766, www.menlynpark.co.za. Mon-Thu and Sat 0900-1900, Fri 0900-2100, Sun 0900-1700. Pretoria's premier mall with 300 shops and restaurants and a 15-screen **Nu Metro** cinema. Its architectural focal point is its tent-like roof that can be seen from far away.

⦿ What to do

Pretoria *p88, maps p90, p93 and p97*
Cricket
SuperSport Park, formerly Centurion Park, 283 West Av, Centurion, 23 km south of the city centre, off the R21 to Johannesburg, enquiries T012-663 3904, www.titans.co.za, tickets booked through **Computicket**, www. computicket.co.za. T011-915 8000, or in South Africa, at any of their kiosks

in the shopping malls or any branch of **Checkers** and **Shoprite** supermarkets. Home to the Nashua Titans cricket team. A modern circular stadium with a capacity of 22,000 and dominated by a huge single grandstand. The rest of the boundary is made up of grass banks which are great for picnics and *braais*.

Golf
Pretoria Country Club, 241 Sidney Av, Waterkloof, T012-460 6241, www. ptacc.co.za. The club was founded in 1910, the 18-hole 72-par course is set in beautiful parkland and the greens are ringed by jacaranda trees.

Rugby
Loftus Versfeld Stadium, Kirkness St, Sunnyside, 5 km east of the city centre, enquiries, T012-420 7000, www. thebulls.co.za, tickets Computicket (see above). A venue for the 2010 FIFA World Cup™, seats 51,000, and home ground to the Vodacom Bulls rugby team and the Mamelodi Sundowns football team.

Tour operators
A standard ½-day tour of Pretoria from Johannesburg takes in sights such as the Voortrekker Monument and Union Buildings. For longer tours, most of the tour operators in Johannesburg (see page 82) can also pick up from accommodation in Pretoria. For details of visiting the Cullinan Diamond Mine see box, page 99.

🚍 Transport

Pretoria *p88, maps p90, p93 and p97*
From Pretoria it is 481 km to the Zimbabwe border (**Beitbridge**), 462 km to **Bloemfontein**, 1499 km to **Cape Town**, 616 km to **Durban**, 1021 km to **East London**, 1058 km to **Harare** (Zimbabwe), 53 km to **Johannesburg**, 540 km to **Kimberley**, 1201 km to **Knysna**, 525 km to **Maputo** (Mozambique), 319 km to **Nelspruit**, and 1140 km to **Port Elizabeth**.

Air
For **OR Tambo International Airport**, see page 27. **Magic Bus**, T011-394 6902, www.magicbus.co.za, **Airport Link**, T011-794 8300, www.airportlink. co.za, and **Airport Shuttle**, T012-348 0650, www.airportshuttle.co.za, drop off at major hotels in Johannesburg and Pretoria.

Bus
Local Municipal buses run along the main roads around the city centre and to the suburbs, 0500-2000, fares are from R10, enquiries T012-358 0839, timetables can be found at www.tshwane.gov.za.

Long distance The bus stand is to the left of the railway station (as you face it) in the 1928 Building, corner of Scheiding and Paul Kruger streets in the city centre. **Translux**, www.translux.co.za, **Intercape**, www.intercape.co.za, and **Greyhound**, www.greyhound.co.za, have offices here. There are departures to all over the country, though on some southern routes, you have to change in Johannesburg. Timetables can be found on the websites and tickets can be booked online through **Computicket**, T011-915 8000, www.computicket.com, or in South Africa, at any of their kiosks in the shopping malls or any branch of **Checkers** and **Shoprite** supermarkets. For more information, see Getting around, page 89.

The **Baz Bus**, reservations Cape Town T021-422 5202, www.bazbus.com, is the best option for backpackers. See Planning your trip, page 10, for full details of the service.

Car hire
For details of car hire companies at **OR Tambo International Airport**, see page 27. Check their websites for other branches in the Pretoria area.

Train
Local The **Gautrain**, call centre T0800-428 87246, www.gautrain.co.za, stations are at the railway station on the corner of Scheiding and Paul Kruger streets in the city centre, and in Hatfield on the corner of Grosvenor Rd and Arcadia St. Trains run 0530-2030, every 12 mins in peak periods, every 20-30 mins off-peak. See also box, page 29. **Metrorail**, services also stop at the railway station (see page 86).

Long distance Long-distance passenger trains are run by **Shosholoza Meyl**, T086-000 888 (in South Africa), T011-774 4555 (from overseas), www.shosholozameyl.co.za. All services depart from Johannesburg (see pages 8 and 86), and the 2 services that stop in Pretoria before/after Johannesburg (roughly 1½ hrs) are **Johannesburg-Komatipoort** on the border with Mozambique (Wed and Fri; Thu and Sun in the opposite direction, 9½ hrs), and **Johannesburg-Musina** near the Beitbridge border for **Zimbabwe** (Wed and Fri; Thu and Sun in the opposite direction, 10½ hrs). For details of luxury trains that service Pretoria, see page 9.

---

❶ Directory

Pretoria *p88, maps p90, p93 and p97*
Embassies and consulates For a full list of foreign representatives in Pretoria, visit the government's Department of Foreign Affairs website www.dfa.gov.za. **Immigration** Dept of Home Affairs, 320 Byron Pl, corner of Nana Sita and Sophie de Bruyn streets, CBD, T012-395 4307, www.home-affairs.gov.za, Mon-Fri 0730-1600. Visa extensions take 10 working days. Onward ticket and proof of funds needed. **Medical services** Netcare, there are more than 30 private Netcare hospitals in Gauteng; for 24-hr medical services and ambulances T082-911, to locate a hospital T011-301 0000, www.netcare.co.za. **Muelmed Medi-Clinic** (private), 577 Pretorius St, Arcadia, T012-440 0600, 24-hr emergency, T012-440 0692, www.mediclinic.co.za.

North West Province

The eastern region of the province gets the lion's share of visitors, thanks to the extravagant attractions of Sun City and the excellent Pilanesberg Game Reserve, where stocks of game readily stand to attention for camera-toting safari enthusiasts. Stretching from the west of Gauteng to the North West's historic town of Rustenburg are the gently rolling Magaliesberg Mountains, which, thanks to their proximity to the urban sprawl of Pretoria and Johannesburg, are a popular weekend retreat. It's a scenic area for sports and outdoor pursuits and the mountains are ideal for hiking.

Magaliesberg Mountains → *For listings, see pages 115-120.*

The Magaliesberg are a range of flat-topped quartzite mountains, which extend roughly from Pretoria to just beyond Rustenburg. The range forms the natural divide between the cool Highveld to the south and the warm bushveld to the north and is about 160 km long, reaching 1852 m at its highest point – which is actually no more than 400 m above the surrounding countryside. The difference in elevation is, however, sufficient to ensure that the hills receive a relatively high rainfall and are far greener than the plains, with some remaining stands of forest. The north-facing slopes are no more than a gentle climb, cut by mountain streams and leafy gorges.

Arriving in the Magaliesberg Mountains

To explore the Magaliesberg there are several routes. The most popular is the old Pretoria–Rustenburg road from Pretoria, the R104 (confusingly in parts also marked the R27), which runs along the shores of Hartbeespoort Dam via Schoemansville before passing over the dam wall and continuing along the northern reaches of the Magaliesberg to join the N4 to Rustenburg, and then on to the R565 to Sun City and Pilanesburg. The R24 or the R512 are more direct routes from Johannesburg to the southern parts of the Magaliesberg. The option here is to also visit the attractions to the northwest of Joburg, including the **Cradle of Humankind**, **Lion Park** or the **Lesedi Cultural Village** (see pages 63-64).

For information, pick up a map for the **Magalies Meander**, www.magalies meander.co.za, at the tourist offices in Gauteng or at the shops and participating venues in the Magaliesberg. Both the map and the website lists craft shops, accommodation, activities and restaurants in the region.

Hartbeespoort Dam → *Altitude: 1200 m.*

The Hartbeespoort Dam was built in 1923 in a narrow gorge where the Crocodile River cuts through the Magaliesberg Mountains. There are two major canals which conduct water away from the dam into a series of smaller canals that irrigate the farmlands around Brits. The old main road from Pretoria runs through the village of **Schoemansville** on the north shore of the lake before crossing the dam wall and continuing to Rustenburg and Sun City.

There is the **Hartbeespoort Dam Snake & Animal Park** ① *T012-253 1162, www.hartbeespoortsnakeanimalpark.co.za, daily 0800-1730, R60, children (3-12) R30, under 3s free, tea garden*, which remains a popular attraction for visiting families from Gauteng but, alongside the collection of reptiles, are chimpanzees, panthers and Bengal tigers, making it unpleasant and zoo-like.

Also near here is the **Harties Cableway** ① *on the R513 towards Pretoria, T0722-412654, www.hartiescableway.co.za, daily 0830-1600, R160, children (4-12)*

The Magaliesberg

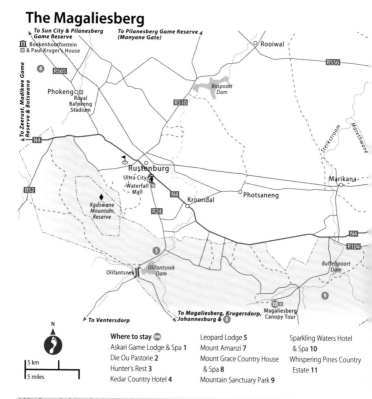

Where to stay 🛏
Askari Game Lodge & Spa **1**
Die Ou Pastorie **2**
Hunter's Rest **3**
Kedar Country Hotel **4**

Leopard Lodge **5**
Mount Amanzi **7**
Mount Grace Country House & Spa **8**
Mountain Sanctuary Park **9**

Sparkling Waters Hotel & Spa **10**
Whispering Pines Country Estate **11**

R90, under 4s free, cafés at the top and bottom cableway stations, a 2.3-km link to one of the highest points of the Magaliesberg. The 1-km Dassie Loop walkway at the top has informative signs to explain points of interest that you can see which include the high-rises in Pretoria on a clear day.

The **Ann van Dyk Cheetah Centre** ① *also on the R513, towards Pretoria, T012-504 9906, www.dewildt.co.za R300, children (6-12) R140, no children under 6, extra fee for a photograph with a cheetah (when available), 3-hr tours Mon, Wed and Fri at 0830 and daily 1330, booking ahead is essential*, was opened in 1971 by founder Ann van Dyk who volunteered her parents' chicken farm when the National Zoological Gardens of South Africa in Pretoria (see page 94) ran out of space to continue their captive breeding programmes. It is now a world-renowned research centre and welcomes visitors, and the three-hour tour begins with a talk about the centre and the genetics of cheetahs, followed by a game drive around the spacious enclosures. On certain mornings when they are exercised, some of the king

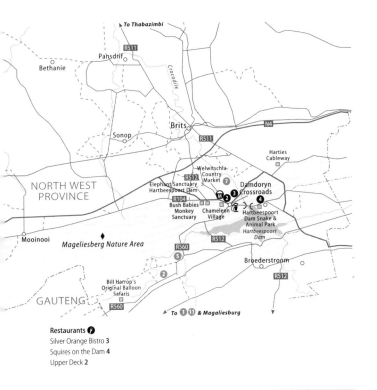

Restaurants 🍴
Silver Orange Bistro **3**
Squires on the Dam **4**
Upper Deck **2**

cheetahs can be seen running at high-speed. Other species bred at the centre to be rehabilitated into the wild include wild dog, brown hyena and vultures.

Once over the dam wall from Schoemansville, the road reaches the Damdoryn Crossroads, which is a hive of activity and a hugely popular spot with day trippers from Pretoria and Johannesburg. It is where the **Welwitschia Country Market** (see page 119), the **Chameleon Village** (see page 119) and a large **curio market** are all located.

From the Damdoryn Crossroads, 2 km along the R104 is the **Elephant Sanctuary Hartbeespoort Dam** ① *T012-258 0423, www.elephantsanctuary. co.za, daily programmes start at 0800, 1000 and 1400, 2½-hr tour R625, children (4-14) R265, under 4s free, 10-15 mins elephant riding R465, children (under 14 and no under 8s) R275*, which is a sister operation of the elephant sanctuaries on the Garden Route and in Hazyview (see page 154). Visitors can feed and interact with the five tame elephants and for an extra fee ride them, and on the 0800 tour can 'brush down' the elephants in their stables. There's a restaurant for a set lunch (pre-book) and guest house accommodation (**$$$**).

Adjacent to the Elephant Sanctuary is the **Bush Babies Monkey Sanctuary** ① *T012-258 9908, www.monkeysanctuary.co.za, 1½-hr tours run on the hour from 0900-1600, R195, children (4-14) R95, under 4s free, coffee shop*, a 7-ha tract of indigenous forest lying in a kloof (gorge) in the mountainside. It's home to a number of species of primate (mostly rescued pets), including bush babies, lemurs and squirrel, spider and vervet monkeys, and the guided tour follows elevated wooden walkways.

Magaliesberg Canopy Tour ① *at the Sparkling Waters Hotel & Spa (see Where to stay, page 115), T014-535 0150, www.magaliescanopytour.co.za, daily 0900-1400, 2½-hr tours depart every 30 mins, R495 per person (no children under 7), including refreshments*, is off the R104, approximately 38 km west of the Damdoryn Crossroads or 16 km southeast of Rustenburg, then 12 km from the main road; it can also be reached from the R24 south of Rustenburg. The tour involves gliding on a steel rope in a harness between 11 elevated platforms that have been built into the mountain rock faces. The longest slide is 170 m and in some places the platforms are 30 m high. The guides talk through the history of the Magaliesbergs and point out the plants and birds.

Rustenburg → *Phone code: 014. Altitude: 1160 m.*

Situated some 120 km northwest of Johannesburg, at the foot of the Magaliesberg, Rustenburg, or 'castle of rest', is one of the oldest towns in the region and was an important centre under the Transvaal Republic. It was founded in 1851 by farmers who, with the Voortrekker leader Andries Pretorius, had settled in the area a decade earlier. During the short existence of the Boer Republic, Rustenburg was the capital before the government moved to Pretoria. Today, much of its old charm has disappeared and it is little more than a scruffy, sprawling crossroads between Gauteng, Sun City and Pilanesberg and the Botswana border. Nevertheless, its proximity to Johannesburg and Pretoria on the one hand, and the Magaliesberg Mountains and the Kgaswane Mountain Reserve on the other, means that the country hotels outside of town are popular. Historical buildings in the town centre include the Anglican Church (1871), the Hervormde or Dutch Reformed Church (1903), and the Statue of a Voortrekker Girl in Plein Street opposite the Hervormde Church.

Interestingly the Royal Bafokeng Stadium, on the R565, 12 km northwest of Rustenburg in Phokeng on the way to Sun City, venue for the 2010 FIFA World Cup™ South Africa, is owned and named after the 300,000 or so baFokeng people in the area. The baFokeng rose to prominence in the 1980s when they won a benchmark legal battle for compensation from the platinum companies mining their land and they now receive annual royalties. They have used this income to build schools, civic buildings, roads, clinics and the large stadium.

Around Rustenburg

Kgaswane Mountain Reserve ⓘ *from Rustenburg take Beyers Naude Rd south for 2 km, which later becomes Helen Joseph Rd, and after 5 km you reach the gate, T014-533 2050, www.parksnorthwest.co.za/kgaswane, Sep-Mar 0530-1930, Apr-Aug 0600-1800, R30, children (2-12) R15, car R10.* This mountain reserve stretches along the summit and the northern slopes of the Magaliesberg, 400 m above Rustenburg. The land was originally part of Rietvallei Farm, which belonged to President Paul Kruger, and now covers 5300 ha. From the top of the reserve you can see the flat bushveld to the south, while the ridge of the mountains disappears east towards the Hartbeespoort Dam and Pretoria. It provides excellent hiking territory, and there are three marked hiking trails in the reserve (5-25 km). Detailed maps are available at the reserve office. A self-drive tarred road links the picnic sites and viewpoints.

Some of the species of antelope found here include grey duiker, klipspringer, mountain reedbuck, impala, oribi, waterbuck, steenbuck, kudu and red hartebeest, and the reserve is famous for the breeding herd of sable which are particularly well suited to the environment. Black-backed jackal, leopard and caracal are also known to live in the mountains but are rarely seen. Nesting pairs of martial and black eagles and an important breeding colony of the endangered Cape vulture live high up along the rocky cliff faces.

Paul Kruger Country House Museum ⓘ *at the Kedar Country Hotel (see Where to stay, page 117), 18 km northwest of Rustenburg, off the R565 towards Sun City, look out for a left turning just after Phokeng, T014-573 3218, 1000-1600, R25, children (under 12) R15.* Boekenhoutfontein is the farm dating to 1841 where Paul Kruger lived as a farmer before he became the president of the Transvaal Republic from 1883 until the end of the Anglo-Boer War. Four buildings have been preserved and restored as museums commemorating the life of Paul Kruger and the earliest farmers in the Transvaal. On display are many of Kruger's possessions along with an assortment of period furniture, and in the gardens is a bronze statue of Paul Kruger that was discovered in Paris in 1919 by General Louis Botha and General Jan Smuts. It is of the president sitting grumpily in his armchair during his last days of exile in France.

Sun City → *For listings, see pages 115-120.*

ⓘ *49 km northwest of Rustenburg on the R565, T014-557 1544, www. suninternational.com, day visitors daily 0800-2100, R60 per person; Valley of the Waves R150, children (4-14) R80, under 3s free, no entrance fees for hotel guests.*
Tucked between dusty plains and rolling bushveld is the surreal highrise, neon-lit resort of Sun City. Much like Las Vegas in the US, the resort was built around gambling and today comprises a vast complex of four hotels with more than 1000 rooms between them and numerous restaurants and fast-food outlets. The extravagant recreational facilities include two golf courses, a water park with a fake sandy lagoon, a man-made tropical rainforest, a crocodile park, an aviary, a lake offering watersports, a massive mock semi-ruined Mayan stone maze, a casino and the Sun City Theatre. The result is both staggeringly impressive and laughably tacky – all good fun if you take it with a pinch of salt. The **Welcome Centre** is in the middle of the complex and is a good place to start and pick up a map. The free skytrain runs throughout the complex.

Background
The first part of the complex was opened in 1979; namely the Sun City Hotel and a golf course designed by Gary Player as well as the adjacent Pilanesberg Game Reserve (see below). Back then, much of Sun City's appeal for wealthy whites was its gambling licence as it was in Bophuthatswana (one of the designated black homelands) where gambling was legal; which it wasn't in South Africa. Like many other casino resorts that were built in the homelands during the Apartheid era, the contrasts between the luxury of the resorts and the impoverished areas around them were (and, to some extent, still are) stark. In 1980 the Sun City Cabanas opened, aimed at families, and in 1984 the third hotel was opened, the five-star Cascades, surrounded by waterfalls, streams and a tract of forest. In 1992 came the icing on the cake: the Lost City and the Valley of the Waves (see Places in Sun City, below).

With the change in gambling laws allowing casinos to be built across the country, visitor numbers to Sun City dropped sharply in the 1990s, but these have crept up again as the focus has switched from gambling to family entertainment, golf and conferences. Although far removed from the culture and landscapes that draw most tourists to South Africa, Sun City's glitz and garishness is fascinating and worth a day's visit.

Places in Sun City
The complex focuses on the most excessive component to Sun City – the **Palace of the Lost City**, a magnificent 338-room hotel with a vaguely Moorish construction characterized by soaring dome-capped towers ringed by prancing statues of antelope. Below the hotel is the **Valley of the Waves**, reached by a bridge that trembles and spouts steam during mock earthquakes (every 30 minutes). This stunning artificial sandy lagoon, complete with desert island and palm-lined soft white sand, has a wave machine capable of creating metre-high waves. Day visitors have to pay extra to enter the Valley of the Waves, but this doesn't seem to put anyone off – the beach gets completely packed at weekends, with noisy music pumping out of loudspeakers and every large wave bringing forth a yell of jubilation from the crowds. Smaller swimming pools dotted around the lagoon are quieter.

A welcome retreat lies around the hotel and lagoon, the impressive 25-ha **man-made forest**. Remarkably lush and quiet, the forest was originally made up of 1.6 million plants, trees and shrubs, and the rainforest component includes three layers with creepers and orchids growing in the canopy. Although the moulded cement rocks and perfectly pruned paths give it a distinctly Disney feel, the plants have attracted prolific birdlife and the walking trails, lasting up to 1½ hours, allow a real sense of isolation from the resort.

Elsewhere, an abundance of activities are available to guests. There are two 18-hole golf courses, including the Gary Player-designed course, home to the annual **Nedbank Golf Challenge**, one of the world's great championships with prizes valuing over US$1.2 million. At **Waterworld**, guests can try parasailing, waterskiing and jetskiing. There is a horse-riding centre, tennis, mini-golf, squash, a gym and spa, mountain-biking trails, jogging routes, 10-pin bowling and swimming pools (the more peaceful of which are located in the hotels).

Close to the entrance is **Kwena Gardens Crocodile Sanctuary** with over 7000 crocs, including the three biggest captive Nile crocodiles in the world. Nearby is the **Cultural Village**, where guests are shown around mock-ups of villages, with dancing and singing, and a *shebeen* serving African cuisine. There's also an aviary, a bird of prey centre, cinemas, a casino, a hall filled with slot machines, and countless restaurants and bars.

Pilanesberg Game Reserve → *For listings, see pages 115-120.*

① *Follow signs for Sun City on the R565 from Rustenburg, or alternatively take the R510 from Rustenburg and after 51 km turn left for a further 5 km to the Manyane*

Gate, T014-555 1600, www.parksnorthwest.co.za/pilanesberg, Nov-Feb 0530-1900, Mar-Apr 0600-1830, May-Aug 0630-1800, Sep-Oct 0600-1830, R65, children (under 14) R20, car R20.

Thanks to the ambitious Operation Genesis in the 1970s, which involved the game-fencing of the reserve to complement the adjacent Sun City, and the re-introduction of many long-vanished species, Pilanesberg is today home to more than 7000 large species of game. It is roughly 160 km northwest of Johannesburg and 150 km northwest of Pretoria and while it can be visited as a long day trip from the cities, most visitors stay at least one night in the region and combine a visit to both Pilanesberg and Sun City. If you're not staying in the reserve, you can book on one of the three-hour game drives that leave Sun City's Welcome Centre (see page 112).

The park encompasses the caldera of an extinct volcano, which is geographically similar to the Ngorongoro Conservation Area in Tanzania. The crater is surrounded by three concentric rings of hills and in the centre is a lake, **Mankwe Dam**, where you can see crocodile and hippo. The hills are broken up with wooded valleys, which gradually give way to open savannah grasslands.

Pilanesberg Game Reserve

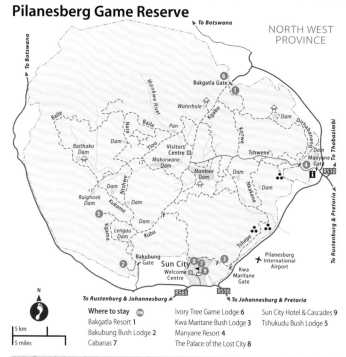

NORTH WEST PROVINCE

Where to stay
Bakgatla Resort 1
Bakubung Bush Lodge 2
Cabanas 7
Ivory Tree Game Lodge 6
Kwa Maritane Bush Lodge 3
Manyane Resort 4
The Palace of the Lost City 8
Sun City Hotel & Cascades 9
Tshukudu Bush Lodge 5

During Operation Genesis, the animals came from all over southern Africa: elephant and buffalo from Addo Elephant National Park; black and white rhino from the Natal Parks Board; eland from Namibia; Burchell's zebra and waterbuck from the Transvaal; and red hartebeest from the Northern Cape and Namibia. As a transition zone between the Kalahari sandveld and the bushveld, it was also the natural habitat for a number of rare species already in existence, including brown hyena and sable antelope. As you drive around the 55,000-ha reserve today you have a good chance of seeing all the large animals, including rhino, elephant, lion, cheetah, buffalo and the occasional leopard. This variety of habitat is also a rewarding birdwatching environment where over 300 species. More than 200 km of excellent tar and gravel roads traverse the park, and a number of walk-in viewing hides have been constructed. Maps and game checklists are available at each of the four gates: Manyane, Bakgatla, Bakubung and Kwa Maritane – the last one being the closest to Sun City.

◎ North West Province listings

For hotel and restaurant price codes and other relevant information, see pages 13-18.

● Where to stay

Magaliesberg Mountains
p107, map p108

$$$$-$$$ Mount Grace Country House & Spa, off the R24, 3 km north of Magaliesberg village, T014-577 5600, www.africanpridehotels.com. Although lying in Gauteng, one of the most luxurious options in the Magaliesberg, with 121 luxury rooms in thatched cottages set in 10 ha of beautiful gardens with lakes and waterfalls. Heated swimming pool, tennis, library, excellent food, and a sumptuous spa with hydro pools which is open to non-guests.

$$$ Askari Game Lodge & Spa, again in Gauteng at the private Plumari Game Reserve, off the R560, 18 km northeast of Magaliesberg village, T014-577

2658/9, www.askarilodge.co.za. Luxury thatched chalets overlooking a dam with wooden patios, Victorian baths, antique furnishings and fireplaces. Restaurant, bar, game activities include daily drives and walks and overnight guests can join the 'wake-up' experience with 2 tame elephants (if they haven't already seen them from their chalet). There's also an interesting collection of Voortrekker ox-wagons. The spa is open to day visitors.

$$$ Whispering Pines Country Estate, also in Gauteng off the R509, 5 km west of Magaliesberg village, T014-577 5901, www.whispering pines.co.za. 14 spacious cottages sleeping 2-4 with a/c, DSTV, patio and fireplace, set on a 14-ha estate with forest walks and garden hammocks, indoor and outdoor pools, bar, restaurant, good country cooking, spa.

$$$-$$ Sparkling Waters Hotel & Spa, off the N4, 16 km southeast of

Rustenburg, then 12 km from the main road, it can also be reached from the R24 12 km south of Rustenburg, T014-535 0019, www.sparklingwaters.co.za. Pleasant country retreat in a clutch of thatched buildings, with 56 spacious a/c rooms and plenty of family-friendly activities, including tennis, swimming pool, mini-golf and the Magaliesberg Canopy Tour (see page 110). The extensive spa and good restaurant are open to day visitors.

\$\$ Die Ou Pastorie, on the R560, 15 km southwest of Damdoryn Crossroads towards Magaliesburg village, T012-207 1027, www.dieou pastorie.com. Upmarket guesthouse with 8 contemporary individually decorated suites with a/c and DSTV, private patios with mountain views, superb gourmet restaurant using home-grown produce and set in an 1880s pastor's homestead, also sells home-made jams, chutneys and pâté in the farm shop.

\$\$ Hunter's Rest, 12 km south of Rustenburg on the R24, T014-537 8300, www.huntersrest.co.za. Affordable family resort with 91 spacious rooms with patios; though a bit of a hike from the furthest room to the restaurant. English-style pub, large swimming pool, well-kept garden, curio shop, and huge range of activities include tennis, hiking trails, horse riding, mountain bike hire, and 9-hole golf course.

\$\$ Leopard Lodge, on the R560, 13 km southwest of Damdoryn Crossroads towards Magaliesburg village, T012-207 1130, www.leopard lodge.co.za. Peaceful spot on a high mountainside with expansive views of Hartbeespoort Dam, a combination of 16 rooms in a guesthouse or thatched log cabins and a 4-bed self-catering house, restaurant with deck and fireplace. Giraffe, zebra, wildebeest and a number of antelope are on the property and Cape vultures can be seen on the cliffs.

\$\$-\$ Mount Amanzi, off the R104, 1.5 km northeast of the Damdoryn Crossroads towards Brits, T021-253 0541, www.mountamanzi.co.za. Large family resort on the banks of the Crocodile River, with 168 basic but comfortable self-catering brick chalets sleeping up to 6, restaurant serving generous buffet meals, bar with pool tables, 3 swimming pools, tennis courts, children's playgrounds and a petting farm. Handy for the local attractions that appeal to kids.

\$\$-\$ Mountain Sanctuary Park, a private nature reserve in the mountains, off the R104, 35 km southeast of Rustenburg, then 10 km from the main road, T014-534 0114, www.mountain-sanctuary.co.za. Simple rest camp, with self-catering chalets sleeping 2-6, fully equipped and furnished (but bring towels and food), and a shady campsite with a thatched lapa and freezer facilities. Stunning pool built from natural stone on the lip of the valley, offering fantastic views. Guests have access to over 1000 ha of hiking country and maps are provided.

Rustenburg *p110, map p108*
The country resorts in the Magaliesberg Mountains are the better bet. There's little choice in town.

$$$-$$ Kedar Country Hotel, 18 km from Rustenburg towards Sun City on the R565, T014-573 3218, www.kedarcountryhotel.com. A peaceful group of cottages next to the historic farm of President Kruger (see page 125), with 62 African-themed rooms with DSTV, the deluxe ones feature open log fires, plunge pools and outdoor showers. Zebra and antelope are within the grounds, restaurant and bar decorated with Boer War memorabilia, and a spa.

$$ Rustenburg Boutique Hotel, 243 Joubert St, T014-592 4645, www.rustenburgbh.co.za. Modern option with 19 smart rooms with kitchenettes, a/c and DSTV, contemporary decor with splashes of colour, bar and lounge, sunny breakfast room, dinner on request.

Sun City *p112*

The whole complex is part of **Sun International**, central reservations T011-780 7810, Sun City T014-557 1000, www.suninternational.com.

$$$$ Cascades. Decorated in a vaguely colonial-style with 243 rooms facing the man-made forest and an ornamental lake with waterfalls. **The Peninsula** is a smart international restaurant with a weekend buffet **The Santorini**, a Mediterranean and seafood restaurant, 2 bars, and large pool with mock-up sandy beach.

$$$$ The Palace of the Lost City. Both impossibly kitsch and beautifully lavish, with 335 rooms spread across a string of airy courtyards, each overlooking fountains and sculptures of game. The entrance is marked by a super-sized sculpture of cheetahs hunting, surrounded by lakes and fountains, while the lobby is a palatial hall lined with vast columns, leading to restaurants and elegant bars. **Plume** offers classic French cuisine, **The Grill Room** has gourmet steaks, live piano and is surrounded by man-made rainforest.

$$$$-$$$ Sun City Hotel. The original hotel with 340 rooms overlooking the swimming pool and lush lawns or the Gary Player Golf Course. The lobby is probably the tackiest with fake palms and boulders and noisy slot-machines and leads to the resort's only remaining casino. There's plenty of choice on the restaurant front including **The Calabash**, a carvery and salad bar, and **The Orchid**, which offers an Asian-inspired menu. There are also 4 cocktail bars.

$$$ Cabanas. The most family-orientated and best-value option with 380 rooms set in neat gardens close to the lake at **Waterworld**, with a kids' petting farm and adventure playground. The **Palm Terrace** is a buffet restaurant with a supervised kids' play area, and the **Treasure Island Snack Bar** is on decks overlooking **Waterworld**.

Pilanesberg Game Reserve
p113, map p114

$$$$ Bakubung Bush Lodge, on the southwest edge of the park, 10 km from Sun City, T014-552 6000, www.legacyhotels.co.za. Large complex with 76 a/c rooms with DSTV, patios or balconies. Rates (mid-range) include breakfast and dinner but game drives are extra. Superb views of the surrounding bush and a waterhole with resident hippos. There's a restaurant, bar, curio shop, tennis courts, swimming pool, and free shuttle to Sun City.

$$$$ Ivory Tree Game Lodge, at the northwest of the park close to the Bakgatla Gate, T014-556 8100, www.ivorytreegamelodge.com. 65 a/c luxury thatched rooms with stone baths, outside showers and patios, the 4 suites have private plunge pools. Central facilities include pool, spa, restaurant, cocktail bar, lounge and open-air boma for dining and Zulu dancing displays. Rates include meals and game drives.

$$$$ Kwa Maritane Bush Lodge, near the gate of the same name, in the south of the park, T014-552 5100, www.legacyhotels.co.za. A smart bush lodge with 90 rooms with a/c, DSTV, high thatched ceilings and a private veranda. Rates (mid-range) include breakfast and dinner, game drives and guided walks are extra. Nearby waterhole with underground hide reached via a 180-m tunnel from the lodge, 2 swimming pools, tennis courts, spa and gym, and free shuttle to Sun City.

$$$$ Tshukudu Bush Lodge, in the middle of the park on the slope of a steep rock outcrop, T014-552 6255, www.legacyhotels.co.za. 6 chalets built into the rock with slate floors, fireplace, beds on an elevated platform, sunken double bath with a view, linked to the main lodge by a steep, winding stone staircase (not for the elderly or less mobile) and from the top you have clear views of the park and a floodlit waterhole. Restaurant, bar, pool. Rates

(very expensive) include meals, game drives and transfers from Bakubung. No children under 12.

$$$-$$ Bakgatla Resort, at the northwest of the park close to the Bakgatla Gate, T014-555 1000, www.goldenleopardresorts.co.za. 58 plain but affordable self-catering chalets sleeping up to 5, with patio and *braai*. Rates include breakfast and if guests don't want to self-cater there's a restaurant offering buffet meals. There are also 5 cheaper en suite safari tents (not self-catering) and a limited number of caravan and campsites (**$**). At the centre of the complex is a large swimming pool, picnic site and kiosk.

$$$-$$ Manyane Resort, 300 m from Manyane Gate, T014-555 1000, www.goldenleopardresorts.co.za. A total of 60 units; 2-bed brick chalets with patio and fridge, and 2- to 4-bed thatched self-catering chalets with patio and *braai*, some with loft rooms for children. Caravan and campsite (**$**) with electric hook-up and shady trees, some pre-erected 2-bed safari tents can be hired. Breakfast is included in the rates for the chalets and safari tents and there's a central restaurant for all meals. Bar, swimming pool, children's play area. There is a day visitors' complex with a shop, picnic area, swimming pool, a couple of walk-in aviaries and mini-golf.

❼ Restaurants

Hartbeespoort Dam *p108, map p108*
The restaurants in the mountain resorts are open to non-guests; many of which offer Sun buffet lunch. There are also a number of farmstalls

throughout the region selling fresh produce, snacks and drinks.

$$$ Silver Orange Bistro, on the R560, 1 km north of Damdoryn Crossroads, T0823-782948, www.silverorangebistro.co.za. Tue-Sun, 1200-1530, Tue-Sat 1800-2230, also open for breakfast Sat-Sun 0900-1100. A chef's school set in a charming farmhouse with antique decor, candelabras and chandeliers. A 2-weekly changing menu with a South African slant, an example might be duck and fig samoosas, followed by seared salmon on lemon-infused mash and traditional malva pudding. A vast selection of Cape wines to choose from plus French champagne.

$$-$ Squires on the Dam, 1 Scott St, Schoemansville, opposite the **Hartbeespoort Dam Snake and Animal Park** (see page 108), T012-253 1001, www.squiresonthedam.co.za. Daily 1000-2300. Popular family steak house with a large bar with TV for sports events and a broad outside deck. Long menu of meat dishes, good-value seafood platters and a kids' menu. Also has 8 plain, en suite motel rooms (**$**).

$ The Upper Deck, at Welwitschia Country Market, Damdoryn Crossroads (see below), T012-253 2586, www.theupperdeck.co.za. Daily 0900-late. Lively spot especially at weekends when there's often a live band on at lunchtime, simple but filling meals such as fried breakfasts, burgers, ribs, chicken and steaks, outside seating on pub-style benches.

Rustenburg *p110, map p108*
There is little choice in the town centre and most restaurants are in the **Waterfall Mall** on the edge of town (see Shopping, below), where there's a predictable range of pasta, steak and fast-food joints. Again, the Magaliesburg resorts and hotels are the better bet.

○ Shopping

Hartbeespoort Dam *p108, map p108*
At the Damdoryn Crossroads after crossing the Hartbeespoort Dam on the R104 from Schoemansville is the **Welwitschia Country Market**, T083-302 8085, www.countrymarket.co.za, Tue-Sun 0900-1700. Over 40 shops, in prefabricated sheds arranged in lanes, sell crafts, clothes, snacks, furniture, toys and all manner of other things aimed at day trippers from the cities. There are also 3 open-air restaurants, a pub and a mini kids' fairground and live (Afrikaans) music at weekends.

Less than 1 km further on the R104 towards Rustenburg, the **Chameleon Village**, T012-253 1451, www.chameleonvillage.co.za, daily 0800-1700, and covering 10 ha, is a similar set-up. There's the enormous indoor **Crafters Market**, and another thatched building with more than 30 home decor shops selling everything from grandfather clocks to lampshades. Both are worth a browse for South African-produced items. There are 8 restaurants with outside seating under thatch and numerous kids' playgrounds.

Rustenburg *p110, map p108*
Waterfall Mall, off the N4 from Pretoria at the junction with the R24, T014-537 3600, www.waterfallmall.co.za.

Mon-Fri 0830-1800, Sat 0900-1700, Sun 0900-1300. Has the usual chain stores, supermarkets and restaurants. Those on their way to self-catering accommodation should stop here.

⏱ What to do

Magaliesberg Mountains
p107, map p108
Most resorts are equipped with a range of sports facilities and each resort has its own hiking trails (some lead further up into the mountains than others).

Balloon rides
Bill Harrop's Original Balloon Safaris, T011-705 3201, www.balloon. co.za. Sunrise 1-hr flights over the Magaliesberg followed by champagne breakfast, R1365-2000 per person depending on group size. Take-off is from a site on the R560 but transfers can be arranged from Johannesburg and Sun City.

Pilanesberg Game Reserve
p113, map p114
Balloon rides
Air Trackers, desk at **Welcome Centre**, Sun City, T014-552 5020, www.air trackers.co.za. 1-hr safari flights from the centre of the reserve, price includes transfers, a glass of bubbly and game drive to, and breakfast at, one of the lodges. R3950 per person.

Safaris
You'll get most out of the park by going on a guided tour, as rangers are in constant contact and monitor movements of the Big Five.

Game Trackers, desk at **Welcome Centre**, Sun City, T014-552 5020, www.gametrac.co.za. If visiting Sun City on a day or over-night trip, 3-hr guided tours leave from the **Welcome Centre** Oct-Mar 0530 and 1700, Apr-Sep 0630 and 1600, R460, children (under16) R225; 3-hr game walks are also on offer in the mornings only, R550, no children under 16.

🚌 Transport

Rustenburg *p110, map p108*
49 km to **Sun City** via R565, 193 km to **Mafikeng**, 130 km to **Zeerust**, 115 km to **Pretoria via N4**, 118 km to **Johannesburg via N14**.

Sun City *p112*
Air
Pilanesberg International Airport, 8 km from Sun City, close to Kwa Maritane Gate, T014-552 1261, www. acsa.co.za. Has international status for flights from neighbouring countries. Currently no scheduled flights, though it is served by charter flights.

Car hire
Most people visit Sun City and Pilanesberg in a car hired from Johannesburg or Pretoria. **Avis**, at the Welcome Centre, T014-552 1501, www.avis.co.za.

ℹ Directory

Rustenburg *p110, map p108*
Medical services Netcare Ferncrest (private) Hospital, Moumo St, T014-568 4399, www.netcare.co.za.

Contents

Footprint features

Kruger National Park & Panorama Region

Kruger National Park

Kruger is the king of South African game parks. The figures speak for themselves: 507 bird species, 114 reptiles, 49 fish, 34 amphibians, 147 mammal and over 23,000 plant species have been recorded here. The region itself is enormous, extending from the Crocodile River in the south to the Limpopo in the north, from the wooded foothills of the eastern escarpment to the humid plains of the Lowveld. It certainly fulfils most visitors' fantasies of seeing magnificent herds of game roaming across acacia-studded stretches of savannah and, of course, is home to the Big Five. The park is 60 km wide and over 350 km long, conserving 21,497 sq km, an area the size of Wales or Israel. Despite its size, it is very well developed, with a good network covering 2600 km of roads and numerous camps, making a Kruger safari relatively hassle free.

Don't expect to have the park to yourself, however. Kruger receives over one million visitors a year and some of the larger public camps cater for up to 5000 visitors a day. Nevertheless, Kruger has managed to maintain its wild atmosphere, and only about 5% of the park is affected by the activities of the visitors.

Arriving in Kruger National Park → *For private reserves, see pages 144-148.*

Getting there and around

Air The four principal airports are **Kruger Mpumalanga International Airport (KMIA)** ① *T013-753 7500, www.kmiairport.co.za,* 42 km from Numbi Gate, 70 km from Phabeni Gate and 68 km from Malelane Gate and gives access to the southern camps; **Skukuza Airport** ① *at Skukuza Rest Camp, T013-735 4265, www.sanparks.org,* within the southern section of the park; **Eastgate Airport** ① *T015-793 3681, www.eastgateairport.co.za,* 68 km from Orpen Gate for the central camps; and **Phalaborwa Kruger Gateway Airport** ① *at Phalaborwa, T015-781 5823,* 3 km from Phalaborwa Gate for Kruger's northern camps.

Road Most people arrive in Kruger by road, either on a tour or in their own vehicle. There are nine entry gates (see box, opposite) and numerous options of approach. Which area you end up staying in will depend to a large extent on

Arriving in Kruger

The nine entrance gates to Kruger are (anti-clockwise from the north): **Pafuri**, T013-735 5574; **Punda Maria**, T013-735 6870; **Phalaborwa**, T013-735 3547; **Orpen**, T013-735 0237; **Kruger**, T013-735 5107; **Phabeni**, T013-735 5890; **Numbi**, T013-735 5133; **Malelane**, T013-735 6152; and **Crocodile Bridge**, T013-735 6012. **Gates open**: October-March, 0530; April-September, 0600.

Gates close: October-February, 1830; March-April, 1800; May-July, 1730; August-September, 1800. Latecomers will be refused entry; however, late entry escorts (R150 per car) are available until 2100 for guests with pre-booked accommodation at certain camps within 10 km distance from the relevant gate. These are Numbi Gate (for Pretoriuskop); Malelane Gate (for Berg-en-Dal and Malelane); Crocodile Bridge Gate (for Crocodile Bridge); Punda Maria Gate (for Punda Maria); and Orpen Gate (for Orpen). The escort for Skukuza, the park's largest camp and HQ, from Kruger Gate (14 km) costs R500. Most of the other camps are at least an hour's drive from the nearest gate so always make sure you arrive in time.

For day visitors, entry into Kruger is on a first come first serve basis and strict quotas of vehicles are applicable for each gate – if these quotas are reached only visitors with pre-booked overnight accommodation are permitted access. This rarely happens in reality except over peak periods such as Christmas and New Year and public holiday long weekends. Nevertheless, day visitors are advised to get to your gate of choice as early as possible.

Alternatively SANParks have now introduced advanced bookings for day visits. You can book no less than one day prior to date of arrival through **SANParks** (see page 126) at an extra cost of R20 per adult and R10 per child on top of the normal conservation fees. You need to arrive at your specified gate not later than 1300 on the day.

Another alternative is to book on a Park & Ride, which currently operate from Numbi, Phabeni and Kruger gates. Visitors park up their own vehicles at the gate and go on a four-hour return game drive, which depart at 0700 and 1400. However, note that these are not official 'guided' trips, but more 'rides', and drivers take you along the main game-viewing circuits and stop off at the picnic sites. On top of the regular conservation fee, they cost R210, children (2-11) half price. To pre-book these, phone T0824-681290 or contact the gates.

where you are coming from. Petrol is available at the larger camps during office hours, and the mark-up on litre prices is not as unreasonable as you'd expect (credit cards aren't accepted). There is a speed limit of 50 kph on the surfaced roads, and 40 kph on the gravel/sand roads in the park. If you breakdown do not get out of your vehicle. Wait for another car to come past or phone SANPark's 24-hour Emergency Call Centre which is based at Skukuza, T013-735 4325. Their breakdown service is not equipped to do any major repairs, but they will tow you to the nearest garage outside the park. You can also use this number if you find yourself in any other emergency and to report any violation of the park rules (like off road driving), or if you see an animal in distress.

Orientation Given its huge size, many visitors to Kruger concentrate on one area of the park on each visit. Unless you are staying for more than a couple of nights, it is impossible to combine effective game viewing and visit all the areas. For the purposes of this guide, the park has been divided into three areas: Southern, Central and Northern, with a description of each of the different camps within these areas.

Best time to visit
The park looks its best after the summer rains when the new shoots and lush vegetation provide a surplus of food for the grazers. Migratory birds are attracted and display their colourful breeding plumage, and this is a good time to see courtship rituals and nesting. The animals look their best thanks to their good diet, and mammals give birth to their young. The disadvantages are that the thick foliage and tall grasses make it harder to spot animals and daytime temperatures can rise to a sweltering 40°C; afternoon rains are also common. The winter months are good for game viewing because the dry weather forces animals to congregate around waterholes and there is less foliage for them to hide in. June, July and August are more comfortable with daytime temperatures of around 30°C, but night temperatures can drop to 0°C. This is a good time of year to visit the northern areas which can be unbearably hot in the summer.

Kruger is at its most crowded during the South African school holidays. Accommodation within the park will be completely full and the heavy traffic on the roads can detract from the wilderness experience.

Cost
Conservation fees per 24 hours are R264, children (2-11) R132, under 2s free. South African and regional residents get a substantial discount.

Malaria
South Africa only has a very low seasonal risk of malaria in the extreme east of the country along the Mozambique border. This includes parts of Kruger where the risk period is usually between December and April. If you are travelling there during this time, consult your doctor or travel clinic about taking anti-malarials and ensure you finish the recommended course. All

SANParks accommodation in the park has insect nets installed on windows and doors, and is sprayed periodically with insecticide. Advice is available from the very useful **Kruger malaria hotline**, T083-900 8424.

Background

The earliest inhabitants of the region were the San and Baphalaborwa peoples, who had little impact on the region's wildlife but did leave their mark in cave paintings throughout the area. The first part of what was to become Kruger National Park was officially protected in 1898 by President Kruger when he established the Sabie Nature Reserve, now in the southern sector between the Crocodile and Sabie rivers. This was an early attempt to preserve an undisturbed wilderness and to protect wildlife from the threat of 'biltong hunters'. A single police sergeant at Komatipoort was given the daunting task of protecting the entire area from poachers.

After the end of the Anglo-Boer War, James Stevenson-Hamilton was appointed as Kruger's game warden; a position he kept until 1946. With two other rangers, he spent the first years patrolling the reserve on horseback and on foot. His deep love of the African bush inspired him to campaign to increase the size of the park and from 1903 the British expanded it to include the area between the Letaba and the Luvuvhu rivers, and the 5000 sq km of unworked ranches between the Sabi and the Letaba rivers.

The new area under protection covered roughly the same area as Kruger does today. However, numerous factions threatened the survival of the park: hunters wanted access to the park, soldiers returning from the First World War expected land for sheep farming; prospectors looking for gold, coal and copper wanted mining rights; and South Africa's vets were campaigning for a mass slaughter of wildlife to prevent the possible spread of tsetse fly.

The seeds of creating a self-financing national park open to visitors were unwittingly sown by South African Railways when they opened a new tour running from Pretoria to Lorenço Marques (today Maputo), which stopped in the reserve for game rangers to take visitors into the bush. The first tourists arrived in 1923 and the visits became such a popular feature of the holiday that park visits were used as publicity by the railways. Public support for a national park empowered the conservationist lobby and public access was finally allowed in 1926. The first cars arrived in 1927 and were able to travel by road through Sabi Bridge between the Olifants and Crocodile rivers. Visitors were expected to fend for themselves and made their own thorn bush camps to stay in. The first camp was built for tourists at Pretoriuskop after the chaos of the early years when tourists had been known to spend the night in trees hiding from predators. By 1946, 38,000 tourists a year were visiting Kruger and in 1947 Princess Elizabeth and Princess Margaret visited the park on their royal tour of South Africa where they stayed in the first luxury lodges. The publicity surrounding the tour ensured that a visit to Kruger became a fixture on every tourist's trip to South Africa. By 1955 over 100,000 people were visiting each year.

Where to stay

While much of the park is designed for self-driving and self-catering using the South African National Parks (SANParks) facilities, it is also possible to stay in either the privately run concessions within the park or the string of top-end private game reserves that stretch between the Olifants and Sabie rivers down the western side of Kruger. The abundance of safari lodges and tented camps at these offer refined luxury in the bush, but at a price. Nevertheless they are hugely popular with first-time visitors as all game drives are led by rangers, so you can leave the animal-spotting to the experts, see page 144, for details.

South African National Parks (SANParks) operates 12 main rest camps, two bush lodges, five bushveld camps and four satellite camps. There are three seasonal brackets for the price of all SANParks accommodation (including campsites); low season is 19 January-24 March; shoulder season is 1 November-9 December and 11 October-31 October; high season is 10 December-18 January and 25 March-10 October. The direct line for each camp is included with the description of the camp. This number can only be used for making a last-minute booking, up to 48 hours prior to arrival. All other bookings should be made through the **SANParks head office** ⓘ *643 Leyds St, Groenkloof, Pretoria, T012-428 9111, www.sanparks.org, Mon-Fri 0730-1545, telephone reservations Mon-Fri 0700-1700, Sat 0800-1300, either in person, online or by phone*. There are also satellite SANParks offices around the country; check the website for contacts.

Price codes listed in the camp descriptions refer to the minimum price per accommodation unit – meaning, for example, a cottage that sleeps six people, can take a minimum of four, so it is these prices that are listed. Expect to pay a little more if you are filling a unit. Disabled travellers should check out the comprehensive Information for People with Disabilities pages on the SANParks website, www.sanparks.org.

Main rest camps
The majority of overnight visitors stay in one of the 12 main rest camps in the park at **Berg-en-Dal**, **Crocodile Bridge**, **Lower Sabie**, **Pretoriuskop**, **Skukuza**, **Letaba**, **Mopani**, **Olifants**, **Orpen**, **Satara**, **Shingwedzi** and **Punda Maria**. Most of the accommodation is in the form of chalets or cottages, which can sleep between two and 12. If you are self-catering, you'll have the choice between a separate fully equipped kitchen, a kitchenette or the use of a communal

kitchen. All accommodation comes with a refrigerator, bedding and towels. If in doubt, always check when booking exactly what you will be getting.

Some of the older camps feel a little outdated, but the grounds are universally clean and well kept. The facilities vary from one camp to the next but in most cases they include a shop selling basic self-catering supplies, a petrol pump, a restaurant or café, launderette, toilets and hot showers, *braai* areas and an office/reception where you check in, book additional activities. During the school holidays, the atmosphere in the larger camps can feel like holiday camps, and you can easily forget you are in the middle of a game reserve.

Bush lodges

The two bush lodges are smaller and more secluded than the main rest camps, but without facilities such as shops, restaurants or petrol stations, although the main rest camps are close enough to visit for supplies. These are ideal for a large group of friends/family, since the whole camp has to be taken with each booking, and are exceptionally good value if the maximum number of people stay. They are **Boulders** (sleeps 12, minimum four), and **Roodewal** (sleeps 16, minimum eight).

Bushveld camps

The five bushveld camps, **Biyamiti**, **Shimuwini**, **Talamati**, **Bateleur** and **Sirheni,** are smaller and more remote than the main rest camps, but again they also have far fewer facilities. Accommodation is in chalets or permanent en suite tents that sleep no more than four, so staying in these camps is one of the best ways to experience Kruger on a more intimate level, but does involve a degree of advanced planning in terms of what to take.

Satellite camps

The four satellite camps, **Balule**, **Malelane**, **Maroela** and **Tamboti**, are similar to the bushveld camps in that they have fewer facilities but again are near enough to the main rest camps for amenities and to get supplies. **Malelane** has cottages, **Tamboti** en suite tents, and Maroela and Balule are campsites.

Campsites

The main rest camps have a separate area for caravans, camper vans and tents. They have hot, clean showers, laundry blocks and the communal kitchens have power points, instant boiling water machines, electric rings and sinks. It is your responsibility to clean up after yourself. Always secure rubbish to minimize the risk of baboons raiding the bins. There are also three separate campsites at Maroela, Balule and Tsendze which are more rustic and isolated but have no generators for lighting or power points. Camping at all of them costs R215-250 depending on season for one or two people, and R72 per extra adult and R36 per extra child, up to a maximum of six people per site.

Eating

The standard camp restaurants are generally open daily for breakfast (0700-1000), lunch (1200-1430) and dinner (1800-2100). All are licensed and some have an additional bar. At smaller camps during low season when there are fewer guests, you will be asked to order your evening meal in advance. Additionally SANParks are currently outsourcing some of their restaurants to the private sector – a little odd to see a branch of a burger chain in a national park, but this does give visitors more choice in terms of eating out. Currently Lower Sabie, Satara, Olifants and Letaba have branches of the national coffee shop/café chain **Mugg & Bean** (0700-2100); at Pretoriuskop there's a **Wimpy** (0700-2100); and at Skukuza a branch of steakhouse chain **Cattle Baron** (1000-2200). Most of the larger camps also organize an evening *braai* in an outside boma or in the bush close to the camp from 1730 onwards, which includes a choice of three meats as well as salads, breads and desserts (average price is R70 and half price for children); book at reception.

Camp shops are open daily April to June 0800-1800; March, September and October 0800-1830; and November to February 0800-1900. The closer you are to Skukuza (the largest camp), the fresher the produce stocked in camp shops. Most shops stock firewood and *braai* lighters, bread, frozen meat, tinned vegetables, jams, biscuits, beer, wines, spirits, cool drinks, books and a few curio items. If you don't have a cool box in your car and you are self-catering, it is still possible to buy all you need for a meal from the shops each day.

Other facilities

There are many **picnic spots** distributed throughout the park. All of these have toilets and at some there are small kiosks for snacks and drinks. At many, visitors can (for a nominal fee) hire a gas *skottel* (mobile frying pans on stands) from the picnic site attendant to *braai* on. All the main rest camps have day visitor areas; the ones at Skukuza and Letaba have swimming pools. The camps with swimming pools for overnight residents are **Berg-en-Dal**, **Lower Sabie**, **Mopani**, **Pretoriuskop**, **Shingwedzi**, **Orpen**, **Satara** and **Skukuza**; a good option if you choose to base yourself at a camp for a few days in summer and want to relax during the midday heat. There is a bank with ATM at Skukuza and another ATM at Letaba, and internet cafés/Wi-Fi hotspots at **Berg-en-Dal** and Skukuza. Note that mobile phone coverage in Kruger is patchy; there is concentrated coverage in the south and around the main camps in the central and northern regions, but there are some sizable gaps in between.

A large proportion of people who visit South Africa do so to see its spectacular wildlife. This colour section is a quick photographic guide to some of the more fascinating mammals you may encounter, including pictures and information about habitat, habits and characteristic appearance to help you when you are on safari. It is by no means a comprehensive survey; there are plenty of other fascinating animals and birds in Kruger National Park.

The Big Nine

It is fortunate that many of the large and spectacular animals of Africa are also, on the whole, fairly common. They are often known as the 'Big Five'. This term was originally coined by hunters who wanted to take home trophies of their safari. Thus it was, that, in hunting parlance, the Big Five were elephant, black rhino, buffalo, lion and leopard. Nowadays the hippopotamus is usually considered one of the Big Five for those who shoot with their camera, whereas the buffalo is far less of a 'trophy'. Equally photogenic and worthy of being included are the zebra, giraffe and cheetah. But whether they are the Big Five or the Big Nine, these are the animals that most people come to Africa to see and, with the possible exception of the leopard, you have an excellent chance of seeing them all.

Below: Hippopotamus

Above: Black rhinoceros
Right: White rhinoceros

■ **Hippopotamus** *Hippopotamus amphibius*. Prefers shallow water, grazes on land over a wide area at night, so can be found quite a distance from water, and has a strong sense of territory, which it protects aggressively. Lives in large family groups known as 'schools'. The river fronts of the camps in Kruger are a great place to look for hippopotamus.

■ **Black rhinoceros** *Diceros bicornis*. Long, hooked upper lip distinguishes it from white rhino rather than colour. Prefers dry bush and thorn scrub habitat and in the past was found in mountain uplands. Males usually solitary. Females seen in small groups with their calves (very rarely more than four), sometimes with two generations. Mother always walks in front of offspring, unlike the white rhino, where the mother walks behind, guiding calf with her horn.

■ **White rhinoceros** *Diceros simus*. Square muzzle and bulkier than the black rhino, they are grazers rather than browsers, hence the different lip. Found in open grassland, they are more sociable and can be seen in groups of five or more. The term 'white' is said to derive from the Dutch word *wijd*, meaning 'wide', in reference to this broader mouth. The populations of both black and white rhino in Kruger have been massively reduced by poaching, but they are monitored carefully and visitors still have a good chance of seeing them at the waterholes. Walking safaris are another option for getting close to them in the bush.

■ **Giraffe** *Giraffa camelopardis*. Yellowish-buff with patchwork of brownish marks and jagged edges, usually two different horns, sometimes three. Found throughout Africa in several differing subspecies.

■ **Common/Burchell's zebra** *Equus burchelli*. Generally has broad stripes (some with lighter shadow stripes next to the dark ones) which cross the top of the hind leg in unbroken lines. As with fingerprints in humans, each individual's stripes are unique. Lives in family units

of up to 20, lead by a stallion. The true species is probably extinct but there are many varying subspecies found in different locations across Africa.

■ **Leopard** *Panthera pardus*. Found in varied habitats ranging from forest to open

Right Giraffe
Below: Common zebra
Opposite page: Leopard

Above: Cheetah
Left: Lion
Bottom: Buffalo
Opposite: Elephants

savannah. They are generally nocturnal, hunting at night or before the sun comes up to avoid the heat. You may see them resting during the day in the lower branches of trees.

■ **Cheetah** *Acinonyx jubatus*. Often seen in family groups walking across plains or resting in the shade. The black 'tear' mark is usually obvious through binoculars. The fastest land mammal, its legs are relatively long compared to its greyhound-like body, and it can reach speeds of 90 kph over short distances. Found in open semi-arid savannah, never in forested country.

■ **Lion** *Panthera leo*. The largest of the big cats in Africa (adult males can weigh up to 200 kg) and also the most common, lions are found on open savannah all over all over eastern and southern Africa. They are often not at all disturbed by the presence of humans and so it is possible to get quite close to them. They are sociable

animals living in prides or permanent family groups of up to around 30 animals and are the only felid to do so. The females do most of the hunting (usually ungulates such as zebra and antelope).

■ **Buffalo** *Syncerus caffer*. Were considered by hunters to be the most dangerous of the big game and the most difficult to track and, therefore, the biggest trophy. Generally found on open plains but also at home in dense forest, they are fairly common in most African national parks but, like the elephant, they need a large area to roam in, so they are not usually found in the smaller parks.

■ **Elephant** *Loxodonta africana*. Commonly seen, even on short safaris, the largest land mammal weighing up to six tonnes with an average shoulder height of 3-4 m. They can live to the age of 70. The massive tusks of older bulls can weigh up to 50 or 60 kg. They form large family groups led by a female matriarch. There are an estimated 13,000 elephants in Kruger and the Elephant Hall is a museum at Letaba rest camp.

Larger antelopes

■ **Nyala** *Tragelaphus angasi*, 110 cm. Slender frame, shaggy, dark brown coat with mauve tinge (males). Horns (male only) single open curve. The female is a different chestnut colour. They like dense bush and are usually found close to water. Gather in herds of up to 30 but smaller groups are likely.

■ **Common waterbuck** *Kobus ellipsiprymnus* and **Defassa waterbuck** *Kobus defassa*, 122-137 cm. Very similar with shaggy coats and white marking on buttocks. On the common variety, this is a clear half ring on the rump and around the tail; on the Defassa, the ring is a filled-in solid white area. Both species occur in small herds in grassy areas, often near water.

■ **Sable** *Hippotragus niger* 140-145 cm, and **roan antelope** *Hippotragus equinus*, 127-137 cm. Both similar shape, with ringed horns curving backwards (both sexes), longer in the sable. Female sables are reddish brown and can be mistaken for the roan.

Top: Waterbuck
Below: Nyala

Above: Sable
Left: Greater kudu
Below: Topi

Males are very dark with a white underbelly. The roan has distinct tufts of hair at the tips of its long ears. Sable prefers wooded areas and the roan is generally only seen near water. Both species live in herds.

■ **Greater kudu** *Tragelaphus strepsiceros*, 140-153 cm. Colour varies from greyish to fawn with several vertical white stripes down the sides of the body. Horns long and spreading, with two or three twists (male only). Distinctive thick fringe of hair running from the chin down the neck. Found in fairly thick bush, sometimes in quite dry areas. Usually live in family groups of up to six, but occasionally larger herds of up to about 30.

■ **Topi** *Damaliscus korrigum*, 122-127 cm. Very rich dark rufous, with dark patches on the tops of the legs and more ordinary looking lyre-shaped horns.

■ **Hartebeest** In the hartebeest the horns arise from a bony protuberance on the top of the head and curve outwards and backwards. **Coke's hartebeest** *Alcephalus buselaphus*, 122 cm, is a drab pale brown with a paler rump; **Lichtenstein's harte-beest** *Alcephalus lichtensteinii*, 127-32 cm,

is also fawn in colour, with a rufous wash over the back and dark marks on the front of the legs and often a dark patch near the shoulder; the **red hartebeest** *Alcephalus caama*, 127-132 cm, is the most colourful hartebeest with black markings contrasting against its white abdomen. All are found in herds, sometimes they mix with other plain dwellers such as zebra.

■ **Blue wildebeest** or **gnu** *Connochaetes taurinus*, 132 cm, only found in southern Africa, is often seen grazing in herds with zebra. Blue-grey coat with a few darker

stripes down the side, black muzzle and buffalo-like horns.

■ **Eland** *Taurotragus oryx*, 175-183 cm. The largest of the antelope, it has a noticeable dewlap and shortish spiral horns (both sexes). Greyish to fawn, sometimes with rufous tinge and narrow white stripes down side of body. Occurs in groups of up to 30 in grassy habitats.

Top: Hartebeest
Above left: Blue wildebeest
Above right: Eland

Smaller antelope

■ **Bushbuck** *Tragelaphus scriptus*, 76-92 cm. Shaggy coat with white spots and stripes on the side and back and two white, crescent-shaped marks on front of neck. Short horns (male only) slightly spiral. High rump gives characteristic crouch. White underside of tail noticeable when running. Occurs in thick bush, near water. Either seen in pairs or on its own.

■ **Klipspringer** *Oreotragus oreotragus*, 56 cm. Brownish-yellow with grey speckles and white chin and underparts with a short tail. Has distinctive, blunt hoof tips and short horns (male only). Likes dry, stony hills and mountains.

■ **Common reedbuck** *Redunca arundinum*, 71-76 cm. Horns (male only) sharply hooked forwards at the tip, distinguishing them from the oribi. Reddish fawn with white underparts and a short bushy tail.

Above right: Bushbuck
Right: Common reedbuck
Bottom: Klipspringer

They usually live in pairs or in small family groups. Often seen with oribi, in bushed grassland and always near water.

■ **Steenbok** *Raphicerus campestris*, 58 cm. An even, rufous brown colour with clean white underside and white ring around eye. Small dark patch at the tip of the nose and long broad ears. The horns (male only) are slightly longer than the ears: they are sharp, have a smooth surface and curve slightly forward. Generally seen alone, prefers open plains, often found in arid regions. Usually runs off very quickly on being spotted.

■ **Springbok** *Antidorcas marsupialis* or springbuck, 76-84 cm. The upper part of the body is fawn, and this is separated from the white underparts by a dark brown lateral stripe. It is distinguished by a dark stripe which runs between the base of the horns and the mouth, passing through the eye. This is the only type of gazelle found south of the Zambezi River. You no longer see the giant herds the animal was famous for, but you will see them along the roadside as you drive through Kruger. They get their name from their habit of leaping stiff-legged and high into the air.

■ **Common (Grimm's) duiker** *Sylvicapra grimmia*, 58 cm. Grey-fawn colour with darker rump and pale colour on the underside. Its dark muzzle and prominent ears are divided by straight, upright, narrow pointed horns. This particular species is the only duiker found in open grasslands Usually the duiker is associated with a forested environment. It's difficult to see because it is shy and will quickly disappear into the bush.

■ **Oribi** *Ourebia ourebi*, 61 cm. Slender and delicate looking with a longish neck and a sandy to brownish-fawn coat. It has oval-

Above: Steenbock
Above right: Oribi
Below right: Duiker
Opposite page: Springbok

Above: Suni
Right: Impala

shaped ears and short, straight horns with a few rings at their base (male only). Like the reedbuck it has a patch of bare skin just below each ear. Found in small groups or as a pair and never far from water.

■ **Suni** *Nesotragus moschatus*, 37 cm. Dark chestnut to grey-fawn in colour with slight speckles along the back, its head and neck are slightly paler and the throat is white. It has a distinct bushy tail with a white tip. Its longish horns (male only) are thick, ribbed and slope backwards. One of the smallest antelope, it lives alone and prefers dense bush cover and reed beds.

■ **Impala** *Aepyceros melampus*, 92-107 cm. One of the largest of the smaller antelope, the impala has a bright rufous-coloured back and a white abdomen, a white 'eyebrow' and chin and white hair inside its ears. From behind, the white rump with black stripes on each side is characteristic and makes it easy to identify. It has long lyre-shaped horns (male only). Above the heels of the hind legs is a tuft of thick black bristles (unique to impala) which are easy to see when the animal runs. There's also a black mark on the side of the abdomen, just in front of the back leg. Found in herds of 15 to 20, it likes open grassland or sometimes the cover of partially wooded areas and is usually close to water.

Other mammals

There are many other fascinating mammals worth keeping an eye out for. This is a selection of some of the more interesting or particularly common ones.

■ **African wild dog** or hunting dog *Lycacon pictus*. Easy to identify since they have all the features of a large mongrel dog: a large head and slender body. Their coat is a mixed pattern of dark shapes and white and yellow patches and no two dogs are quite alike. They are particularly vicious when hunting. They are very rarely seen and are seriously threatened with extinction; there may be as few as 4000 left. Kruger is home to a quarter of this number, but seeing them is still a matter of luck.

Spotted hyena *Crocuta crocuta*. High shoulders and a low back give the hyena its characteristic appearance. The spotted variety, larger and brownish with dark spots, has a large head and rounded ears. The brown hyena, slightly smaller, has pointed ears and a shaggy coat, and is more noctural. Although sometimes shy animals, they have been know to wander around campsites stealing food from humans.

Rock hyrax *procavia capensis*. The rock hyrax lives in colonies amongst boulders and on rocky hillsides, protecting itself from predators like eagle, caracal and leopard by darting into the rock crevices.

Caracal *felis caracal*. Also known as the African lynx, it is twice the weight of a domestic cat, with reddish sandy-coloured fur and paler underparts. Distinctive black stripe from eye to nose and tufts on ears. Generally nocturnal and with similar habits to the leopard. It is not commonly seen, but is found in hilly country.

Vervet monkey *Chlorocebus pygerythrus*, 39-43 cm. A smallish primate and one of the most recognized monkeys in Africa and often seen at campsites and lodges. Brown bodies with a white underbelly and black face ringed by white fur, and males have blue abdominal regions. Spends the day foraging on the ground and sleeps at night in trees.

Left: African wild dog
Below: Vervet monkey
Bottom left: Spotted hyena
Bottom right: Rock hyrax
Next page: Caracal

Game viewing

There are no longer fences between Kruger and the private reserves, so game can roam freely between them vastly increasing an area of wilderness that is now referred to as Greater Kruger. The fences between the countries bordering South Africa have also come down in the last few years, and today Kruger and Mozambique's Limpopo National Park and Zimbabwe's Gonarezhou have created the Great Limpopo Transfrontier Park, a conservation area straddling a staggering 35,000 sq km.

The majority of game viewing is undertaken independently from a vehicle. The best times are after dawn and just before dusk, as animals tend to rest during the heat of the day. Kruger is only open to self-drivers during daylight hours, so plan your drives to start at first light and to return to camp just before the gates shut as it gets dark. There is a network of tarred and gravel or sand roads linking the camps and looping through the best game-viewing areas; all of which are navigable in a normal car unless it's particularly wet.

Since you are left to your own devices (and may never have been on safari before) it's a good idea to arm yourself with some identification guides for animals, and if you're interested, birds and trees. The Kruger shops sell a wide choice of their own publications, including the indispensable map of the park. The highest concentrations and variety of game are usually around Lower Sabie, Satara and Skukuza, but there are seasonal changes across the park; always ask at the entrance gates or camps in which direction you should head, and each has a frequently updated map of where animals have recently been spotted (which you can add to if you like).

Game viewing takes time and it is best to drive below 20 kph to maximize your chances of spotting animals. Although there is a temptation to head for the most isolated dirt tracks and to neglect the tarred roads, this can be a mistake as cars are quieter on tarred roads and the animals living near them are more used to traffic. The run-off from tarred roads also makes the vegetation greener and attracts more animals. Driving around Kruger can be very tiring, so it's a good idea to visit one of the get-out points or picnic sites (marked on park maps).

Game drives
Even if you drive yourself to and around Kruger, an additional game drive with an experienced guide can increase your chance of seeing animals and provides a deeper understanding of the wilderness. Most camps offer popular guided three- to four-hour day and night drives, which should be booked at camp reception as soon as you arrive. They cost from R210-380, children (2-11) half price, depending on the camp and time of day.

Morning drives leave at around 0430 in summer and 0530 in winter, so accommodation must be booked for the previous night at the camp as they

Game-viewing rules

• Keep on the well-marked roads and tracks; off-road driving is harmful because smoke, oil and destruction of the grass layer cause soil erosion.

• For your own safety, stay in your vehicle at all times; it serves as a blind or hide, since animals will not usually identify it with humans. It is forbidden to leave the vehicle except in designated places, such as a picnic site or hide.

• Never harass the animals. Make as little noise as possible; do not flash lights or try and attract the animals' attention by calling out or whistling.

• Never chase the animals and always let them pass unhindered; they always have right of way.

• Do not feed the animals; the food you provide might make them ill, and, worse still, once animals learn that food is available from humans they can become aggressive and dangerous.

• Do not throw any litter, including used matches or cigarette butts; this increases the fire risk in the dry season and some animals will eat whatever they find.

• Do not disturb other visitors. If you discover a stopped vehicle and you want to check what they are looking at, never hinder their sight or stop within their photographic field. If there is no room for another car, wait patiently for a car to leave.

• Do not drive too fast; the speed limit is 40 kph and speeding damages road surfaces, increases noise and raises the risk of running over animals.

• Remember all animals are wild; despite their beauty their reactions are unpredictable so don't expose yourself to unnecessary risks.

depart before the gates officially open. Sunset drives leave camp in the mid-afternoon (depending on the time of sunset) and get back once the sky is dark. Night drives are an added attraction as private vehicles are not allowed outside the camps after sundown, and these usually depart around 1700. Make sure you have warm clothing as temperatures drop in the evenings. The drives finish in time for guests to have an evening meal at the camp restaurant.

Game walks

Most camps also offer two- or three-hour walks in the morning or afternoon accompanied by an armed game ranger from around R450 per person, no children under 13. Groups are kept small – up to eight people – and the rangers are trained in field guiding. These provide an excellent way of getting close to smaller animals and are a thrilling way of exploring the bush. Again like the game drives, the early morning walks depart before the gates officially open so accommodation must be booked for the previous night at the camp.

Wilderness trails

Seeing the park on foot is the most exciting way to experience the wilderness, and the seven SANParks wilderness trails are three-day guided walking safaris. A maximum of eight people go on each trail and they are accompanied by an armed ranger. Hikers spend each night at the same rustic bush camp with huts or tents (bedding and towels provided), flush toilets and gas-powered showers, and rates include all meals. A reasonable level of fitness is required as up to 20 km may be walked per day, although at a leisurely pace and broken up by brunch and a siesta back in camp. The trails start on either a Wednesday afternoon to a Saturday morning or a Sunday afternoon to a Wednesday morning, and check-in is at the nearest main rest camp (where you can leave your car). They cost R4000 per person (no children under 12) and bookings through SANParks can be made up to a year ahead and places fill up quickly. The best time of year for hiking is March to July when the weather is dry and daytime temperatures are cooler. The wilderness trails are Bushman (check in at Berg-en-Dal); Napi (Pretoriuskop); Metsi-Metsi (Skukuza); Nyalaland (Punda Maria); Olifants (Letaba); Sweni (Satara); and Wolhuter (Berg-en-Dal).

Backpacking trails

These are different to the wilderness trails in that hikers cover around 45 km over four days and three nights but camp in a different place each night. As such, hikers have to carry packs with tents and sleeping gear, and all their own cooking equipment and food, which they cook themselves. These are tough hikes – 10-15 km a day carrying heavy packs, and additionally the trails are designed on a 'take in, take out' basis – hikers need to be fit and show a medical certificate of good health. A maximum of eight and a minimum of four people are permitted and are accompanied by two armed rangers. Departures are every Wednesday and Sunday between 1 February and 31 October, and cost R2350 per person (no under 12s). Orientation (and pack-checking) is at the nearest rest camp (where you can leave your car), before hikers are transferred by vehicle to a remote region of the park. The backpacking trails are Lonely Bull (departure from Shimuwini); Mphongolo (from Shingwedzi); and Olifants River (from Olifants).

Southern Kruger

Kruger's historic southern region is bordered by the Crocodile River in the south and the Sabie River in the north. In the east, along the border with Mozambique, the Lebombo Moutains form a rugged and scenic low ridge. The greatest concentrations of game and most of Kruger's large camps are in the south and many visitors only ever see this section of the park. The landscape here is far more varied than the rest of the park and therefore supports a wider range of animals. The 43-km road between Skukuza, the park's headquarters and its largest camp, and Lower Sabie, one of the most popular and picturesque camps, is the most popular game-viewing road in the whole of Kruger. If you don't mind the crowds and your interests lie predominantly in ticking off the Big Five than head to the south.

Arriving in southern Kruger

The entrance gates at **Crocodile Bridge** and **Malelane** are on the southern boundary of the park and are clearly signposted from the N4 running between

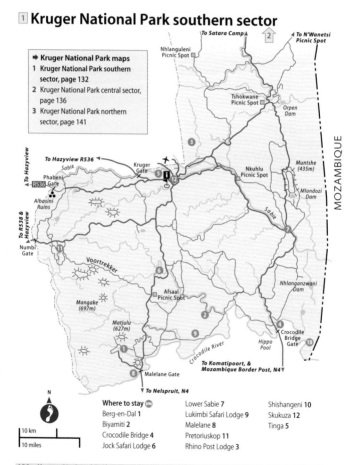

1 Kruger National Park southern sector

➡ **Kruger National Park maps**
1 Kruger National Park southern sector, page 132
2 Kruger National Park central sector, page 136
3 Kruger National Park northern sector, page 141

To Satara Camp
To N'Wanetsi Picnic Spot

Nhlanguleni Picnic Spot

Tshokwane Picnic Spot

Orpen Dam

MOZAMBIQUE

To Hazyview R536
To Hazyview
Sabie
R536 Gate
Phabeni Gate
Kruger Gate
Albasini Ruins
To R538 & Hazyview
Numbi Gate
Voortrekker
Mangabe (697m)
Matjulu (627m)
Afsaal Picnic Spot

Nkuhlu Picnic Spot
Muntshe (435m)
Mlondozi Dam
Sabie
Nhlanganzwani Dam
Crocodile River
Hippo Pool
Crocodile Bridge Gate

To Komatipoort, & Mozambique Border Post, N4
Malelane Gate
To Nelspruit, N4

N

10 km
10 miles

Where to stay 🛏
Berg-en-Dal **1**
Biyamiti **2**
Crocodile Bridge **4**
Jock Safari Lodge **6**

Lower Sabie **7**
Lukimbi Safari Lodge **9**
Malelane **8**
Pretoriuskop **11**
Rhino Post Lodge **3**

Shishangeni **10**
Skukuza **12**
Tinga **5**

Nelspruit and Komatipoort (the Mozambique border). The entrance gates at **Numbi**, **Phabeni** and **Kruger** are on the southwestern boundary. Numbi Gate is signposted off the R538 between White River and Hazyview; Phabeni and Kruger gates are on the R536 from Hazyview.

Berg-En-Dal ⓘ *12 km from Malelane Gate, T013-735 6106.* This large, modern camp has a rather austere, institutional feel to it, but is set in a hilly landscape, wooded with acacia, marula and jackalberry overlooking the Matjulu Dam. Facilities include a swimming pool, in-camp trail, environmental centre showing wildlife films, petrol, shop, restaurant and launderette. There are two guest houses (**$$$**) sleeping six or eight, 23 **cottages** (**$$$**) which are slightly larger than at the other camps and sleep six to eight people, 69 three-bed **bungalows** (**$$**) and 72 camping and caravan sites.

Biyamiti ⓘ *26 km from Crocodile Gate, T013-735 6171.* This bushveld camp is in the far south of Kruger on the banks of the Mbiyamiti River set in an area of crocodile thorn thicket. The camp has 15 one- or two-bed **cottages** (**$$$-$$**).

Crocodile Bridge ⓘ *At Crocodile Gate which is 10 km north of Komatipoort on the N4, T013-735 6012.* This small camp is set in acacia woodland on the northern bank of the Crocodile River next to the park's southern gate. There is a hippo pool on the dirt road to Malelane where elephant and other animals come to drink. The camp has 20 two- or three-bed **chalets** (**$$**), eight **safari tents** (**$**) with communal ablution and kitchen units, and 15 camping and caravan sites. Facilities include petrol, shop, café and launderette.

Lower Sabie ⓘ *53 km from Kruger Gate, T013-735 6056.* The region around Lower Sabie is part of a classic African savannah landscape, with grasslands, umbrella thorn and round-leaf teak stretching off into the distance. Game is attracted here by water at the Mlondosi and Nhlanganzwani dams and the camp overlooks the Sabie River. The accommodation is impersonal but the camp itself is fairly peaceful. Facilities include a **restaurants**, a bar, shop, petrol, launderette and swimming pool. Accommodation is in large two or five-bed **cottages** (**$$$-$$**); two- or three-bed **chalets** (**$$**); two-bed **rondavels** (**$$**) with fridge; two-bed **huts** (**$$**) with fridge; small, two-bed **cottages** (**$$**) with fridge and communal ablutions; one-bed **safari tents** (**$$**) with communal ablution and kitchen units; one-bed **huts** (**$**) with fridge and communal ablution and kitchen units; plus camping and caravan sites.

Malelane ⓘ *At Malelane Gate which is 5 km north of Malelane on the N4, T013-735 6152.* Malelane is a satellite camp to Berg-en-Dal, set in a rugged area of mountain bushveld on the banks of the Crocodile River on the southern boundary of the park near the Malelane Gate. It has five three- and four-bed cottages (**$$**), with bathroom and solar-powered communal kitchen facilities, plus camping and caravan sites.

Pretoriuskop ⓘ *9 km from Numbi Gate, T013-735 5128.* This is the oldest camp in Kruger and is also the third largest, with a fairly institutional feel. The game drives around Pretoriuskop pass through marula woodland and tall grassland, with good game-viewing areas to the north along the Sabie River and to the south along the Voortrekker Road, which follows the original wagon route through the veld. Facilities include a restaurant, café, swimming pool made out of natural rock, petrol, shop and launderette. There are 142 sleeping units: six-, eight- and nine-bed **cottages** (**$$$**), with two bathrooms; four-bed **cottages** (**$$$-$$**) with one bathroom; two- to four-bed **bungalows** (**$$**); two-, three-, five- and six-bed **huts** (**$**) with with communal ablution and kitchen units, plus 45 camping and caravan sites.

Skukuza ⓘ *12 km from Kruger Gate, 39 km from Phabeni Gate, T013-735 4152.* Located on the south bank of the Sabie River, Skukuza is Kruger's largest camp and the administrative centre of the park. The camp has grown to such an extent that it resembles a small town and you may forget that you're in a national park. Despite its size, Skukuza is at the centre of Kruger's prime game-viewing area; the road heading northeast towards Satara is said have one of the densest concentrations of lion in Africa – and the densest population of cars in Kruger. Facilities here cater to almost every need and include a supermarket, petrol, car wash, two restaurants, bank, post office, internet café, two swimming pools, doctor and launderette, and an airport. There is also an open-air cinema showing wildlife videos in the evenings, a good information centre and library, and a nursery that cultivates indigenous plants including baobabs, which for a small fee you can visit. Skukuza accommodates over 1000 people in four-, six- and eight-bed **cottages** (**$$$$**), with two bathrooms; two-, three- and four-bed **cottages** (**$$$**) with one bathroom; two- three-bed **chalets** (**$$**) two- and four-bed **safari tents** (**$**) with communal ablution and kitchen units, plus 80 camping and caravan sites. The **Skukuza Golf Course** ⓘ *clubhouse T013-735 5543*, was originally built in 1972 as a course for Kruger staff. Today this 19-hole 18-tee course is open to all, but you'll need your own golf clubs. Given that it's unfenced and winds its way around a central lake, uninvited spectators are a common sight, including hippo, impala, warthog and baboon. Tee-off times are between 0700 and 1200, nine-holes R210, 18 holes R290; book in advance.

Central Kruger

Central Kruger is a little quieter than the south, with large areas of flat mopane woodland and the abundance of excellent browsing trees sustain the largest buffalo, giraffe, wildebeest, zebra, waterbuck and sable populations in the park. As such these attract more than half of Kruger's lion population plus sizeable numbers of cheetah and hyena. The central region is a good place to spot predators especially around Satara, the second largest camp in Kruger, while any exploration of the river roads, especially along the Olifants and Letaba rivers, can produce some of the best game-viewing in the park.

Arriving in Central Kruger

Orpen Gate and **Phalaborwa Gate** are on the western boundary. Orpen Gate is off the R40 just south of Klaserie on the border with Mpumalanga and Limpopo provinces, and Phalaborwa Gate is on the R71 3 km east of Phalaborwa on the route from Polokwane and Tzaneen in Limpopo.

Balule ⓘ *86 km from Orpen Gate, 96 km from Phalaborwa Gate, 11 km from Olifants where visitors must check in, T013-735 6606.* Balule is on the banks of the Olifants River and is one of Kruger's wildest camps. It is little more than a patch of cleared bush surrounded by an electrified chain-link fence; visitors can see animals wandering by only metres away. There are six three-bed **huts ($)**, with communal ablution and kitchen units but no electricity, though there are gas stoves and lanterns are provided, and 15 basic caravan and camping sites, with ablution block and *braai* sites; firewood is on sale here. The smell of barbecued meat attracts hyenas who patrol the fence all night in search of scraps (but don't under any circumstances feed them).

Boulders ⓘ *54 km from Phalaborwa Gate; 31 km from Mopani where visitors must check in, the camp must be booked as a single unit, minimum 4, maximum 12.* This unfenced private camp is set among massive granite boulders in an area of acacia, knobthorn and mopane woodland, and blends in beautifully with its environment. The five thatched **bungalows ($$$$)** are raised on stilts and have a veranda from which to observe the wildlife wandering through the camp. Each sleeps two and there's a communal kitchen and solar power.

Letaba ⓘ *51 km from Phalaborwa Gate, 119 km from Orpen Gate, T013-735 6636.* Letaba is one of the larger camps in central Kruger and is pleasant and neatly laid out on the banks of the Letaba River. The restaurant is in a magnificent setting for watching game come down to drink, and there is good game viewing to the east along the river and at Engelhardt Dam. Facilities include a shop, restaurant, swimming pool, launderette, petrol, museum with exhibits on Kruger's elephants, and TV lounge showing wildlife films. Accommodation is in six-, eight- and nine-bed **cottages ($$$)**; two- and three-

2 **Kruger National Park central sector**

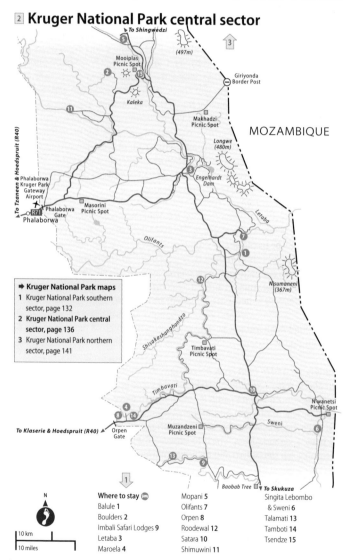

To Shingwedzi

(497m)

3

Mooiplas
Picnic Spot

2

15

Giriyonda
Border Post

Kaleka

Makhadzi
Picnic Spot

MOZAMBIQUE

11

Longwe
(480m)

3

*Engelhardt
Dam*

Letaba

Phalaborwa
Kruger Park
Gateway
Airport

Masorini
Picnic Spot

7

Phalaborwa
Gate

R71

Phalaborwa

Olifants

1

Ntsumaneni
(367m)

12

➡ **Kruger National Park maps**
1 Kruger National Park southern
  sector, page 132
2 **Kruger National Park central
  sector, page 136**
3 Kruger National Park northern
  sector, page 141

Shisakashonghondzo

Timbavati
Picnic Spot

Timbavati

10

N'wanetsi
Picnic Spot

4

8 **14**

To Klaserie & Hoedspruit (R40)

Orpen
Gate

Muzandzeni
Picnic Spot

Sweni

6

13

9

Baobab Tree **To Skukuza**

N

Where to stay	Mopani **5**	Singita Lebombo
Balule **1**	Olifants **7**	& Sweni **6**
Boulders **2**	Orpen **8**	Talamati **13**
Imbali Safari Lodges **9**	Roodewal **12**	Tamboti **14**
Letaba **3**	Satara **10**	Tsendze **15**
Maroela **4**	Shimuwini **11**	

10 km

10 miles

bed chalets (**$$**); three-bed bungalows (**$$**); four-bed huts (**$$**) with fridge; and four-bed safari tents (**$**) with communal ablutions and kitchen units, plus a large campsite, with 35 camping and caravan sites.

Maroela and Tamboti satellite camps ⓘ *4 km from Orpen Gate where visitors check in.* These are both satellite camps to Orpen. Maroela's large campsite is on the south bank of the Timbavati River, and has 20 camping and caravan sites, ablution blocks and kitchen units. There are no other facilities here, but there is a shop at Orpen where you check in and where you can also arrange day walks and night drives. Not far from Maroela, **Tamboti ($$-$)** is a tented camp on the banks of the Timbavati River, offering 35 furnished safari tents for two to four people, either fully equipped or sharing communal kitchen, ablutions and eating boma. This is the ideal spot for people looking for a complete bush experience without having to bring all the equipment. There is no restaurant or shop.

Mopani ⓘ *76 km from Phalaborwa Gate, T013-735 6535.* This is set on a seemingly endless plain of mopane shrub overlooking the Pioneer Dam and is only a few kilometres south of the Tropic of Capricorn. The accommodation at Mopani has been made from natural materials and is more pleasant and spacious than some of the older camps. Choose from an eight-bed cottage (**$$$$**); six-bed cottages (**$$$**); or two- and three-bed bungalows (**$$**). Facilities include swimming pool, nature trail, petrol, shop, restaurant, bar overlooking the dam, café and launderette.

Olifants ⓘ *82 km from Phalaborwa Gate, 94 km from Orpen Gate, T013-735 6606.* Olifants is one of Kruger's most attractive and peaceful camps in a spectacular setting high on a hill overlooking fever trees and wild figs lining the banks of the Olifants River. The game drives in the immediate area pass through flat mopane woodland in the north and a hilly area of rocks and woodland in the south. Facilities include a restaurant, shop, wildlife films, petrol and launderette. A thatched game-viewing veranda perched on the edge of the camp looks down into the river valley. The thatched accommodation, shaded by large old sycamores and sausage trees, encompasses eight-bed cottages (**$$$$**); four-bed cottages (**$$$**); two-bed chalets (**$$**); and two- or three-bed bungalows (**$$**).

Orpen ⓘ *At Orpen Gate, which is 45 km east of Klaserie and the R40, T013-735 6355.* Orpen is a small camp past the entrance gate on the western central plains, set amongst acacias, marulas and aloes. The road passing along the Timbavati River offers a chance of seeing game, and the area around the camp is known as the habitat of predators. There are six-bed cottages (**$$$**), and three-bed bungalows (**$$**). Facilities include petrol and shop.

Kruger's feathered friends

Kruger straddles a variety of ecosystems and so birdwatching throughout the entire park is excellent, and is an ideal activity to accompany game viewing, especially during quiet moments of animal activity. Kruger is home to almost 500 of South Africa's 860 plus bird species, and is a superb place to see woodland and savannah birds. Numbers are greatest in summer, when all the Palaearctic and intra-African migrants are present. The numerous rivers and waterholes, as well as the rest camps and picnic sites, are exceptionally rewarding vantage points. Hornbills, starlings, vultures, rollers, bee-eaters and shrike typify the ubiquitous dry bushveld, and birdwatchers can look forward to pursuing the Big Six: saddle-billed stork, kori bustard, Martial eagle, lappet-faced vulture, Pel's fishing owl and ground hornbill. By and large restricted to the Kruger region, these six species are easily indentified and instantly recognizable (with the exception of the Pel's fishing owl, which is seldom seen, because of its nocturnal habits). Eagles are also common and, as well as the Martial, bateleur, black-chested snake, brown snake, African hawk, African fish and tawny eagles, are all regularly seen, and in summer, there are Wahlberg's, steppe and lesser-spotted eagles too.

Roodewal ⓘ *75 km from Orpen Gate; check in at Satara, 44 km, or Olifants 28 km, the camp must be booked as a single unit, minimum 6, maximum 16.* This secluded bush lodge is an unfenced private camp on the banks of the Timbavati River and the riverine plant life like Natal mahogany and jackalberry trees create a picturesque view from the *braai* area and elevated game-viewing deck. The camp must be booked as one unit (**$$$$**) and it has one two-bed two-bathroom cottage and three twin bungalows with lofts for children. There's a communal kitchen with gas stove and solar power.

Satara ⓘ *48 km from Orpen Gate, 104 km from Kruger Gate, T013-735 6306.* Satara, Kruger's second-largest camp looks rather like a motorway service station in the middle of the bush, although the institutional atmosphere of the accommodation is softened by its trees and lawns. Satara is set in the flat grasslands of the eastern region, which attract large herds of wildebeest, buffalo, kudu, impala, zebra and elephant. There is good game viewing on the road from Orpen. Accommodation is available in guest **cottages** (**$$$$**) sleeping six, eight or nine, with one or two bathrooms; two- or three-bed **bungalows** (**$$**); two- or three-bed **bungalows** (**$$**) with bathroom and communal kitchen; and 87 camping and caravan sites. Facilities include petrol, car wash, shop, café, restaurant, launderette and swimming pool.

Shimuwini ⓘ *52 km from Phalaborwa Gate, T013-735 6683.* Overlooking the Shimuwini Dam, this bushveld camp is set in a region of bushwillow and mopane woodland, with less of a concentration of wildlife compared to the south but still with a good variety of species. The road leading to Shimuwini follows the Letaba River where elephant can sometimes be seen bathing and the riverine forest around the camp is good for birdwatching. There is a hide here from which to see crocodiles, hippo, waterbuck and waterbirds. The camp has four- and six-bed thatched **cottages ($$$)** shaded by appleleaf trees and acacias.

Talamati ⓘ *28 km from Orpen Gate, T013-735 6343.* This rustic bushveld camp is set on the banks of the Nwaswitsonto River, which is normally dry. The grassland and acacia woodland along the western boundary attract kudu, giraffe, sable and white rhino, and there are two hides in the camp for game viewing and birdwatching. Accommodation is in two-, four- and six-bed **cottages ($$$)**.

Tsendze ⓘ *69 km from Phalaborwa Gate, 7 km from Mopani, where visitors check in.* This is Kruger's newest rustic campsite set among stands of ancient and beautiful leadwood, mopane and apple leaf trees. Two prominent seasonal water courses, the Tsendze River and Nshawu Creek, run through this area that is known for large buffalo herds and lone elephant bulls. The 30 sites are placed in two circles around the ablution and kitchen facilities, but there is no electricity although it has gas geysers to warm the open-air showers and solar lights.

Northern Kruger

This is a dry and remote region that is the least popular part of the park for visitors. Much of it is blanketed in shrub mopane and packets of sand forest making it difficult to spot animals and as there is no year-round water supply, there isn't the same density of animals as in the south of Kruger. But the area does support animals unique to this part of Kruger, including Sharpe's grysbok, tsessebe, sable and nyala, and it's known for its huge pythons that thrive in the thick forests, and some of the largest crocodiles in Kruger can be seen in the Luvuvhu River. It is also one of the most rewarding areas for birdwatchers, as many species are attracted to the fruit trees. The north is considered by some as the most enchanting and wild, and will appeal to those that enjoy seeing the smaller and lesser-known creatures and birds.

Close to the Luvuvhu River, in the northern corner of the park, is the late Iron Age site of **Thulamela**; an important archaeological site which lies on the top of a sub-plateau which is reached after a steep 25-minute climb. It is estimated that more than 1500 people lived here some 400-500 years ago.

The stone enclosure was a royal palace, which, during its heyday in the Khami period, was an important commercial centre of a powerful agro-pastoral kingdom. Evidence collected at Thulamela points towards a thriving metal-working community producing spearheads and hoe blades in iron, as well as more delicate items from copper and gold. Guided walking tours to Thulamela depart from the Pafuri picnic spot twice daily. Bookings can be made at Sirheni, Shingwedzi, Punda Maria and Pafuri.

Arriving in Northern Kruger
Punda Maria Gate and **Pafuri Gate** are in the far north of the park in Limpopo. Punda Maria Gate is on the R524 and can be reached from Louis Trichardt on the N1. Pafuri Gate can be reached on the R525 which leaves the N1 between Louis Trichardt and Musina.

Bateleur ⓘ *74 km from Punda Maria Gate, T013-735 6843.* Bateleur is an isolated bushveld camp surrounded by a vast area of mopane and acacia woodland with the Phonda Hills (400 m) lying to the north. Visitors to the camp have exclusive access to the two nearby dams, Rooibosrand and Silverfish, both of which are good areas for game watching, especially for sable and nyala. There is a viewing platform overlooking a waterhole. The camp is solar powered and accommodates up to 34 visitors in four- and six-bed **cottages ($$$)**.

Shingwedzi ⓘ *73 km from Punda Maria Gate, T013-735 6806.* The best game viewing in this area is around Kanniedood Dam and the riverine forest along the banks of the Shingwedzi. Waterbuck, nyala, kudu and elephant are often seen here and the bird life is prolific. The thatched units here are arranged in two large circles, looking in on an open area, which has no grass, but a shady area of short mopane trees. Accommodation comprises one four-bed **cottage ($$$$)**; two-bed **chalets and bungalows ($$)**; three-bed **huts ($)**, with fridge, veranda, and communal ablution and kitchen units. Facilities include a restaurant, café, shop, petrol, swimming pool and launderette. The restaurant has a pleasant outside terrace where you can sit during the day and look out over the Shingwedzi River. The campsite is well away from the cottages and chalets, and while it has plenty of space, there is limited shade and virtually no grass.

Punda Maria ⓘ *8 km from Punda Maria Gate, T013-735 6873.* This peaceful camp, hidden by dense woodland, is the northernmost large rest camp in Kruger and by far the most pleasant. It is situated in an area of sandveld dotted with baobabs, white seringa and pod mahogany. There are spectacular views of the surrounding landscapes from the top of Dzundzwini (600 m) and good game viewing on the Mahonie Loop and up by the Witsand windmill. It's a good area to see nyala, kudu, roan, sable and tsessebe, and the bridge over the Luvuvhu River is a top place for birdwatchers. Accommodation is in four-bed **cottages** (**$$$**); two-bed **chalets** (**$$**); two-bed **bungalows** (**$$**) with bathroom, fridge and communal kitchen, plus camping and caravan sites.

③ Kruger National Park northern sector

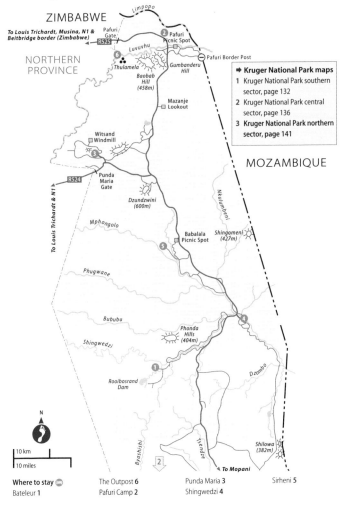

➡ **Kruger National Park maps**
1 Kruger National Park southern sector, page 132
2 Kruger National Park central sector, page 136
3 Kruger National Park northern sector, page 141

Where to stay 🛏
Bateleur **1**
The Outpost **6**
Pafuri Camp **2**
Punda Maria **3**
Shingwedzi **4**
Sirheni **5**

Note that this is a small camp and is often fully booked at weekends. Facilities include restaurant, bar, shop and petrol.

Sirheni ① *48 km to Punda Maria Gate, T013-735 6860*. This is a bushveld camp overlooking Sirheni Dam, surrounded by mopane and acacia woodland. This region is better known for birdwatching than game viewing but the road approaching the camp from the south passes through the alluvial plains and riverine forest of the Mphongolo River, inhabited by leopard, nyala and waterbuck. The camp has four- and six-bed **cottages** (**$$**).

Kruger concessions

Nine concessions have been granted by SANParks to privately owned camps within the boundaries of Kruger. These are exclusive-use, unfenced areas where the general public are not permitted, while guests also have uninhibited access to the surrounding Kruger road network. The safari experience is similar to the private game reserves on the western edge of the park (page 144) and rates include game drives, bush walks and all meals. Also like the lodges in the private game reserves, rates are expensive and all firmly in the **$$$$** price bracket; over R3000 per person per night rising to R14,000 per person per night at some.

Arriving in Kruger concessions

Access to the Kruger concessions is obviously via the park gates (see Arriving in Kruger box, page 123), and once in the park, the concessions are clearly signposted. The standard SANParks daily conservation fees apply. On a self-drive holiday around Kruger, there's no reason why you can't mix it up a little and stay in midrange to budget SANParks camps on some nights, and treat yourself to a night or two of luxury at the concession lodges on others. If you don't have your own vehicle, transfers to the concessions from the nearest airport (see page 122) can be arranged, including Skukuza Airport within the park.

Imbali Safari Lodges ① *37 km from Orpen Gate, 80 km from Kruger Gate, T011-516 4367, www.imbali.com*. This collection of luxury lodges are located in central Kruger on the banks of the N'waswitsontso River within the 10,000 ha Mluwati concession. The **Imbali Safari Lodge** has 12 suites with jacuzzis or plunge pools; **Hoyo-Hoyo Tsonga Lodge** has 6 'beehive' suites around a waterhole; while **Hamilton's Camp** (named after James Stevenson-Hamilton, Kruger's first warden) has six tents on elevated platforms among jackalberry trees.

Jock Safari Lodge ① *40 km from Malelane Gate, midway between Skukuza and Berg-en-dal, T041-407 1000, www.jocksafarilodge.com*. Lying in an area of mixed woodland at the confluence of the Mitomeni and Biyamiti rivers in the southeast of the park, the 6000-ha Jock of the Bushveld concession is named after the gutsy Staffordshire terrier in the classic animal novel (see box, page 156). 12 luxurious thatched suites with plunge pools in the main camp, while the exclusive **Fitzpatrick's Lodge** sleeps six adults and four children. As well as the normal activities, a two-day walking safari is on offer using a mobile camp.

Lukimbi Safari Lodge ① *26 km from Malelane Gate, 32 km from Crocodile Bridge Gate, T011-431 1120, www.lukimbi.com.* Located on the 15,000 ha Lwakahle concession in the south of the park bordering the Crocodile River, this has easy access from the N4 between Nelspruit and Mozambique. The lodge has 16 suites, some with a splash pool and extra bedroom, and is one of the more family-friendly concession lodges with a children's activity programme.

Pafuri Camp ① *24 km from Pafuri Gate, 60 km from Punda Maria Gate, T011-257 5111, www.wilderness-safaris.com.* This remote 24,000-ha concession is in the extreme north of Kruger between the Limpopo and Luvuvhu rivers. The camp is set under giant ebony trees and has 20 river-facing tents on raised platforms under thatch, some sleep families of four, also organizes three-day walking safaris using mobile camps.

Rhino Post Lodge ① *30 km from Kruger Gate, 10 km northeast of Skukuza, T011-467 1886, www.isibindiafrica.co.za.* This 12,000-ha concession shares a 15 km unfenced boundary with Mala Mala in Sabi Sands, and has eight thatch and canvas suites that are raised on stilts on the banks of the Mutlumuvi River under magnificent tamboti trees. As well as game drives, offers multi-day walking safaris utilizing both the lodge and simple bush camps.

Shishangeni ① *18 km from Crocodile Bridge Gate, T011-028 0882, www.shishangeni.com.* This 15,000 ha private concession in the southeast of Kruger is bordered by the Crocodile River to the south and Mozambique in the east. Larger and less expensive than some, Shishangeni comprises of three camps: Shishangeni Private Lodge has 22 chalets, while Camp Shonga has five thatched rooms and Camp Shaw has five tents.

Singita Lebombo and Sweni ① *70 km from Orpen Gate, 32 km east of Satara, T021-683 3424, www.singita.com.* A 15,000 ha concession on the remote eastern boundary of Kruger near the Mozambique border on the banks of the Sweni River and backed by the Lebombo Mountains. **Lebombo** has 15 suites, and **Sweni** six, and are modern, stylish and very expensive; a fashionable alternative to the usual colonial or ethnic themes. **Singita** also has two lodges in Sabi Sands, and this collection constitutes the most luxurious safari offerings in the whole of South Africa.

The Outpost ⓘ *10 km from Pafuri Gate, 80 km from Punda Maria Gate, T011-327 3920, www.seasonsinafrica.com.* In Kruger's northern tip and part of the 26,500 ha Makuleke concession which is bordered to the north by the Limpopo River's floodplains and Zimbabwe. A contemporary steel and concrete lodge, the 12 suites are set on the side of a hill overlooking the Luvuvhu River, all connected by a 500-m-long walkway made of Zimbabwean teak. Walking safaris for up to three nights on offer using bush camps.

Tinga ⓘ *13 km from Kruger Gate, 7 km northwest of Skukuza, T011-880 9992, www.tinga.co.za.* Tinga borders Sabi Sands and has a 5000-ha concession on the game-rich Sabie River and has two luxurious and very expensive lodges set close together under jackalberry trees, each with nine vast suites with plunge pools. Close to the airport and other facilities at Skukuza.

Private game reserves

There are numerous private game reserves fringing the western border of Kruger that stretch in a continuous unbroken block from the Olifants River in the north to the Sabie River in the south. Some are in the Limpopo Province, but the best-known of these are included here together with the Mpumalanga reserves. Confusingly, within some of the reserves are several smaller ones; over the years these have been incorporated into a single wilderness area but some still retain their original name – for example, Mala Mala Game Reserve and Londolozi Game Reserve are now both part of the much larger Sabi Sands Game Reserve. There are no longer any fences between the western boundary of Kruger and these reserves, which has helped, in part, to restore natural east-west migration routes for the game. This has also created a vast joint area under conservation, and together Kruger and the adjoining private game reserves is most often dubbed Greater Kruger; a region considered to be around 20,000 sq km in size.

Arriving in private game reserves
Access to the private reserves is straightforward. Guests are collected from the airports (see page 122); namely **Phalaborwa Kruger Park Gateway Airport**, **Eastgate Airport** at Hoedspruit, or **Kruger Mpumalanga International Airport** (KMIA) near Nelspruit (scheduled flights or charter flights are usually included in packages) and driven by safari vehicle to the lodge. Alternatively, you can drive yourself. In addition to the overnight rates at the lodges, the reserves

Greater Kruger private game reserves

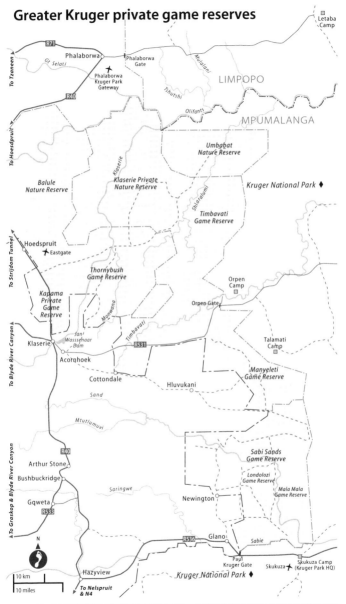

Walk on the wild side

Similar to the Wilderness and Backpacking Trails run by SANParks within the park (see page 126), **Transfrontiers Wildlife Walking Safaris**, T015-793 0719, www.transfrontiers.com, offer four- or five-day walking safaris in the private reserves accessed from Hoedspruit. The five-day safari (R7400) starts on Monday and the four-day safari (R5600) starts on Friday, and for an extra fee transfers to and from Johannesburg can be arranged; there's a maximum of eight people so early booking is advised. Accommodation is in two simple bush camps with pre-erected walk-in tents with twin beds, and communal ablution facilities, and daily walks leave from these. Each camp has an honesty bar and a dining tent, and costs include all meals. No children under 16 and you need to be reasonably fit. Many of the luxury lodges in the private reserves also offer walking safaris with overnights in mobile bush camps away from the main lodge. Highly recommended for a peaceful, authentic and informative bush experience well away from the crowds.

charge a daily conservation fee; these vary but expect to pay around R50-150 per person and R200 per vehicle if driving in.

Lodges

Each private game reserve in turn is home to countless safari lodges and tented camps (far too many to list individually here). Each is unfenced and has its own secluded setting, providing an enjoyable 'in the wild' experience. Here you have the chance of seeing the Big Five and exploring the natural environment of Kruger from the comfort of a 4WD on private tracks were no public vehicles are allowed. Of course game viewing is always dependent on luck, and staying in a five-star lodge does not mean that you will be guaranteed better animal sightings than if you were travelling around Kruger in a hire car and staying in a SANParks campsite. But the benefits are that you will have a personal and knowledgeable guide and you're unlikely to come across too many other tourists – and with the promise of luxury accommodation and superb cuisine at the end of the day.

Most guests spend between two and three days at a lodge to get the most out of the experience. Days normally begin with an early-morning drive, returning in mid- to late-morning for brunch. When the worst of the day's heat has passed, the vehicles set off on another game drive, returning for dinner. Optional night drives are usually also available. In between outings you can appreciate the full extent of your surroundings: most camps have platforms overlooking a waterhole or a river, there are usually comfortable lounge areas, libraries of books and magazines about wildlife, most lodges have swimming pools and some have them have spas.

Daily rates at the lodges in all private game reserves falls into the highest accommodation price bracket (**$$$$**) and start from R3000 per person per night, though rates at many can soar to over R20,000. However prices include all meals, game walks and game drives, and special deals are often available; it is worth looking out for fly-in packages and discounts out of peak season. Be sure to shop around; the reserves themselves have excellent websites, as do the individual lodges within them.

Kapama Private Game Reserve ⓘ *Gate is 18 km south of Hoedspruit on the R40. 4 luxury lodges, T012-368 0600, www.kapama.co.za.* This reserve in Limpopo Province covers approximately 13,000 ha of prime big game territory of savannah and riverine forest. A highlight here are the elephant-back safaris offered at **Camp Jabulani**, the first of now many operations of its kind in South Africa. The reserve also offers game drives and walks, birdwatching from a bird hide on the banks of a large dam, sundowner cruises and hot-air ballooning. Additionally there's a separate sumptuous spa for guests from all the four lodges.

Timbavati Game Reserve ⓘ *Gate is 7 km south of Hoedspruit off the R40. 12 luxury lodges and camps, T015-793 2436, www.timbavati.co.za.* Also in Limpopo, Timbavati extends from Orpen to the region just south of the Olifants River. The open savannah, riverine forest, acacia, marula and mopane woodlands support a tremendous variety of wildlife, including large herds of elephant, giraffe, blue wildebeest, zebra and impala, and this area is known for its white lions, although these have largely become assimilated in to the larger lion population.

Thornybush Game Reserve ⓘ *The access road (known as Guernsey Rd) is just north of Klaserie on the R40. 9 luxury lodges, T011-253 6500, www.thornybush collection.co.za.* Sharing a border with Timbavati, Thornybush is one of the oldest private game reserves that started life as a private farm before it was converted into a private game reserve of 13,500 ha in 1955. Back then it was fenced, and was the location of the first translocation of an entire herd of elephant from Kruger, although today without fences, all game wanders around in the full extent of the area. There are broad tracts of savannah grassland making it easier to spot the numerous animals and more than 250 bird species have been recorded including many raptors.

Klaserie Private Nature Reserve ⓘ *7 km south of Hoedspruit off the R40, then to Timbavati Gate but head north into Klaserie not into Timbavati proper.*

3 camps, T015-793 3051, www.klaseriereserve.co.za. This reserve is located on the Klaserie River which even when dry, creates a number of waterholes shaded by established marula, wild teak and umbrella thorn trees. Klaserie is perhaps the least commercially developed of all the private reserves, simply because as yet it only has three camps and they are not in the top-end of the luxury category. It will appeal to those who want a more rustic experience without excessive frills.

Sabi Sands Game Reserve ⓘ *There are 3 entry gates: in the south, Shaws and Newington gates are accessed off the R536 between Hazyview and Kruger Gate, in the north Gowrie Gate is off the R40 north of Hazyview, turn off at Acornhoek. 30 luxury lodges and camps, T013-735 5102, www.sabi-sands.com.* Sabi Sands is made up of a block of contiguous reserves north of the Sabie River and lies entirely in the Lowveld of Mpumalanga; the name comes from the Sabie River and the Sand River flowing through it. It is the largest of the reserves and has the highest density of lodges and game-viewing vehicles and is slightly more crowded than say Timbavati or Thornybush. But it covers a vast area of 65,000 ha, it shares a non-fenced boundary of 50 km with Kruger, and the Sabie River has water all year round, which attracts large numbers of game. Most of the famous private concessions are within Sabi Sands, including Lion Sands, Londolozi, Mala Mala, Singita and Ulusaba, and some of the fashionable and contemporary lodges couldn't be more different than the large Skukuza national park rest camp across the Sabie River.

Panorama Region

Closer to Maputo in Mozambique than Pretoria, Nelspruit, capital of the Mpumalanga province, has a sleepy, tropical feel with broad, streets lined with acacias, bougainvillea and jacaranda trees. Although as a modern industrial town there's little to keep you here, it has excellent road links to Mpumalanga's major tourist attractions. The nearest entrance gates to Kruger are less than 80 km away on the N4 and the shopping centres in town are convenient for stocking up on food and supplies.

The R40 road north of Nelspruit gradually climbs up into the eastern Drakensberg, generally referred to as the Panorama Region; a scenic area dotted with small towns popular with tourists for the craft shops and restaurants, but the main reason for a visit is the spectacular Blyde River Canyon. These mountains provide blessed relief from the heat on the plains of the Lowveld, and anyone visiting Kruger should schedule the region into their itinerary.

Nelspruit and around → *For listings, see pages 161-172. Phone code: 013.*

Nelspruit developed around the railway when the line between Pretoria and Lourenço Marques (now Maputo) was completed in 1891. Briefly the capital of the Transvaal Republic after Paul Kruger abandoned Pretoria in 1900 during the Boer War, it is now the industrial centre of the Lowveld and a processing point for the surrounding citrus and beef farms. Nelspruit has grown rapidly in recent years and it has a prosperous air with a new sprawl of well-off suburbs surrounding the city centre. New business parks and a number of shopping malls have been built in the area, especially along the road to White River.

Arriving in Nelspruit

Kruger Mpumalanga International Airport (KMIA) ⓘ *airport enquiries, T013-753 7500, www.kmiairport.co.za*, is 25 km from the centre of Nelspruit towards Kruger off the R538. Nelspruit is 373 km or 4½ hours from Johannesburg along the N4 toll road, a smooth highway that continues east to Maputo, Mozambique's capital. **Greyhound** and **Intercape** operate services from Johannesburg and Pretoria to Maputo in Mozambique, which stop in Nelspruit.

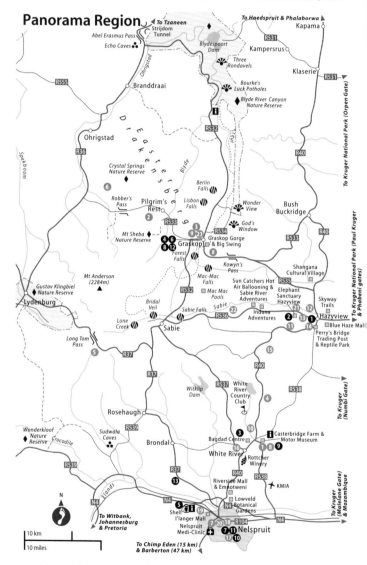

Fri 0800-1700, Sat 0800-1500, is the main tourist office for the entire region. It can organize car hire, safaris, game drives and accommodation in Kruger.

Where to stay 🛏

Casterbridge Hollow Boutique **1**
Crystal Springs Mountain Lodge **6**
Flycatcher Castle **3**
Funky Monkey Backpackers **7**
Graskop **9**
Greenway Woods Resort **10**
Hazyview Adventure Backpackers **11**
Highgrove House Country Hotel **15**
Hippo Hollow Country Estate **12**
Hulala Lakeside Lodge **4**
Karula **16**
Loerie's Call **17**
Misty Mountain **5**
Mount Sheba **2**
Nelspruit Backpackers **18**
Panorama View Chalets **8**
Perry's Bridge Hollow Boutique **14**
Promenade **19**
Rissington Inn **13**
Sabie River Sun Resort **21**
Sheppard Boutique **20**
Timaroon Lodge **22**
Valley View Backpackers **23**

Restaurants 🍴

Caninambo **4**
Halls Farm Stall Coffee Shop **5**
Harrie's Pancakes **6**
Jock & Grill Pub **7**
Loco & Coachman Grill **8**
Magnolia **9**
Orange **10**
Pioneer's Butcher & Grill **1**
Saffron **11**
The Silver Spoon **12**
Summerfields River Café & Kitchen **2**
Zannas Flavour Junction **3**
Zest **13**

Mpumalanga Tourism ① *5 km west of Nelspruit on the R104, turn off at the Hall's Gateway Shell petrol station, 013-759 5300, www.mpumalanga. com, Mon-Fri 0800-1630*, is the provincial office, which again has numerous leaflets and maps on the surrounding area, and can make bookings and give advice on Kruger.

➤➤ *For details, see Transport, page 171.*

Places in and around Nelspruit

Lowveld National Botanical Gardens ① *1 km north of Nelspruit on the R40, T013-752 5531, www. sanbi.org, Sep-May 0800-1800, Apr-Aug 0800-1700, R24, children (under 16) R12, restaurant*, are relatively small but are attractively shaped by the Crocodile and Nels rivers, which converge in the gardens below a pretty series of waterfalls that can be viewed at the Cascades and the Nels viewpoints. There's also a boardwalk which takes you through a 3-ha section of tropical rainforest, an open area of marshland which is good birdwatching country, a collection of indigenous cycads, and the Riverside Trail – a 1-km walk along the banks of the Crocodile River, with a suspension bridge linking the two sides.

The Jane Goodall Institute's **Chimp Eden** ① *15 km south of Nelspruit off the R40 towards Barberton, T079-777 1514, www.chimpeden.com. Daily 1-hr tours depart at 1000, 1200 and 1400, R160, children (under 12) R80, the Chimp Chow Café is open 0800-*

1600 for meals before or after the tour, was established in 2006 as a facility to care for and provide a home to rescued chimpanzees and is the only chimp sanctuary in South Africa. It's currently home to 35 chimps that live in spacious semi-wild enclosures with plenty of trees. Although chimps do not naturally live in South Africa, the enclosure is made up of vegetation similar to that of their indigenous homes. Many of them have arrived here as a result of being rescued from the bushmeat trade or as pets from other parts of Africa. The interesting tours take you to shaded observation platforms from where you can watch the chimps socialize, play and swing through the branches.

White River → *For listings, see page 161-172. Phone code: 013.*

Just 20 km north of Nelspruit on the R40, this country town is at the centre of a citrus fruit-growing area; fresh local produce includes macadamia nuts, pecans, cashews, avocados, lychees and mangoes. The first settlers here were Boer cattle ranchers who arrived in the 1880s; at the end of the Anglo-Boer War a settlement was created to accommodate a new farming community made up of newly demobilized soldiers. **Lowveld Tourist Information** ① *T013-750 1073, www.lowveldtourism.com, Mon-Fri 0900-1700, Sat 0900-1500,* has a small helpful office on the Hazyview road, at Casterbridge Farm (see below), which can give local advice and make reservations for lodges in Kruger.

Casterbridge Farm ① *2 km from town on the Hazyview road/R40, T013-750 1540, www.casterbridge.co.za, Mon-Fri 0900-1630, Sat-Sun 0900-1600, restaurant hours vary,* is a very attractive old farmstead that has been converted into a shopping centre for arts and crafts. One of the shops is an outlet for **Rottcher Wineries**, a macadamia nut farm and orange winery in the nearby valley that produces a range of orange liquors. There are also a number of restaurants, a little cinema, the Barnyard Theatre for local productions, a farmer's market every Saturday morning, a plant nursery and a pleasant garden café, and the **Casterbridge Hollow Boutique Hotel** (see Where to stay, page 162).

Also here is the **Casterbridge Motor Museum** ① *T013-750 2196, daily 0900-1630, R20, children (under 12) R10,* which has small displays on local history, but more impressive is the collection of over 60 vintage cars on three floors of exhibition space. They are owned by a private collector, though it's still quite astonishing to see such a comprehensive collection of beautifully restored classic cars in such a backwater location. Among the oldest vehicles to be displayed are those built in 1911, not too long after the introduction of the automobile or 'horseless carriage' as it was then known. Of interest is the 1924 seven-seater Packhard Phaeton with a giant eight-cylinder engine, bought new by Lord Delamere and discovered on his Kenyan estate in the 1970s, and a 1936 Jaguar SS100, which is one of only 314 ever built. There are several interesting racing cars, including the Fatman, an MG single-seater racing car built in Durban in 1954, and a replica of Ayrton Senna's 99T Honda Formula 1 car. One of the most remarkable cars on display is a 1912 Willy's Overland, which was purchased by a Mr Brandt in 1924. Legend has it that he parked his beloved car in a room in his house and, presumably in an eccentric effort to preserve it, bricked up all the doors and the windows. Many years later, after his death, Mr Brandt's grandson unearthed the vehicle and it was restored in 1997.

Hazyview → *For listings, see page 161-172. Phone code: 013.*

To the northeast of White River via either the R40 (48 km) or the R538 (41 km), Hazyview lies on the banks of the Sabie River in the hot Lowveld country on the south-western border of Kruger. It is surrounded by banana plantations and the shimmering blue haze over the Sabie River Valley and the hills beyond lends this busy little town its name. Six roads, coming from all directions, converge at Hazyview, and it was established as a trading post in 1955 when a post office and petrol station opened. Today the town is a convenient stop on the way to Kruger, and is only 20 km to Numbi Gate via the R538 south, and 15 km to Phabeni Gate and 44 km to Kruger Gate, both via the R536 east. There is a wide range of accommodation around Hazyview from caravan parks to luxury private game reserves, useful if you'd rather not stay in the park itself. Information is available from **Tours & Tickets** ⓘ *Rendezvous Tourism Centre, Main Rd/R40, T013-737 8191, www.toursandtickets.co.za, Mon-Fri 0800-1700, Sat 0800-1400*, which acts as an agent for a range of tour operators and safari lodges in the region and can book adventure activities.

Perry's Bridge Trading Post ⓘ *corner Main St and Sabie Rd (R40), T013-737 6929, www.perrysbridge.co.za, daily 0900-1630*, is set in attractive colonial buildings on a former citrus estate. It has a collection of quality gift and curio shops as well as a deli, a number of restaurants and the **Perry's Bridge Hollow Boutique Hotel** (see page 163).

Perry's Bridge Reptile Park ⓘ *T013-764 1177, daily 1000-1700, 45-min snake demo 1100 and 1500, R85, children (5-13) R50, under 5s free*, houses snakes including pythons, black and green mambas, boomslangs and cobras, as well as leopard tortoises, crocodiles and many colourful lizards and frogs. Children will also enjoy petting the farmyard animals including pot-bellied pigs.

Also at Perry's Bridge is the office and departure point for **Skyway Trails** ⓘ *T013-737 6747, www.skywaytrails.com, daily departures 0830, 0930, 1230 and 1330, R480 per person, children under 10 may need to be assisted and no under 3s*, a 1.2-km-long aerial forest canopy ride between 10 elevated platforms in the trees as you descend down into the Sabie River Valley. The excursion takes around 2½ hours. It's a similar setup to the **Magaliesberg Canopy Tour** in the Magaliesberg Mountains (see page 110).

Elephant Sanctuary Hazyview ⓘ *on the R536, 5 km from Hazyview towards Sabie, T013-737 6609, www.elephantsanctuary.co.za, daily programmes start at 0800, 1000, 1300 and 1500, 1½-hr tour R545, children (4-14) R275, under 4s free, elephant riding R350, children (under 14 and no under 8s) R275*, is run by the same outfit that established the elephant sanctuaries on the Garden Route and Hartbeespoort Dam (see page 110). The **Trunk-in-Hand** experience is a 1½-hour interaction with the elephants, including a walk through the bush holding on to their trunks, an informative talk on African elephants and an optional 20-minute elephant ride. Visitors can also brush down the elephants and accompany them to their stables at the end of the day.

Shangana Cultural Village ⓘ *on the R535, 5 km from Hazyview towards Graskop, T013-737 5805, www.shangana.co.za, 0900-1600, tea garden, 1-hr tour R120, tour and lunch R260, evening festival R425, children (4-12) ½-price, under 4s free*, celebrates the culture of the Shangaan people, whose origins date back to the 18th century and are a combination of Zulu, Tsonga and other smaller ethnic groups. This is not a typical 'tribal village' experience as the resident family are keen to preserve their traditional lifestyles. One-hour tours take place throughout the day and follow a path from the **Marula Market** (a cut-above-the-rest curio market) to the village, and a guide explains traditional practices such as farming, food preparation, hut building and clothing, and there is ample opportunity to interact with the family members. On the midday tour a traditional lunch is included, and in the evening a festival dinner is served and the history of the Shanganas is presented by singers and dancers, which begins with drumming and a procession of flaming torches. The food is quite delicious; crocodile in groundnut sauce, baked vegetables, salads, venison and oxtail stews and fresh fruit.

Sabie → *For listings, see page 161-172. Phone code: 013.*

Once a gold-mining town, Sabie has little left to show of its glistening age and is now a prosaic timber-processing centre. Nevertheless, it has a pretty setting, ringed by mountains, pine and eucalyptus plantations, and it attracts a fair number of visitors who flock to its main road, lined with pleasant craft and coffee shops.

Due to its high altitude the hills of Sabie have always been malaria-free, and as such early pioneers used the area for their base camps when hunting and exploring down into the Lowveld. During an expedition in 1871, led by famous big-game hunter Henry Thomas Glynn, a stray bullet chipped a rock and revealed a rich gold reef. This led to an influx of fortune hunters who came and camped on the banks of the Sabie River. In the process, many indigenous forests were chopped down to meet the demand for mine props and firewood. Fortunately, the far-sighted mine manager, Joseph Brook Shires,

Sabie

Sabie

To Mac Mac Falls & Pools, Graskop (28 km) & Pilgrim's Rest (34 km)

Sabie River

Sabie Falls

Power

Lydenburg

To Lone Creek Falls

Main (R532)

Ford

Lea

Malíveld

Simmons

Sabie Hospital

Quick Spar

Michael

Pol

Church

Forestry Museum

Malíveld

Engen 1 Stop & Wimpy

Glynn

10 th

6 th

Town Hall & Library

ABSA

St Peter's

7th La

6th

Nugget Ave

Spar Supermarket

Woodsman Centre

To Hazyview (45 km)

BP

Market Square

Mphozeni Arts & Crafts

Percy Fitzpatrick & Jock plaque

Louis Trichardt

R536

Cyclejunkies

3rd La

R537

Main (R532)

2nd La

1st La

2nd La

Nelson

Andrew

To White River (48 km)

Caltex

Potgieter

Big Sky Fly-fishing & Outdoor

To Lydenburg (56 km) via Long Tom Pass (R37)

N

200 metres
200 yards

Where to stay
Villa Ticino Guest House 4
Woodsman & Restaurant 6

Restaurants
Wild Fig Tree 1

realized that man-made forests were necessary and planted the first trees in 1876. Today, Sabie lies in one of the largest man-made forests in the world. Driving around this region, the roads pass through endless tracts of neat rows of commercially planted trees – impressive, but only a very few patches of indigenous forest remain.

In **Market Square** is the lovely little Anglican church of St Peter's designed by Sir Herbert Baker, who also designed India's government buildings in Delhi and the Union Buildings in Pretoria. Jock of the Bushveld, South Africa's most famous dog is commemorated by a plaque in the square marking the arrival of Percy Fitzpatrick and Jock in 1885. **Sabie Information** ① *T013-764 3599, www.sabie.co.za, Mon-Fri 0800-1630, Sat 0900-1300*, is also in the square.

Forestry Museum ① *Ford St, T013-764 1058, www.komatiecotourism. co.za, Mon-Fri 0800-1630, Sat 0800-1200, R5, children (under 14) R2*, has displays on the development of South Africa's plantations and the timber industry, including an interesting cross-section of a 250-year-old yellowwood tree, which highlights aspects of South African history on its rings. The museum is also a satellite office of **Komatiland Forestry**, T013-764 1392, which has information on hiking and mountain-bike trails in the region.

Mac Mac Falls and **Mac Mac Pools** ① *14 km from Sabie on the R532*

Jock of the Bushveld

In many places around the Panorama Region and southern Kruger, you will encounter references to Jock of the Bushveld. Jock was a Staffordshire bull terrier dog, who was the companion of Percy FitzPatrick during the 1880s. Percy wrote about their adventures and *Jock of the Bushveld* became one of the best-loved children's books ever published.

In 1884, Percy left his home in the Cape in search of fortune in the Transvaal where gold had been discovered. But he wasn't a lucky prospector and instead bought a wagon and some oxen and began life as a transport rider. It was a hard life; the days were scorching hot, the nights freezing cold, the roads were simple dirt tracks, and the teams of oxen had to be fed, watered and protected from wild animals. In 1985, Percy decided to get a dog to keep him company and act as an extra pair of eyes in the bush. He ended up accepting the runt of the litter, but it seemed the bull terrier puppy knew that Percy had saved him, perhaps from a drowning in a bucket of water, and became a loyal companion from day one.

Jock grew from a weak little runt into a great and fearless dog that was well-liked, well-respected and well-behaved. Percy and Jock worked on the supply route through the Lowveld, from the Lydenburg and Pilgrim's Rest goldfields, through what are now the Graskop and Sabie areas, to Lourenço Marques on the coast (now Maputo in Mozambique). The dog never strayed from Percy's side, and they had many adventures, which included them getting lost in the bushveld, having a fight with a baboon and crossing crocodile-infested rivers.

Percy and Jock did this work for five years, and then all their oxen got infected by tsetse fly and died. Percy moved to Johannesburg but couldn't take Jock with him, and instead gave Jock to a trader who lived in Mozambique. Jock had already lost his hearing after a kudu had kicked him, and his deafness is attributed as the main reason he died. He could not hear when his new owner called for him to get out of the way and was mistakenly shot because he was thought to be a stray dog killing chickens. In fact Jock had already killed the other dog responsible.

Jock had been so brave and loyal, Percy began to tell his children about their adventures as bedtime stories. Rudyard Kipling, a close friend, used to take part in these story-telling evenings and it was him who persuaded Percy to put the stories together in a book. After it was published in 1907, it was reprinted four times within the first year and has never been out of print since.

to Graskop, daily 0700-1800, R5 per person, car R10, are 65 m high and drop dramatically into a series of crystal clear pools. The viewing platform is just beyond the large curio market but swimming in the deep pool at the base of the tumbling water is not allowed. However Mac Mac Pools are about 2 km before you get to the falls, where for a small fee you can also use the *braai* area and picnic site. Over 1000 miners rushed to the falls in 1873 after gold was discovered above them. Originally there was a single fall, but in their eagerness to get to gold, some miners tried to divert the waterfall's flow and an over-enthusiastic application of dynamite created the second fall. The name of Mac Mac Falls originates from the large numbers of Scottish miners who came here. The tourist office has leaflets on day hikes which visit these and other local waterfalls: **Bonnet Falls**, **Maria Shires Falls** and **Forest Falls**.

Pilgrim's Rest → *For listings, see pages 161-172.*

Pilgrim's Rest, a tiny mining town dating from the late 19th century, has been totally reconstructed as a living museum to preserve a fascinating part of South Africa's cultural heritage. It's a pretty spot: lining the main street, a row of miners' cottages with their corrugated-iron roofs and wooden walls nestles in a lush, leafy and utterly quiet valley. It's easy to imagine how it must have once looked, with a magistrate's court, church, local newspaper and schoolhouse. Although most of the buildings are strung out along one long street, the settlement has a very clear division between Uptown and Downtown, and today many of the reconstructed cottages house gift shops and cafés, and there's a large craft market at the entrance to the village.

Background
The history of Pilgrim's Rest is a fascinating tale of gold fever in southern Africa during the late 19th century, as prospectors opened up new areas in search of a fortune. The town was named by one of the first prospectors, William Trafford, because he believed that his wandering days in search of gold had finally ended and yelled out "the pilgrim is at rest!" The first gold was found by Alec 'Wheelbarrow' Patterson, in a fertile valley then known as Lone Peach Tree Creek, in September 1873. Once Trafford announced that he had also found gold, the newspapers quickly spread the word and by the end of the year more than 1500 prospectors had pitched their tents along the creek. Life was far from easy for these fortune seekers, who slept on grass mattresses in makeshift tents, often sick with malaria and exposure, in a place where lawlessness and violence was rife.

Although some of the best finds were made in 1875, the region continued to produce gold until 1972, when the last mine was closed. In 1986 Pilgrim's Rest

Pilgrim's Rest

To ③ ④, Robber's Pass (12 km) & Lydenburg (58 km)

R533

Blyde

Joubert Bridge

DOWNTOWN

⑤

To Alanglade House Museum

Highwayman's Garage

Main

③

Bypass

Historic Cemetery

Dredzen Shop & House Museum ▥

Pilgrim's Creek

④ ⓢ FNB ▥ House Museum

☒

② ▥ Pilgrim's Rest Museum

(Pol)

Old PO □

Printing Museum ▥

P

Town Hall □

UPTOWN

R533

Diggings Site Museum ▥

P

To Graskop (16 km)

200 metres
200 yards

Where to stay 🛏
Crystal Springs
  Mountain Lodge **3**
Mount Sheba **4**
Royal **2**

Restaurants 🍴
Pilgrim's Pantry **3**
Scott's Café **4**
The Vine **5**

was declared a National Monument and restoration of the old mining buildings began.

Places in Pilgrim's Rest

Historical displays and exhibits on gold-panning techniques can be found at the **Pilgrim's Rest Information Centre and Museum** ① *Main St, Uptown, T013-768 1060, www.pilgrims-rest.co.za, daily 0900-1600.* There are several other small village museums, housed in old miners' cottages, within walking distance; each is open 0900-1245, 1345-1600, and entry fee for each one is R12, children (under 16) R6, tickets from the tourist office.

Both in Uptown, the **House Museum** is a wooden and corrugated-iron structure typical of Pilgrim's Rest and displays Victorian furniture, while the **Printing Museum** has some old printing presses from the 1900s when news of the expanding goldfields was distributed to interested stockbrokers, prospectors and the Boer government in the *Gold News* newspaper which was established 1874. In Downtown, the **Dredzen Shop & House Museum**, has been fitted out as it would have been when it was built as a general dealers in the 1930s, with bicycles and brooms hanging from the ceiling, and the house of the proprietor has furnishings typical of a middle-class family of the period.

Diggings Site Museum ① *daily tours 1000, 1100, 1200, 1400 and 1500 with gold-panning demonstration, R12, children (under 16) R6, tickets from*

Robber's Pass

From Downtown Pilgrim's Rest follow the R533 to this scenic road rising 650 m in only 12 km opening up views of rusty-red cliffs, rolling grasslands, cattle ranches and the wheat-growing country of central Mpumalanga. Now an easy-going tarred road it follows a historical transport route, and once gold bullion and mail from Pilgrim's Rest was taken over the mountain to the commercial banks in Lydenburg by coach twice a week. The first major robbery took place on the pass in 1899 when two masked gunmen on horseback held up the stagecoach and made off with £10,000 worth of gold bullion. The second robbery in 1912 was not as successful. Although Tommy Dennison, a local barber, managed to rob a coach of £129 in silver coins, when he returned to Pilgrim's Rest to celebrate, he was soon arrested and spent five years in jail in Pretoria.

the tourist office, is at the top of Uptown where the tour coaches park. A visit here helps visitors gain an insight into the lives of the diggers and prospectors during the gold rush at the end of the 19th century, before the first gold mining company took control of the town. Gold panning is demonstrated and visitors can have a go themselves.

Alanglade Period House Museum ① *guided tours only and at least 30 mins' notice needed, daily 1100 and 1400, R20 per person, tickets from the tourist office,* is north of the village on the Mpumalanga escarpment. Built in 1915, the house is typically early 20th century and was the official mine manager's residence for Pilgrim's Rest until 1972. Today it is furnished with Edwardian, art nouveau and art deco pieces.

Graskop → *For listings, see pages 161-172. Phone code: 013.*

Back on the R532, this small town lies just south of the Blyde River Canyon, but despite having a large selection of holiday accommodation, restaurants and craft shops, it remains surprisingly quiet and makes a peaceful base from which to explore the region. Graskop attracts fame as being home of the South African stuffed pancake – the famous **Harrie**'s restaurant started it all, and the stuffed sweet and savoury pancakes are renowned throughout the country. Local residents have capitalized on this reputation, and there is now a line of pancake houses along the main street.

The R533 east towards Hazyview and Klaserie goes over **Kowyn's Pass** a few kilometres from Graskop. Before descending towards the Lowveld it passes **Graskop Gorge**, where adrenalin junkies try out the **Big Swing** (see What to do, page 169), and there are views looking up to **God's Window** (see below) as well as a curio market. This is a fruit-growing area of mangoes and lychees, which are sold at stalls on the side of the road in season.

Berlin Falls and **Lisbon Falls** are north of Graskop on the R532. Berlin Falls are 45 m high, and the water cascades into a circular pool surrounded by forest. At 92 m, Lisbon Falls are the highest in the area, and the river is separated into three streams as it plunges into the pool below. One of the wettest regions in South Africa, most of the rain falls during torrential thunderstorms in the summer months, and so this is the best time of year to see the waterfalls; the force of the water crashing into the pools below is spectacular.

Blyde River Canyon → For listings, see pages 161-172.

While the definition of 'largest canyon' is imprecise, as a canyon can be large by its depth, length, or the total area of the canyon system, the Blyde River Canyon is largely regarded as the third largest in Africa after the Blue Nile Gorge in Ethiopia and the Fish River Canyon in Namibia. It is the product of the Blyde River, which tumbles down from the Eastern Drakensberg escarpment to the Lowveld over a series of waterfalls and cascades that spill into the **Blydespoort Dam** at the bottom. Blyde means 'river of joy', and the river was so named after Hendrik Potgieter and his party returned safely from Delagoa Bay (Mozambique) in 1844. Voortrekkers, who had stayed behind at their camp, first named the river Treur River ('river of mourning'), under the mistaken impression that the party had been killed, so when Pogieter returned, they had to rename it.

The winding canyon is 26 km in length and is joined by the similarly spectacular 11 km **Ohrigstad Canyon** near Swadini. The 29,000-ha **Blyde River Canyon Nature Reserve** stretches for 60 km from just north of Graskop, up to the Abel Erasmus Pass on the R36, which marks the border with Limpopo Province. The canyon drops down to 800 m, and for most of its length it is inaccessible. There are no roads crossing the reserve or linking the top and bottom of the canyon, but there are some short walking trails, and a number of viewpoints snake off the along the R532 and overlook the Canyon and Lowveld beyond. Do take the time to drive down to the viewpoints, as you can't see much of the spectacular canyon if you stick to the R532.

Viewpoints

The most famous of the viewpoints is **God's Window**, right on the edge of the escarpment overlooking an almost sheer 300-m drop into the tangle of forest below. The views through the heat haze stretch over the Lowveld as far as Kruger. At the top of the hill there is a tiny patch of rainforest, which survives in the microclimate on the very tip of the ridge. At 1730 m, **Wonder View** is the highest viewpoint accessible from the road and **Pinnacle Rock** is a 30-m-high quartzite 'needle' that rises dramatically out of the fern-clad ravine. From here it is possible to see the tops of the eight waterfalls that take the Blyde River down 450 m in a series of cascades to the dam.

The most developed viewpoint is at **Bourke's Luck Potholes** ⓘ *35 km north of Graskop on the R532, daily 0700-1700, R30, children (under 12) R20, car R20, kiosk serving snacks*, an unusual series of rock formation resembling Swiss cheese. The smooth rock has been moulded and formed by the swirling action of whirlpools where the Treur and the Blyde rivers meet, creating spectacular dips, hollows and holes. The name 'Bourke's Luck' comes from Tom Bourke, a prospector who worked a claim here in the vain belief that he would find gold. The visitor centre includes an exhibition outlining the geological history of the area. From here, a 700 m wooden walkway winds around and over the potholes. A short drive further north, the viewpoint at the **Three Rondavels** is by far the most dramatic. At the car park by the walkway is a small craft market and some toilets. From here, a walkway leads out onto the lip of the canyon, with the vast cleft in the rock opening out in front of you, and **Blydespoort Dam** shimmering intensely blue at the bottom. The Three Rondavels easily recognized as the three circular rocky peaks opposite, capped with grass and vegetation and looking distinctly like thatched African rondavel huts.

◉ Panorama Region listings

For hotel and restaurant price codes and other relevant information, see pages 13-18.

◉ Where to stay

Nelspruit and around
p149, map p150
Being so close to Kruger and the Panorama Region, it makes little sense to stay in town, but nevertheless there's a good range of accommodation.
$$$ Loerie's Call, 2 Du Preez St, T013-744 1251, www.loeriescall.co.za.
Boutique-style guesthouse with 9 beautifully decorated rooms with all mod cons, set in a modern building with terraces from where there are

views across the Crocodile River Valley. There's a pool in landscaped gardens and the excellent **Orange** restaurant and wine bar (see page 165).
$$$-$$ Sheppard Boutique Hotel, 23 Sheppard Dr, T013-752 3394, www.sheppardboutique.co.za.
Another smart offering with 17 tasteful suites with antique furnishings, stylish prints and low-key lighting. Elegant, old-fashioned lounge and dining room serving good South African cuisine. Swimming pool and tennis courts. No children under 8.
$$ Hotel Promenade, corner Samora Machel Dr and Henshall St, T013-753 3000, www.hotelpromenade.co.za.

Once Nelspruit's original town hall, this historic hotel is one of the town's most prominent landmarks and is the best option in the centre. 71 modern and well-equipped rooms with a/c and Wi-Fi, restaurant, bar with courtyard terrace dotted with palms around the swimming pool.

$$ Mercure Inn, corner of Graniet St and N4, T013-741 4222, www. mercure.com. A good family option with 104 modern self-catering units sleeping up to 6 with DSTV, a/c and Wi-Fi, bar and restaurant and attractive pool area (it's the largest pool in Nelspruit).

$ Funky Monkey Backpackers, 102 Vanwijk St, T013-7441310, www. funkymonkeys.co.za. Good set-up offering dorms and doubles spread through a spacious house adorned with bright artwork. Swimming pool, bar, kitchen, meals available, secure parking and Wi-Fi. Can organize day trips to Chimp Eden (page 151) and other local sights, and longer safaris to Kruger.

$ Nelspruit Backpackers, 9 Andries Pretorius St, T013-741 2237 www. nelback.co.za. Mix of dorms, double rooms and camping in a good location next to a nature reserve. Kitchen, bar, swimming pool, close to restaurants and pubs in the Sunpark Centre. Can organize day trips to Blyde River Canyon and Kruger.

White River *p152, map p150*
$$$ Hulala Lakeside Lodge, 22 km from White River on the R40 towards Hazyview, T013-764 1893, www. hulala.co.za. Lovely location on a peninsula in a lake that gives the feeling of being on an island. 28 rooms with fireplace, DSTV, secluded patios overlooking the garden or lake, fine dining in the restaurant, a pool and 2 bars. Choice of canoes, rowing boats, or the nightly sundowner cruise.

$$ Casterbridge Hollow Boutique Hotel, Casterbridge Farm (see page 152), T013-737 7752, www. seasonsinafrica.com. Stylish modern block with 26 standard and 4 family a/c comfortable rooms with DSTV, Wi-Fi and balconies or terraces centred around a large rim-flow pool, a short stroll to restaurants, shops and attractions at Casterbridge Farm.

$$ Greenway Woods Resort, 7 km north of town on the R40, T013-536 6600, www.threecities.co.za. Large well-run country resort focused on the 18-hole golf course at the adjacent **White River Country Club**. 80 rooms and 25 3-bed self-catering chalets set in brick double-storey buildings, each with a/c and DSTV and some with fireplaces. Swimming pool, mountain bikes for hire, African-themed restaurant and bar.

$$-$ Karula Hotel, Old Plaston Rd, 1 km from town centre, T013-751 2277, www.karulahotel.co.za. An old-fashioned family-run country hotel with 46 slightly dated but comfortable rooms set in garden blocks with TV, restaurant, bar, swimming pool, tennis courts and billiard room. Rates include good traditional set 3-course dinners.

Hazyview *p153, map p150*
$$$$ Highgrove House Country Hotel, on the R40 between Hazyview

(18 km) and White River (27 km), T083 6-751500, www.highgrove.co.za. One of the finest country hotels in the region set on a 64 ha avocado and macadamia farm with a historic homestead dating to 1993. 8 sumptuous suites with fireplaces, privates verandas or courtyards, some have splash pools, 5-course gourmet dinners, hiking and mountain bike trails and there's a spa.

$$$ Hippo Hollow Country Estate, 3 km north of Hazyview off the R40, T013-737 6628, www.seasonsinafrica.com. Set in lush grounds overlooking the Sabie River – watch the hippos on the lawn at night – 37 thatched 2- to 4-bed cottages with kitchenettes and 54 hotel rooms, stylish, understated decor, 2 swimming pools, good restaurant, bar and curio shop. Offers day tours to Kruger and excursions to the local attractions.

$$$ Rissington Inn, 2 km from Hazyview off the R40 towards White River, T013-737 7700, www.rissington.co.za. Country inn with 17 comfortable rooms in cottages or in a thatched former barn with Victorian baths and verandas overlooking neat gardens and river. Swimming pool, excellent à la carte restaurant and pub that is also open to non-guests.

$$$-$$ Sabi River Sun Resort, 1 km west of town off the R536, T013-737 4600, www.tsogosunhotels.com. Good-value all-round family resort on the Sabie River with 60 rooms in double-storey blocks or thatched chalets, spa, no fewer than 5 swimming pools, 18-hole golf course (see page 170), children's

entertainment programme, tennis, bowls, mountain bike hire and there are hippo and bird-viewing hides.

$$ Perry's Bridge Hollow Boutique Hotel, at **Perry's Bridge Trading Post** (see page 153), corner Main St and Sabie Rd (R40), T013-737 6784, www.seasonsinafrica.com. Attractive modern hotel with 34 stylish a/c rooms with DSTV, outdoor showers, patios, set in expansive gardens of acacia and fig trees with large pool. Next to restaurants and shops at the **Trading Post**.

$ Hazyview Adventure Backpackers, 5 km south of town on the R40 towards White River, T0838-59 0212, www.hazybackpack.weebly.com. Pleasant bush setup with a family chalet, dorm bunks in wooden huts and dome tents for 2 with camp beds and linen. Swimming pool, hammocks, nightly bonfires and the **Jungle Café** pub and restaurant. Organizes local excursions and day trips to Kruger.

Sabie *p154, maps p150 and p155*
$$$$ Timaroon Lodge, 25 km from Sabie on the R536 towards Hazyview T013-492 0033, www.timamoonlodge.co.za. An expensive but undeniably special retreat in the Sabie River Valley. The 6 massive suites feature Indian, Moroccan or Zanzibar style decor, 4-poster beds, sunken baths, outside showers or rim-flow pools. The restaurant and bar is fashioned like a Bali temple surrounded by ponds. Can organize picnics next to the river or Kruger safaris.

$$ Misty Mountain, Long Tom Pass, 24 km from Sabie on the R532, T013-

764 3377, www.mistymountain.co.za. 27 self-catering or B&B chalets sleeping 2-6 in a beautiful mountain setting, all linked to a cosy pub and restaurant, veranda with small infinity pool and stunning views, the endangered blue swallow nests on the site.

$$ Villa Ticino Guest House, Louis Trichardt St, T013-764 2598, www.villaticino.co.za. Well-regarded guesthouse right in the middle of town and next door to **The Wild Fig Tree** restaurant (see Restaurants, page 167). 6 B&B rooms with balconies or patios, comfortable TV lounge, pool, pleasant gardens with views across the valley and forests. The friendly owners are a mine of information about what to see in the local area.

$ The Woodsman, 94 Main St, T013-764 2204, www.thewoodsman.co.za. An uninspiring brick block, but 12 excellent value B&B rooms with smart dark wood furniture, TV, claw-foot baths and some have balconies with views over the valley. Next door to the pub and restaurant of the same name (see Restaurants, page 167).

Pilgrim's Rest
p157, maps p150 and p158

$$$-$$ Crystal Springs Mountain Lodge, 11 km north of Pilgrim's Rest on the R533, T013-768 5000, www.crystalsprings.co.za. An award-winning resort in a dramatic location at the top of **Robber's Pass** (see box, page 159) on a 5000-ha mountain reserve, which is home to zebra, giraffe, wildebeest and antelope. 100 self-catering thatched cottages and 42 hotel rooms, restaurant and pub, hiking, tennis, squash, birdwatching, spa, gym, 4 swimming pools and game drives.

$$$-$$ Mount Sheba, 12 km from Pilgrim's Rest turn left off the R533 after Crystal Srings and Robber's Pass, then it's 7 km up to the resort on a good gravel road, T013-768 1241, www.mountsheba.co.za. Another mountain retreat high up in the hills in the Mount Sheba Nature Reserve with 25 double-storey self-catering chalets, **Owl & Trout** pub, restaurant, pool, tennis courts and can organize trout fishing. Rates include dinner and breakfast. Also has 10 campsites (**$**); tremendous views but can get very cold in winter.

$$ The Royal Hotel, Main St, Uppertown, T013-768 1100, www.royal-hotel.co.za. Dating from the gold rush, this historical hotel with corrugated-iron roof and wooden walls, has 50 charming rooms set around courtyards or in miner's cottages spread around the village, featuring period-style antique furniture, floral fabrics, claw-foot baths, wash-stands, and very rickety brass beds. Great restaurant and bar (see Restaurants, page 167).

Graskop *p159, map p150*

$$$ Flycatcher Castle, 4 Hugenote St, T013-767 1114, www.flycatchercastle.com. Hugely atmospheric, this quirky sandstone modern-built castle is decorated with a mixture of antiques reminiscent of an English stately home, Art Deco windows and light fixtures from old buildings in

downtown Johannesburg, and edgy modern art of spiritual themes and the human body. The 6 suites, named after classical composers, are stunning – one features a round bathroom in a tower room, another has a 4-m-high mirrored ceiling. The food is also superb and includes elaborate 5-course dinners. Day visitors can take a peek for R40 which includes a cup of tea and slice of cake; phone ahead.
$$ Graskop Hotel, Hoof St, T013-767 1244, www.graskophotel.co.za. An excellent renovated hotel in the centre of town, decorated with an attractive mixture of modern and African furniture, with 15 garden rooms with patios, and 19 individually themed 'artists" rooms which have funky splashes of colour and modern art by contemporary South African artists. Restaurant, bar with large fireplace, swimming pool in the gardens.
$ Panorama View Chalets, 2 km from town on the R533 towards Kowyn's Pass, T013-767 1091, www.panoramaviewchalets.co.za. 24 very basic but spotless self-catering chalets and camping sites with a kitchen block, kiosk selling provisions, coffee shop serving breakfast, TV and pool room. Well worth mentioning because the highlight here is the amazing rock swimming pool perched right on the edge of the escarpment with an incredible view of the Lowveld; the mist rising above the valley first thing in the morning is magical.
$ Valley View Backpackers, 47 De Lange St, T013-767 1112, www.valley-view.co.za. Overlooking the Graskop Valley and set in neat landscaped

gardens, dorms, doubles, and a self-catering rondavel and cottage, plus space for camping. Kitchen, TV room. Arranges a wide variety of activities in the area and rents out mountain bikes.

Blyde River Canyon *p160, map p150*
$$-$ Forever Resorts Blyde Canyon, T013-769 8005, www.foreverblyde canyon.co.za. Huge family resort in a great setting, with 93 self-catering chalets, campsite (**$**), restaurant, shop selling provisions, bar, swimming pool and viewpoints across to the Three Rondavels. Gets packed during school holidays, but out of season it's peaceful and handy for exploring the sights.

❼ Restaurants

Nelspruit *p149, map p150*
$$$ Orange, 2 Du Preez St, T013-744 9507, www.eatatorange.co.za. Mon-Sat 1200-1500, 1800-2200, Sun 1100-1600. A fine contemporary restaurant at the upmarket **Loerie's Call** guesthouse (page 161) with great views over Nelspruit from the terrace and a glass-walled kitchen to watch the team of chefs. Has a modern international menu and good choice of South African wine.
$$$ Zest, 11 km from Nelspruit on the R37 towards Lydenburg T013-742 2217, www.zestrestaurant.co.za. Tue-Sat 0900-2130, Sun 0900-1530. Worth coming out of town to this farmhouse on the hills above Nelspruit for the country atmosphere and gourmet cuisine. The menu changes seasonally but expect the likes of duck, salmon,

venison or rack of lamb. Opens early for breakfast (**$**) and there's accommodation (**$$**) in 5 peaceful garden cottages.

$$ Saffron, 56 Ferreira St, T013-744 0324, www.saffronnelspruit.co.za. Tue-Sat 1200-1500, Mon-Sat 1800-2100. A bistro-style restaurant with shady terrace and an interesting and well-thought out tapas menu of dishes from the Mediterranean and South America – ideal to make up a platter to share. Attached to **Chez Vincent Guest House** (**$$**) which has 11 neat rooms around a swimming pool.

$$-$ Jock & Grill Pub, 23 Ferreira St, T013-755 4969, www.jockpubandgrill. co.za. Daily 1100-2330. Informal place with lively bar and good pub grub including monster steaks, platters of Mozambique seafood and a good value Sun lunch. Often has live music and gets packed when there's an important rugby match on.

Cafés

Halls Farm Stall Coffee Shop, at the Shell Halls Gateway Centre on the R104/N4 5 km west of town, T013-752 2605. Daily 0800-1700. A good stop on the way in or out of town and set in a mock-Cape Dutch thatched building with vintage decor and lush gardens. Coffees, breakfasts, cakes and home cooked meals like chicken pie. Also sells fruit and vegetables, nuts, biltong, honey, jams, marmalades and souvenirs.

White River *p152, map p150*
$$$-$$ Magnolia, **Casterbridge Farm**, 2 km from town on the Hazyview road/R40 (see page 152), T013-751 1947, www.mag-nolia.co.za. Daily 0700-2200. Beautifully styled contemporary decor with large murals of flowering magnolias, mixed menu with a take on French bistro-style, like quail, lamb shank or rib-eye steak. Less formal café menu during the day when the garden tables with kids' play area are a good option.

Cafés

Zannas Flavour Junction, **Bagdad Centre**, across the road from Casterbridge Farm, T013-750 0469. Daily 0800-1700. Café and deli with bustling outside tables, offering breakfasts, sandwiches, wraps, salads, quiches and to-die-for chocolate brownies and lemon meringue pie. The gourmet deli items and frozen home-made ready meals are good options if self-catering in Kruger.

Hazyview *p153, map p150*
$$$-$ Summerfields River Café & Kitchen, 4 km on the R536 to Sabie, next to the Elephant Sanctuary, T013-737 6500, www.summerfields. co.za. Tue-Sun 0800-1100, 1200-1500, 1830-2100, no dinner on Sun. A lodge and spa where the 2 delightful restaurants, the **River Café** and the Kitchen, are open to all for breakfast, light lunches and formal dinners in a beautiful spot next to the Sabie River. Perfectly presented dishes with all the trimmings, expect the likes of tiger prawn curry or rosemary lamb cutlets and crème brûlée and pavlova for dessert. The **Rose Spa** is also open to day visitors and it's not unheard of to

spot hippo from the open-air treatment rooms, while the **River Lodge ($$$)** has 12 luxury tented suites.

$$-$ Pioneer's Butcher & Grill, at the **Rendezvous Tourism Centre**, Main Rd/R40, T013-737 7397, www.pioneersbutchergrill.co.za. Daily 1000-2100. Broad choice of grills and seafood, children's playground and indoor play room where they have their own 'young pioneers' menu, and sells aged steaks, boerewors and lamb and pork chops to pick up for *braais* in Kruger.

Sabie *p154, maps p150 and p155*
$$ The Wild Fig Tree, Main St, T013-764 2239. Daily 0800-2100. Quality restaurant serving light lunches and more ambitious meals in the evening. Choice of cool interior or shaded veranda. Fresh trout, guinea fowl, crocodile, warthog and some delicious home-made desserts, good choice for vegetarians. Attached curio shop.
$$-$ The Woodsman, 94 Main St, T013-764 2015, www.thewoodsman.co.za. Daily 0900-2300. Attached to a B&B (page 164) and craft centre, emphasis on Greek food and wine, try the *stifadho* (a rich stew made from beef, onions, red wine and spices), also local trout and ostrich steaks and cheaper pub grub, great valley views from the terrace.

Pilgrim's Rest
p157, maps p150 and p158
$$$-$$ The Vine, Main St, Downtown, T013-768 1080. Daily 1100-2100. Old-world restaurant with **Johnny's Bar** next door, very popular

and typical of the town, filled with tour groups during the day. Hearty steaks and other typical local fare such as bobotie, ostrich-neck *potje*, and oxtail and samp.
$$-$ The Royal Hotel (page 164). Daily 1000-2230 (last meal orders 2030). There are 2 atmospheric restaurants here serving excellent traditional meals; the more formal Peachtree and the historical **Church Bar** which is filled with Victorian memorabilia.

Cafés
Pilgrim's Pantry, Main St, Downtown, T013-768 1129. Daily 0800-1700. Local baker, also acts as a coffee shop and is well known for its pies, pancakes and waffles and local dishes like *babotie* and *melktart*. Also sells home-made jams, mustards, and pickles, and has pretty outdoor tables in a shady courtyard and a craft shop.
Scott's Café, Main St, Uppertown, T013-768 1061. Daily 0800-1800. Salads and hot dishes, quality country cooking using local fruit and vegetables, afternoon teas with scones and fresh cream, also an art gallery.

Graskop *p159, map p150*
$$ Canimambo, Louis Trichardt St, across the road from the **Graskop Hotel**, T013-767 1868, www.canimambo.za.net. Daily 1200-2100. Charming family-run Portuguese/Mozambican restaurant with colourful interior, roaring fire, and separate bar with leather couches, serving traditional bean stew with chorizo sausage, peri-peri chicken and prawns and beef *espetada*.

$ Harrie's Pancakes, Louis Trichardt St, T013-767 1273, www.harries pancakes.com. Daily 0800-1730. Graskop's original pancake house that went on to establish a countrywide reputation. A wide selection of pancakes with sweet and savoury fillings; try the chicken, mushroom and cashew nut, spicy butternut, and mouth-watering banana and caramel or chocolate mousse and milk tart ice-cream.

$ Loco & Coachman Grill, in the old converted railway station, T013-767 1961. Daily 1200-2300. Popular pub decorated with railway memorabilia, beer garden with kid's playground, good-value menu of pub grub like *eisbein*, spare ribs, burgers, steak and chicken and chips, and some seafood.

$ The Silver Spoon, corner of Louis Trichardt and Church streets, T013-761 1039, www.silverspoon.org. Daily 0700-1900. More pancakes, also has huge burgers, salads and famous Black Forest cake that's made from a German recipe. There's a pleasant deck overlooking the street or a cosy interior with a roaring fire in winter.

⊛ Festivals

Pilgrim's Rest
157, maps p150 and p158
Sep The **South African Gold Panning Championships**, www.sagoldpanning. co.za. Held annually in Pilgrim's Rest and attract about 700 participants. Anyone can enter, including small children, and there's also a parade, a wheelbarrow race, and a pub crawl up and down the main street.

○ Shopping

Nelspruit *p149, map p150*
If you haven't got all you need to go on safari in Kruger, both malls below have branches of **Cape Union Mart** (www.capeunionmart.co.za) for camping gear, outdoor clothing and shoes, and the likes of mosquito repellent, torches and binoculars.
I'langa Mall, on the R104 2 km west of town, corner Bitterbessie and Flamboyant streets, T013-742 2293, www.ilangamall.com. Mon-Sat 0900-1800, Sun 0900-1500. Nelspruit's newest mall with banks, restaurants and 110 shops, including a large branch of **Pick n' Pay** and a **Woolworths** food shop; both ideal for stocking up for self-catering in Kruger if driving through.
Riverside Mall, 5 km north of town on the White River road (R40), T013-757 0080, www.riversidecentre.co.za. Mon-Sat 0900-1800, Sun 0900-1500. 150 shops including large branches of the supermarket chains, plus restaurants and next door is the **Emnotweni Casino** (www.emnotweni.co.za), which also has an 8-screen cinema.

Hazyview *p153, map p150*
Blue Haze Mall, corner of the R40 and the R536 towards Kruger, www. bluehazemall.co.za. Daily 0900-1900. Currently the largest shopping centre in Mpumalanga with more than 200 shops, including **Superspar**, **Pick 'n Pay** and **Woolworths** food, which couldn't be better placed for self-catering provisions for Kruger – the Phabeni Gate is 12 km from here.

Marula Market, **Shangana Cultural Village** (see page 154), on the R535, 5 km from Hazyview towards Graskop. Daily 0900-1700, tea garden open until 1600. Traditional market arranged in a circle of huts with a good range of curios, including wooden sculptures and contemporary metalwork. Many of the artists work at their homes in nearby villages.

Sabie *p154, maps p150 and p155*
Mphozeni Arts & Crafts, Woodsman Centre, Main St, T013-764 2015. Daily 0900-1700. A treasure-trove of a shop next to the Woodsman restaurant with a large selection of African arts and crafts, jewellery and fabrics including hand-painted cloth, wall hangings and batiks.

Graskop *p159, map p150*
There's a large curio market at Graskop Gorge, 2 km south of town on the R533, and another 3 km west on the R532 towards Pilgrim's Rest. Both also sell astonishingly large amounts of clay pots that are unique to the area.
Africa Silks, Louis Trichardt St, T013-767 1655, www.africasilks.com. Daily 0900-1700. Fine selection of handwoven silk products, including hand-dyed scarves, clothes, cushion covers and bedspreads.

○ What to do

Nelspruit *p149, map p150*
Local tour operators can organize a wide range of day and overnight trips to the local sights including Kruger, Blyde River Canyon and Chimp Eden,

and will pick up from any hotel in Nelspruit. A day tour to Kruger costs in the region of R1400 per person, and longer 3-day 2-night Kruger tours start from around R4600. Both **Funky Monkey Backpackers**, and **Nelspruit Backpackers**, see Where to stay, page 162, offer tours.
Kruger Park South Safaris, T082-887 0666, www.krugersouthsafaris.co.za.
Place of Rock, T013-751 5319, www.placeofrock.co.za.
Vula Tours, T031-741 2238, www.vulatours.co.za.

Panorama Region *p149, map p150*
Tours & Tickets, Rendezvous Tourism Centre, Main Rd/R40, Hazyview, T013-737 8191, and Louis Trichardt St, Graskop, T013-767 1573, www. toursandtickets.co.za. Acts as an agent for a range of tour operators and safari lodges in the region and can book adventure activities.

Adrenalin activities
Big Swing & Foefie Slide, Graskop Gorge on the R533, 2 km out of Graskop, T0722-238155, www.big swing.co.za. Daily 0900-1700, weather permitting. R320 or R400 with the Foefie Slide, or slide on its own R1000. You can also jump tandem for a reduced rate per person. Similar to a bungee jump, but with more of an outward swing on the descent. The free fall is 68 m and lasts 3 secs. Once the bungee cord has reached its optimum length, you are lowered down into the rainforest at the bottom of the gorge, before a 10-min walk back to the top. The 131-m Foefie

Slide goes across the gorge at a height of 80 m.

Ballooning
Sun Catchers Hot Air Ballooning, T0878-062079, www.suncatchers. co.za. There are 2 launch sites for sunrise 1-hr balloon flights; on the front lawn at **Sabie River Adventures** (see Whitewater rafting, below), 11 km from Hazyview on the R536 towards Sabie, for flights over the Sabie Valley; and at **Otter's Den River Lodge**, 17 km from Hoedspruit on the R531, for flights over the Lowveld and base of the Blyde River Canyon. Costs are R3249 per person, no children under 1.2 m tall, and include refreshments. Transfers are available from the towns, and some of the Kruger gates and private game reserves.

Fishing
Big Sky Fly-fishing & Outdoor, 19 Main St, Sabie, T013-764 2682, www. bigskyoutdoor.co.za. Mon-Fri 0830-1700, Sat 0830-1300. A fishing and outdoor gear shop and also rents out rods and arranges angling and *braai* excursions to trout dams on local farms.

Golf
Sabi River Sun Resort, 1 km west of Hazyview off the R536, contact the resort (see page 163), or phone the **Pro Shop** T0748-418138. This lovely Par 72 course is next to the Sabie River; there's a hippo pond at the 16th hole. Challenging in that there are water hazards on all but 4 of the 18 holes. Green fees for non-guests of the resort are R530.

White River Country Club, 7 km north of White River, off the R40 towards Hazyview, T013-751 3781, www.whiterivercountryclub.co.za. Attractive 18-hole Par 72 course designed by Gary Player and Reg Taylor surrounded by woodland on the banks of the White River, green fees are around R300. It's adjacent to the **Greenway Woods Resort** (see page 162).

Helicopter flights
Mpumalanga Helicopter Co., based at **Hippo Hollow Country Estate** (see page 163), T0845-052052, www. mhelicopter.co.za. Like ballooning above, the Blyde River Canyon region and the Sabie Valley look even more impressive from the air. Helicopter trips from 45 mins to 2½ hrs fly right into the canyon and dip down to the various waterfalls. It's an exhilarating experience but prices are steep, from R9100 for 2 people, and R1300 each for a 3rd and 4th person.

Horse-riding
Induna Adventures, 10 km from Hazyview on the R536 towards Sabie, T013-492 0071, www.induna adventures.com. Guided horse trails through indigenous forests, citrus farms and blue gum plantations between Hazyview and Sabie. Daily except Sun; 1-hr, R220, 2-hrs, R400, and 4-hrs R630. Suitable for novice and experienced riders but no children under 12.

Mountain biking
Popular in the forests around Sabie and several self-guided trails have been

marked out by the forestry department, **SAFCOL**, including challenging ascents and downhill runs over loose shale and eroded gullies. Information can be found at the **Forestry Museum** (see page 155), T013-7641058, www. komatiecotourism.co.za, and you can download information and maps from the website.

Cyclejunkies, corner Main Rd and Louis Trichardt St, Sabie T013-764 1149, www.cyclejunkies.co.za. Mountain bike hire from R60 for 3 hrs/ R300 per day, information and maps for routes from Sabie from 15-40 km, guided day tours and booking agent for popular multi-day mountain-bike events and races in the region.

Valley View Backpackers, in Graskop (see Where to stay, page 165), rents out mountain bikes from R170 for a full day of cycling in the forests around Graskop and Sabie with maps and permits.

Whitewater rafting

Sabie River Adventures, 11 km from Hazyview on the R536 towards Sabie, T013-492 0071, www.sabieriver adventures.co.za. Offers 4-hr 8-km Grade 3-4 rafting trips on the Sabie River using 2-man inflatable 'crocs'. R390, children (under 12) R250; the minimum age for children depends on water levels of the river. It's a pleasant excursion with good views of the wooded banks that are rich in birdlife and there's time for swimming and 'bum-sliding' on the rocks. Drinks and snacks included.

⊖ Transport

Nelspruit *p149, map p150*
From Nelspruit it is 693 km to Durban, 90 km to Graskop, 60 km to Hazyview, 153 km to Hoedspruit, 356 km to Johannesburg, 207 km to Maputo (Mozambique) and 61 km to Sabie.

Air

Kruger Mpumalanga International Airport (KMIA) is 25 km from Nelspruit towards Kruger's Numbi Gate, off the R538, T013-753 7500, www.kmiairport.co.za. The airport has ATMs, cafés, car rental desks and a desk for **Mpumalanga Tourism**.
Lowveld Link, T013-750 1174, www. lowveldlink.com, provide shuttle transfers to/from the airport to Nelspruit, the towns in the Panorama Region and all the private games reserves in the southern Kruger area.
South African Airways (SAA), KMIA T013-750 2531, central reservations T011-978 1111, www.flysaa.com. Operated by SAA's subsidiary, **SA Airlink**, daily flights to/from **Johannesburg** and **Durban**.

Bus

Greyhound, www.greyhound.co.za, and **Intercape**, www.intercape.co.za, stop in Nelspruit on the route between **Johannesburg** (4 hrs 25 mins) and **Pretoria** (5 hrs 55 mins) and **Maputo** in Mozambique (4½ hrs). The buses stop outside the **Hotel Promenade** on Samora Machel St (see page 161). Full timetables can be found on the websites, and tickets can be booked online through

Computicket, T011-915 8000, www.computicket.com, or in South Africa, at any of their kiosks in the shopping malls or any branch of **Checkers** and **Shoprite** supermarkets. For more information, see Transport, page 11.

Car hire
All offices are at the Kruger Mpumalanga International Airport (KMIA): **Avis**, T013-750 1015, www.avis.co.za; **Budget**, T013-751 1774, www.budget.co.za; **Europcar**, T013-750 2871, www.europcar.co.za; **First Car Rental**, T013-750 2538, www.firstcarrental.co.za; **Hertz**, T013-750 9150, www.hertz.co.za; **Thrifty**, T013-751 3052/3, www.thrifty.co.za.

Panorama Region *p149, map p150*
Avis, at Perry's Bridge Trading Post (see page 153), corner Main St and Sabie Rd (R40), Hazyview, T013-737 8539, www.avis.co.za.

⊙ Directory

Nelspruit *p149, map p150*
Medical services Nelspruit Medi-Clinic, 1 Louise St, off the R40 in Sonheuwel, 3 km south of town, T013-759 0500, 24-hr emergencies, T013-759 0645, www.mediclinic.co.za. This is the principal private hospital in the region.

Sabie *p154, maps p150 and p155*
Medical services Sabie Hospital, Hospital St, T013-764 1222, although in the event of a medical emergency, if possible it's best to go to **Medi-Clinic** in Nelspruit (above).

Contents

Footnotes

Index → *Entries in **bold** refer to maps.*

Join us online...

Follow **@FootprintBooks** on Twitter, like **Footprint Books** on **Facebook** and talk travel with us! Ask us questions, speak to our authors, swap stories and be kept up-to-date with travel news, exclusive discounts and fantastic competitions.

Upload your travel pics to our **Flickr** site and inspire others on where to go next.

And don't forget to visit us at footprinttravelguides.com